Spinoza's Political Psychology

Spinoza's Political Psychology advances a novel, comprehensive interpretation of Spinoza's political writings, exploring how his analysis of psychology informs his arguments for democracy and toleration. Justin Steinberg shows how Spinoza's political method resembles Renaissance civic humanism in its view of governance as an adaptive craft that requires psychological attunement. He examines the ways that Spinoza deploys this realist method in the service of empowerment, suggesting that the state can affectively reorient and thereby liberate its citizens, but only if it attends to their actual motivational and epistemic capacities. His book will interest a range of readers in Spinoza studies and the history of political thought, as well as readers working in contemporary political theory.

JUSTIN STEINBERG is Associate Professor of Philosophy at Brooklyn College and the City University of New York Graduate Center. He has published articles in journals including the *British Journal of the History of Philosophy, History of Philosophy Quarterly, Journal of the History of Philosophy,* and *Pacific Philosophical Quarterly.*

Spinoza's Political Psychology

The Taming of Fortune and Fear

Justin Steinberg

Brooklyn College and the City University of New York Graduate Center

CAMBRIDGE
UNIVERSITY PRESS

University Printing House, Cambridge CB2 8BS, United Kingdom

One Liberty Plaza, 20th Floor, New York, NY 10006, USA

477 Williamstown Road, Port Melbourne, VIC 3207, Australia

314–321, 3rd Floor, Plot 3, Splendor Forum, Jasola District Centre, New Delhi – 110025, India

79 Anson Road, #06-04/06, Singapore 079906

Cambridge University Press is part of the University of Cambridge.

It furthers the University's mission by disseminating knowledge in the pursuit of education, learning, and research at the highest international levels of excellence.

www.cambridge.org
Information on this title: www.cambridge.org/9781107141308
DOI: 10.1017/9781316493465

© Justin Steinberg 2018

First published 2018

Printed and bound in Great Britain by Clays Ltd, Elcograf S.p.A.

A catalogue record for this publication is available from the British Library.

ISBN 978-1-107-14130-8 Hardback

To the memory of my father, Harvey Steinberg, a paragon of *generositas*.

Contents

Figures and Tables

Figures

Tables

Acknowledgments

While this book is not a revised dissertation, it is the outgrowth of work on Spinoza's political philosophy that began almost a decade and a half ago at Boston University. Consequently, I want to thank those who helped set me on this course. Aaron Garrett was an unfailingly cheerful, sharp-witted, and supportive advisor, and he has continued to be a repository of good advice – professional and cinematic – throughout my early academic career. Knud Haakonssen introduced me to early modern political thought, which enabled me to appreciate the extent to which Spinoza was doing something quite original. Knud's historically exacting teaching and scholarship stimulated me to challenge dominant narratives and led me to cultivate a healthy anxiety about anachronism – though I don't always retreat from this anxiety. I also want to thank Henry Allison, in whose Philosophy of Religion class I was first introduced to Spinoza's *Tractatus Theologico-Politicus*. In this and the Kant seminars that I took with Henry, he exemplified how philosophical rigor could be joined to historical sensitivity. Don Garrett was an unparalleled external reader. He was extremely generous with his time, commenting in detail with characteristic perspicacity on multiple drafts of the dissertation and travelling to Boston for the prospectus and dissertation defenses. Finally, I am grateful to have been at Boston University with a supportive group of peers and mentors. Had Boston University not been such a hospitable place, I probably would not have completed graduate study. Here I should single out David Roochnik, DGS for much of my tenure, who provided much-needed confidence boosting at various stages. Every graduate program needs a David Roochnik.

I want also to thank my colleagues – first at The College of Wooster and Colby College, and now at Brooklyn College, CUNY – who have contributed to my generally positive experience in academia. Some of my colleagues at Wooster were also my undergraduate professors, and if I can inspire and support my students in anything like the ways that Ron Hustwit, Hank Kreuzman, and Garrett Thomson inspired and supported me, I should consider myself profoundly successful. Whether or not I have had that kind of impact, I can't imagine a more gratifying place to teach philosophy than Brooklyn College, where the students – especially the philosophy majors – are motivated, inquisitive, independent-minded, and generally delightful to be around. I am honored to be a part of this estimable institution, even while it remains lamentably underfunded.

This manuscript owes much to the spirited and wonderful community of Spinoza scholars, many of whom read and commented on chapters of this manuscript. In addition to the anonymous referee at Cambridge University Press, the following people supplied valuable feedback: Ed Curley, Michael Della Rocca, Don Garrett, John Grey, Karolina Hübner, Matthew Kisner, Eugene Marshall, John Morrison, Steven Nadler, Alan Nelson, Hasana Sharp, Ericka Tucker, Valtteri Viljanen, and Andrew Youpa. Hübner deserves special thanks for organizing and hosting a workshop at the University of Toronto in April 2017 devoted to my manuscript, where Nadler, Nelson, Sharp, and Youpa presented excellent commentaries. And Viljanen deserves a medal of some sort for his role as a stalwart and astute interlocutor. He read the entire manuscript – in disparate stages of refinement – and provided sharp feedback at every turn. I feel fortunate that I can count luminous colleagues like Karolina and Valtteri among my friends. Other Spinozists who have contributed to my scholarly development in manifold ways, and whose work I greatly admire, include Susan James, Michael LeBuffe, Yitzhak Melamed, Jon Miller, and Michael Rosenthal.

I also benefitted from the perspective of non-Spinozists, including the bright students in my Spring 2017 Spinoza Seminar at the CUNY Graduate Center, who read and scrutinized much of the manuscript, and Jamie T. Kelly and Samir Chopra, who provided helpful comments on the Introduction. I also owe thanks to Enrique Chavez-Arvizo, Torin Doppelt, William Edelglass, Shelley Weinberg, and Charles Wolfe for organizing events in which I tested out some of this material. The editorial team at Cambridge University Press – Hilary Gaskin, in particular – has been superb. Hilary was responsive, encouraging, and judicious throughout the entire process. Would that all institutions had such a steady hand at the helm.

Finally, I want to express my appreciation to my family. My parents supported my interest in philosophy, even when it brought out my cantankerousness. Much love to my mom, Karen, and to my dad, Harvey, who passed soon after I started writing this book. I dedicate it to his memory. My deepest gratitude goes to Meg Toth, a remarkable scholar of American literature and film, who has endured my many fits of frustration and self-doubt as I completed this work, providing reassurance and encouragement throughout. Perhaps more importantly she ensured that I remained alive to the world outside of my work, joining me on many small adventures and diversions that kept the creep of stultifying scholarly despair at bay. Our cats Edmund and Henry (and the late, beloved Moogie) helped with this as well.

Note on Primary Sources and Abbreviations

All Latin passages refer to:

> *Spinoza Opera*. Edited by Carl Gebhardt, 4 vols. Heidelberg: Carl Winter, 1925.

English translations refer to:

> *The Collected Works of Spinoza*, vols. I–II. Translated and edited by Edwin Curley. Princeton, NJ: Princeton University Press, 1985 and 2015.

References to the *Ethics* open with numerals, which indicate the Part, followed by specifying information based on the following abbreviations:

a	Axiom
app.	Appendix
alt. dem.	Alternate Demonstration
c	Corollary
d	Demonstration
D	Definition
DA	Definition of the Affects (end of Part 3)
L	Lemma
post.	Postulate
s	scholium

For example, 5p10s refers to *Ethics* Part 5, proposition 10, scholium.

References to the *Tractatus Theologico-Politicus* open with an abbreviated reference to the work – TTP – followed by the chapter and section in the Curley translation and the references to the Gebhardt volume and page.

For example, TTP 3.28, iii.50 refers to chapter 3, section 28, Gebhardt vol. 3, p. 50.

References to the *Tractatus Politicus* open with an abbreviated reference to the work – TP – followed by the chapter and section (identical in Curley and Gebhardt).

For example, TP 4/1 refers to chapter 4, section 1.

Other Works by Spinoza

CM	*Metaphysical Thoughts (Cogitata Metaphysica)*
Ep.	*Correspondence (Epistolae)*
KV	*Short Treatise on God, Man, and His Well-Being*
TdIE	*Treatise on the Emendation of the Intellect (Tractatus de Intellectus Emendatione)*

Other Abbreviated References

CLPB	Grotius, Hugo. *Commentary on the Law of Prize and Booty.* Edited by Martine Julia van Ittersum. Indianapolis: Liberty Fund, 2006.
CSM	Descartes, René. *The Philosophical Writings of Descartes*, vols. 1–2. Edited and translated by John Cottingham, Robert Stoothoff, and Dugald Murdoch. Cambridge University Press, 1985.
CSMK	Descartes, René. *The Philosophical Writings of Descartes*, vol. 3. Edited and translated by John Cottingham, Robert Stoothoff, Dugald Murdoch, and Anthony Kenny. Cambridge University Press, 1991.
CWO	Machiavelli, Niccolò. *The Chief Works and Others* (3 vols.). Translated by Allan Gilbert. Durham: Duke University Press, 1965.
DCG	Sidney, Algernon. *Discourses Concerning Government.* Edited by Thomas G. West. Indianapolis: Liberty Fund, 1996.
De Cive	Hobbes, Thomas. *On the Citizen.* Edited and translated by Richard Tuck and Michael Silverthorne. Cambridge University Press, 1998.
Dissertation	Van Velthuysen, Lambert. *A Dissertation: Wherein the Fundamentals of Natural or Moral Justice and Decorum are State, according to the Principles of Mr. Hobbes. By a Learned Pen.* Translated anonymously. London, 1706.
DJB	Grotius, Hugo. *The Rights of War and Peace* [*De Jure Belli ac Pacis*] (3 vols.). Edited by Richard Tuck. Indianapolis: Liberty Fund, 2006.

DO	Pufendorf, Samuel. *On the Duty of Man and Citizen* [*De officio hominis et civis juxta legem naturalem*]. Translated by Michael Silverthorne and edited by James Tully. Cambridge University Press, 1991.
EL	Hobbes, Thomas. *The Elements of Law*. Edited by J. C. A. Gaskin. Oxford University Press, 1994.
EW	Hobbes, Thomas. *The English Works of Thomas Hobbes* I–XI. Edited by William Molesworth. London: John Bohn, 1839–45.
HBLN	*Hobbes and Bramhall on Liberty and Necessity*. Edited by Vere Chappell. Cambridge University Press, 1999.
HP	Long, A. A. and D. N. Sedley (eds.). *The Hellenistic Philosophers, Vol. 1: Translations of the Principal Sources, with Philosophical Commentary*. Cambridge University Press, 1987.
Lev.	Hobbes, Thomas. *Leviathan*. Edited by Richard Tuck. Cambridge University Press, 1996.
MW	Bacon, Francis. *The Major Works*. Oxford University Press, 1996.
OHWP	Grotius, Hugo. *Ordinum Hollandiae ac Westfrisiae Pietas* (1613). Edited by Edwin Rabbie. New York: Brill, 1995.
Prince	Machiavelli, Niccolò. *The Prince*. Translated by Russell Price. Edited by Quentin Skinner. Cambridge University Press, 1988.
République	Bodin, Jean. *On Sovereignty: Four Chapters from the Six Books of the Commonwealth* (*Les Six Livres de la République*). Edited and translated by Julian H. Franklin. Cambridge University Press, 2005.
TI	De la Court, Pieter. *The True Interest and Political Maxims, of the Republic of Holland*. Translated by John Campbell. New York: Arno Press, 1972.

Introduction

> [O]ne is never to offer at propositions or advice that we are certain will not be entertained. Discourses so much out of the road could not avail anything, nor have any effect on men whose minds were prepossessed with different sentiments. This philosophical way of speculation is not unpleasant among friends in a free conversation, but there is no room for it in the Courts of Princes where great affairs are carried on by authority." – "That is what I was saying," replied [Hythloday], "that there is no room for philosophy in the Courts of Princes." – "Yes, there is," said I, "but not for this speculative philosophy that makes everything to be alike fitting at all times: but there is another philosophy that is more pliable, that knows its proper scene, accommodates itself to it, and teaches a man with propriety and decency to act that part which has fallen to his share.
> – The character of Thomas More in More's *Utopia*.[1]

For much of the past half-century, Anglo-American political philosophy has been dominated by juridical concerns: questions of right, law, duties, and justice. The towering figure during this period is John Rawls, for whom deontological questions, or questions of right, are normatively prior to, and constrain, concerns about the good. As he puts it, justice is "the first virtue of social institutions, as truth is of systems of thought."[2] Rawls's *A Theory of Justice* spawned a cottage industry of critiques and extensions in its wake, works that focused on matters of right and justice. This set the terms and agenda for much of the political philosophy that followed, which focused on such issues as: the nature and scope of political authority; rights and self-ownership; justice in war; global justice; and the status and function of international law. Juridical discourse has held hegemonic sway over the field.

A second feature of contemporary political philosophy, which is non-accidentally related to the first, is idealism. Philosophers have appealed to idealized conditions in order to arrive at accounts of authority, right, and justice.[3] Rational Choice Theory, for instance, with its narrow utility-maximizing conception of

[1] More 1997, p. 22.
[2] Rawls 1971, p. 3n9.
[3] See Habermas 1996; Cohen 1989.

1

human rationality – insulated from the quirks and heuristics of actual human reasoning – has served as a model of human motivation and action.[4] The assumption is that by conceiving of how we would reason if we were not subject to biases, affective disturbances, imperfect epistemic conditions, asymmetric power relations, and so forth, we can arrive at models of perfect justice or full democratic authority. The idealist method yields an ideal theory, an archetype that can guide us as a lodestar. As Rawls puts it, "once we have a sound theory for this [ideal] case, the remaining problems of justice will prove more tractable in the light of it."[5]

However, a number of political philosophers have expressed dissatisfaction with ideal theory and its attendant methodology. Critics have noted that it is a mistake to assume nonideal theory should be modeled on ideal theory, or that in suboptimal conditions the best thing to do is to mirror or approximate what would be best under ideal conditions. In an ideal society, the best way to promote true ideas might be through rational deliberation; but if one lives in a society in which reason-giving is less effective than emotional demagoguery, it is not obvious that the best thing for one to do is to approximate the ideal. This is an example of the problem of "second-bests."[6] To acknowledge the problem of second-bests is to concede that there might not be a clear derivation of the nonideal from the ideal. The best real-world condition might not be a mere modification of the ideal; indeed, it might not resemble the ideal in any significant way.

In her formidable book, *The Imperative of Integration*, Elizabeth Anderson makes a strong case for nonideal theory. In addition to the problem of second-bests, which she acknowledges ("knowledge of the better does not require knowledge of the best"),[7] Anderson cites three further reasons for pursuing nonideal theory. First, "we need to tailor our principles to the motivational and cognitive capacities of human beings."[8] In order to provide useful guidance, norms must satisfy what Owen Flanagan calls the Principle of Minimal Psychological Realism: "Make sure when constructing a moral theory or projecting a moral ideal that the character, decision processing, and behavior are possible, or are perceived to be possible, for creatures like us."[9] A second reason for embracing nonideal theory is that starting with ideal theory leads one to seek to "clos[e] the gaps" between the ideal and the real before adequately diagnosing the problems, "like a doctor who prescribes sleeping pills and aspirin to the patient who complains of fatigue, insomnia, and headaches."[10] And,

---

[4] See e.g. Rawls 1971; Gauthier 1986.
[5] Rawls 1971, p. 8.
[6] For a helpful analysis, see Brennan and Pettit 2005.
[7] Anderson 2010, p. 3.
[8] Ibid.
[9] Flanagan 1993, p. 32.
[10] Anderson 2010, p. 4.

finally, ideal theory is epistemically disabling, as it prevents us from recognizing sources of injustice. Ideal theory takes a too narrow, legalistic view of inequality, failing to apprehend the actual structures and conditions that initially give rise to oppression and discrimination.

Charles Mills critiques ideal theory in a similar fashion. He, too, points to the problem of second-bests, disapproving of the way that "ideal theory either tacitly represents the actual as a simple deviation from the ideal, not worth theorizing in its own right, or claims that starting from the ideal is at least the best way of realizing it."[11] Against this view, Mills claims, rather provocatively, that "the best way to bring about the ideal is by recognizing the nonideal ... by assuming the ideal or the near ideal, one is only guaranteeing the perpetuation of the nonideal."[12] If we are to overcome unjust conditions, we must confront injustice as it actually exists.

Raymond Geuss, another prominent critic of political idealism, makes the case in his *Philosophy and Real Politics* for taking socio-historical particulars very seriously. He advances four principles that ought to structure a political theory:

1. It should be realist, concerning itself "not with how people ought ideally (or ought 'rationally') to act ... but, rather, with the way the social, economic, political, etc., institutions actually operate in some society at some given time, and what really does move human beings to act in given circumstances."[13]
2. It should recognize that politics is fundamentally about action, not merely belief.
3. It should be historically situated.
4. It should acknowledge that politics is "more like the exercise of a craft or art, than like traditional conceptions of what happens when a theory is applied."[14]

In advocating a psychologically attuned, historically situated approach to politics, Geuss seeks to bridge the yawning gap that separates political theory from political action.

Of course, the divide between theory and practice, philosopher and statesperson, was not always so vast. The psychological-grounded political theory advocated by Anderson, Mills, Geuss, and others harks back to a mode of theorizing that was prominent among Renaissance humanists.[15] Indeed, the very dialectic

---

[11] Mills 2005, p. 168.
[12] Ibid., p. 182.
[13] Geuss 2008, p. 9.
[14] Geuss 2008, p. 15.
[15] Brennan and Pettit are particularly attuned to this, acknowledging that "incentive-compatibility" was a feature of "neo-Roman" thought (Brennan and Pettit 2005, p. 264).

that I've briefly sketched between juridical-idealists and psychological-realists roughly parallels a shift from the late medieval into the early Renaissance period. Perhaps political philosophy is on the verge of another renaissance.

From Medieval Ideal Theory to Renaissance Realism

Much medieval political thought was juridical, delineating the bounds of authority and determining the meaning, scope, and justification of law. Perhaps the central concept – and certainly one of the most ambiguous – was that of "right" (*ius*), which divided into at least two broad families of conceptions. On the one hand, there was the conception of right as the object of justice, designating that which is right or just (Aquinas, *Summa Theologiae*, IIaIIae 57). This sense of right – dubbed the "objective" sense – was closely bound up with natural law (*ius naturalis*): right reason determines *ius*, which, when prescribed, takes the form of *lex*.[16] On the other hand, there is the subjective sense of right, so called because it is imputed to subjects rather than to states of affairs, consisting in a kind of moral power (*potestas*) or title. These two senses of *ius* grounded accounts of authority (*imperium*), property, and justice in war, giving rise to a scheme of duties.[17] These rights and duties were, by and large, determined independently of questions of utility and the probability of compliance, resulting in ideal theories of authority and justice.

This is the backdrop against which Renaissance political thought developed. Renaissance civic humanists typically sought a practicable approach to political theory. This period was typified by the rise of the scholar-statesman, the celebration of the *vita activa*, an increased emphasis on virtue and utility rather than right, the flourishing of rhetoric and the language arts, and the corresponding conceptualization of politics as a craft. Let's briefly consider these in turn.

Many prominent civic humanists were also political agents of some sort. To cite just a few familiar examples, Niccolò Machiavelli (1469–1527) had been second chancellor of the Republic and secretary to the Ten of War during the brief flourishing of the Florentine republic at the end of the fifteenth century. He was just one in a line of Florentine scholar-statesmen, including the Chancellor Coluccio Salutati (1331–1406) and his successor to the post, Leonardo Bruni (1370–1444). In the north, Erasmus (1466–1536) sought to proffer advice to King Charles of Spain in his *Education of a Christian Prince*. Thomas More (1478–1535) became Lord Chancellor of England, before his fatal conflict with Henry VIII. Like the character of More in *Utopia*, the

---

[16] Aquinas frequently uses *ius nature* and *lex naturalis* interchangeably. R.W. Dyson notes that for Aquinas "lex is not the same as right, properly speaking, but an expression of the idea of right" (Aquinas 2008, p. 158n2.)
[17] See McGrade 1982, pp. 740–1.

historical More espied a "more pliable" model of political philosophy in which the philosopher is also a kind of actor who must learn to play his (or her) part (see Epigraph). Even Montaigne, who famously withdrew from public life, left his tranquil tower to serve two terms as mayor of Bordeaux and to advise king Henry of Navarre (Henry IV).[18]

The rise of the scholar-statesman was mirrored by a celebration of the life of *negotium*, or the *vita activa*, over the life of *otium*, the *vita contemplativa*. Civic humanists rejected the Aristotelian view that while the political life is good, the life of contemplation was divine. Some, like Petrarch and More, drew inspiration from the Platonic alternative, which conceded that the active life is intrinsically undesirable to men of wisdom, but insisted that the wise and the virtuous take on this burden in order to heal the city.[19] Others were more enthusiastic about civic life. Machiavelli advanced perhaps the most vigorous defense of the active life as a condition for liberty in his *Discourses*, despite having failed to obtain a public post after the Medici returned to Florence in 1513. Machiavelli's encomium to the *vita activa* captured the prevailing ethos of a certain civic strand of humanism: a useful life was to be preferred to a life of idle learning. This was true irrespective of whether one lived in a republic or served a prince.

As political theorists increasingly joined the ranks of political actors, enacting and glorifying the *vita activa*, rhetoric took on a greater philosophical significance.[20] The medieval *ars dictaminis*, the skill of composing persuasive speeches and diplomatic letters, helped to elevate the status of rhetoric, long regarded as inferior to logic in the *trivium*.[21] But it was in the Renaissance period, with the rediscovery of Cicero's letters and speeches and Quintilian's *Institutio Oratoria*, that rhetoric became a prized part of the humanist program, uniting theory and practice, inquiry and argumentation.[22] Rhetoric was especially important to moral philosophy, since a skilled writer or orator, especially one endowed with a good character, could stimulate the cultivation of virtue, adding affective force to what might otherwise be a cold, intellectual appreciation of that which is honorable (*honestas*). It also served as a model for political life in which, in Geuss's terms, the aim is action and not mere belief.

These three related aspects of Renaissance civic humanism – the emergence of the scholar-statesman, the celebration of the *vita activa*, and the elevated position of rhetoric – contributed to the shift from the language of rights to that of utility and virtue, the promotion of which made psychology an essential component of political theory. If philosophers are to lead lives of public influence and

---

[18] For an analysis of how his political engagement informs his *Essays*, see Fontana 2008.
[19] See, for instance, Petrarch's letter to Carrara. For analysis, see Nelson 2007; More 1997, pp. 17–22.
[20] See Seigel 1966; Pocock 1975.
[21] See Copenhaver and Schmitt 1992, p. 25ff.
[22] See Skinner 1978, pp. 88–9; Seigel 1966.

persuasion, they must be savvy judges of their audiences. One cannot simply appeal to reason to discern *ius* and *lex*; one must find *useful* laws and institutions that foster loyalty and conduce to the stability and, indeed, glory of the state. In order to advance effective laws and institutions, one must accurately assay the prevailing cognitive–affective make-up of one's subjects and one's readers.

Finally, in this period, governance is conceived of as a craft, akin to medicine.[23] Both practices drew on the rhetorical method, using maxims as guides, while accommodating these rules to suit the particular constitutions or "humors" of their subjects.[24] Knowledge of the humors was regarded as just as important for politicians as it was for doctors. Machiavelli stresses the need to balance the opposing humors of competing factions of society.[25] Justus Lipsius, in his *Politica*, maintains that "the humor and inclination of the subjects ought to be as well knowne to the Prince, who commandeth over them, as if he were one amo[n]gst them."[26] And Francis Bacon, too, cites the need to espy "the predominancy, what humour reigneth most, and what end is principally sought."[27] Just as in the "medicining of the body" one must first "know the divers complexions and constitutions, secondly the diseases, and lastly the cures," so too "in medicining of the mind, after knowledge of the divers characters of men's nature, it followeth in order to know the diseases and infirmities of the mind, which are no other than the perturbations and distempers of the affections."[28] As humors and tempers vary, good governance must be adaptive, prescribing treatments that match the diagnoses. And, like medicine, governance is stochastic: even when practiced unimpeachably, it may fail to achieve its goal. Circumstances shift; fortune intrudes.

Spinoza and Renaissance Realism

I propose that we understand Spinoza's political philosophy within the lineage of Renaissance civic humanism. At first blush, this may be surprising. Spinoza is positively hostile toward "humanism" in the sense of conceiving of human beings as fashioned in God's image and possessing unique dignity.[29] He also seems to privilege the *vita contemplativa* over the *vita activa* both in theory[30] and in practice – declining, for instance, to abandon his "private and solitary life" for a professorship at the University of Heidelberg (*Epistle 48 to Fabritius*, March 30, 1673). Moreover, Spinoza was writing in a time when many philosophers like him, who were impressed by the power of reason and the promise

---

[23] See Fontana 2008, p. 13.
[24] See Pender 2005.
[25] Machiavelli, *Prince*, Ch. XIX, pp. 71–2; cf. *Discourses* 1.4 in *CWO* 1.
[26] Lipsius 1970.
[27] Bacon, *The Advancement of Learning*, Book II in *MW*, p. 275.
[28] Bacon, *The Advancement of Learning*, in *MW*, pp. 258–9.
[29] Mirandola, *De Hominis Dignitate*. Melamed 2010; Sharp 2011.
[30] Hannah Arendt criticized Spinoza on precisely this point. See Kahn 2014, p. 140n70.

of scientific advancement, took a suspicious view of rhetoric, associating the art of arguing *pro et con* with obscurantism and skepticism. We see this in Thomas Sprat's enthusiastic heralding of a new scientific language, marked by a "primitive purity" and "Mathematical plainness," shorn of "all the amplifications, digressions, and swellings of style" (*The History of the Royal Society*, 1667) as well as in Descartes's suggestion that clear, rational argumentation has persuasive force without the need for adornment (*Discourse on Method*, AT VI, 7; 114). The geometrical method of *Ethics* certainly looks like a model of a purely rational language, stripped of rhetorical ornamentation.

Nevertheless, Spinoza shares a basic orientation with Renaissance political thinkers – and, indeed, with contemporary nonideal theorists – in seeking to construct a theory of governance suited to humans "as they are" not as one "want[s] them to be" (TP 1/1).[31] Since Spinoza grounds his analysis of governance in his account of human psychology, I begin my study of his political philosophy by looking at his theory of motivation (Chapter 1). In this chapter, I maintain that the activity of finite things is fixed entirely by their affects, leaving no independent motivating role for reason. Furthermore, I show that while, in some sense, "everyone shares a common nature" (TP 7/27), this nature may be constituted in radically different ways, reflecting the influence of socio-political structures. The state, in particular, plays an outsized role in regulating the behavior of its subjects.

The subsequent three chapters examine the aims of the state. In Chapter 2, I argue that Spinoza adopts a juridical vocabulary only to strip it of its normative import. He disavows any non-prudential sense of obligation, embracing instead the position associated with the academic skeptic Carneades that *utilitas* alone is the measure of right. This sets the stage for a psychologically attuned analysis of political organization in the mode of Renaissance political theorists. In Chapter 3 I seek to show that in the absence of juridical side-constraints, the state has a single directive: to liberate or empower its citizens as far as possible. Chapter 4 examines the affective side of liberation or empowerment, defending the internal coherence of Spinoza's insistence that hopeful citizens are freer, less constrained, and more willing than their fearful counterparts. Civil liberation requires the promotion of hope, trust, and peace.

Chapter 5 looks at the method by which this end is advanced. Spinoza conceives of governance as the craft of accommodating institutions and laws to the affective make-up, or *ingenia*, of subjects. While I argue for the continuity of ethical and political *aims* in Chapter 3, this chapter makes the case for the continuity of ethical and political *methods*. This throws into sharp relief Spinoza's

---

[31] Throughout this manuscript I have generally tried to avoid using gendered pronouns when referring to generic subjects. In those instances where I have adopted gendered pronouns, I have typically preferred the feminine "she/her/hers." However, in instances in which the subject that Spinoza has in mind seems paradigmatically male – as with the "citizen-subject," since Spinoza's exclusion of women from his model democracy suggests that full civil rights were reserved only for males – I have adopted the masculine "he/him/his."

affinity with Renaissance civic humanists, as he conceives of governance as a rhetorical, adaptive craft. Spinoza's account of the aim and method of governance yields a form of what I call "dynamic realism": civic institutions and laws are suited to existing *ingenia* (realism), with the goal of reconstituting or reshaping these very *ingenia* (dynamism).

The subsequent two chapters explore Spinoza's proposals for institutional design. These chapters loosely trace the protective and the constructive aspects of *ingenia* reform, respectively. Chapter 6 sketches Spinoza's multipronged attempt to diminish superstition and intolerance, which are rooted in one particular civic institution: a politicized and powerful clergy. Consequently, Spinoza seeks to dismantle clerical power, first by restricting the domain over which clerics could preside, and then by depriving them of authority altogether. Chapter 7 examines Spinoza's endorsement of deliberative, democratic, and relatively egalitarian civil institutions. Behind the apparently tidy veneer of Spinoza's democratic egalitarianism lies a complex, psychologically rich understanding of the relationship between political participation, affective buy-in, and individual and collective rationality.

I conclude the book (Chapter 8) by considering the extent to which the state can contribute to salvation and beatitude. Here I advance an interpretation of intellectual perfection as the strengthening or potentiation of adequate ideas, showing how the imagination can serve the intellect and, consequently, how the state can promote intellectual perfection. I also attempt to make sense of why Spinoza, who privileges the eternal order of things over the temporal order, devotes much of the last decade of his life to working on political treatises that are precisely concerned with ephemeral things in the diminished temporal order. I argue that one's determinate, temporal existence is the only condition about which it makes sense to care. This reinforces Spinoza's connection to a secular strain of Renaissance civic humanism.

Even though Spinoza did not lead the active life of the scholar-statesman – a role that was certainly not available to an apostate Jew with a scandalous reputation – he recognized the transience of human flourishing, its shifting and historical character, and the roles of adaptive governance and civic engagement in its production. In short, he viewed governance as a kind of praxis aimed at promoting virtue, and he adopted a mode of theorizing that was, in accordance with Geuss's requirements, realist, action-oriented,[32] historically situated, and craft-like.

Methodology

My interpretation proceeds by way of close readings of Spinoza's texts, attending to their dialectical aims and the intellectual and political contexts

---

[32] I shall argue that he denies that there is a sharp distinction between belief and action (Section 6.5).

from which they emerge. My approach to some degree straddles the lines – to the extent that such lines truly exist – between intellectual history, history of philosophy, and philosophy, leaving me susceptible to what John Dunn aptly described as the "persistent tension between the threats of falsity in its history and incompetence in its philosophy."[33] But while methodological purists may regard my approach as insufficiently committed, I cannot easily separate out my philosophical engagement with Spinoza from my historical interest in his texts. While my own interests are primarily philosophical, and certainly not antiquarian, I believe that situating historical texts in their proper contexts – seeing them as dependent on, and arising out of, somewhat alien sets of concerns and belief-systems – expands our repository of philosophical resources and affords reflective distance from where we can better appreciate our own shibboleths and biases.[34] Sensitivity to history and historicity is indispensable to philosophy.

In developing a reading of Spinoza's political philosophy, I seek to preserve the strangeness of his perspective, which challenges certain contemporary sensibilities. And while I don't linger too much on how contemporary political philosophers can benefit from Spinoza – this is, after all, primarily an interpretative work – I hope that readers will find in my interpretation provocations to think Spinozistically about contemporary civic affairs.

When it comes to conceiving of the relationship between Spinoza's mature philosophical works – the *Ethics*, the *TTP*, and the *TP* – I am a lumper, not a splitter. Despite differences of style and emphasis, I see these works as fundamentally of a piece, each filling out a crucial part of Spinoza's normative program. Lumping is somewhat out of fashion. Intellectual history promotes splitting, not only because it provides the historian with endless opportunities for reconceptualization, but also because the capacity to descry differences between texts and figures is seen as a mark of subtlety and erudition.

Unsurprisingly, we find many splitters when it comes to understanding how Spinoza's two political treatises hang together. Étienne Balibar insists that "what is most striking are the points not of continuity but of contrast" between the two works, claiming that they "seem to belong to two entirely different worlds ... Both the logic of the theory that Spinoza advances [in the TP] and its political implications are significantly different from those of the earlier work."[35] Lewis Feuer reaches a similar assessment for almost diametrically opposed reasons – while Balibar thinks that Spinoza becomes more democratic in the later treatise, Feuer thinks he becomes less so (see Chapter 7). And, when justifying her approach to reading the earlier works in relative isolation from the later political treatise, Susan James raises some concerns about those

---

[33] Dunn 1968, p. 85.
[34] Skinner 1996, p. 15.
[35] Balibar 1998, p. 50.

who indiscriminately mine Spinoza's corpus to build a comprehensive interpretation: "Spinoza's texts are far from forming a seamless whole. Written for various audiences and diverse purposes, they operate on a number of levels and use different methods to win the agreement of their readers."[36]

These commentators are right, in a sense. There are indisputable differences between these two works. The TTP was published anonymously, for a particular audience – chiefly, liberal theologians – and can be reasonably understood as an intervention in a particular theologico-political dispute (see Chapter 6). By contrast, the TP, which was unfinished at the time of Spinoza's death in 1677, is a thoroughly philosophical work written for a philosophical audience. Given Spinoza's own principle of linguistic accommodation (see Section 5.2), we should expect to find variations between these texts. And we do. Rhetorically, these works do occupy different worlds.

However, *pace* Balibar, what is remarkable to me is how consistent the two works are when it comes to normative political theory. The TP, which reflects Spinoza's most considered political views, reproduces and recasts many of the core arguments of the TTP in more compact and consistent forms. Where there are deviations, they are typically clarificatory or elaborative. As I will show, this is true of both of the alleged points of distinction between the works that Balibar alludes to: the abandonment of the social contract in the TP and the shift in the declared purpose of the state from freedom to peace.[37] Because of the broad consistency, I do not hesitate to juxtapose texts from these two works – despite James's caution against this practice[38] – as there are observations and elucidations in one treatise that are absent from the other. Indeed, I would insist that, by and large, reading texts from the TTP alongside texts for the TP yields a more comprehensive understanding of Spinoza's positions.

Of course, this leaves me to answer why Spinoza wrote a second political treatise, if he didn't radically change his mind on matters of substance. My answer is that these works are concerned with distinct aspects of *ingenia* reform. The TTP seeks to protect the citizenry from ideological corruption by curbing the power of the clergy and limiting the scope of sovereign interest, while the TP aims to identify institutions that promote civic integration and collective rationality.[39] While there is a lot of overlap in the overall theoretical

---

[36] James 2012, p. 5.

[37] Balibar 1998, pp. 50–1.

[38] "The context in which a point is made alters its valency, so that it can be dangerous to uproot an argument from one text and plant it in another" (James 2012, p. 5).

[39] Consider for instance the fact that Spinoza does not repeat much of the analysis of religion in the TP. This is not evidence that he has disavowed this material. On the contrary, he omits this material precisely because "In the *Theological-Political Treatise* we showed fully enough what we think about Religion" (TP 8/46). Nevertheless, he supplements the discussion of the TTP with some new material, for which the TTP "wasn't the place to discuss" (TP 8/46).

framework, these two works focus on different aspects of the project of *ingenia* reform.

Ultimately, I hope to show not only that the two political treatises complement one another, but further that Spinoza's political writings and the *Ethics* are mutually supportive, collectively constituting a comprehensive vision of human empowerment and the methods by which this end is promoted. The *Ethics* in general, and the metaphysical psychology in particular, provides the theoretical foundations for many of the observations and arguments of the political treatises, and it illuminates the aims of these works. And the political works explicate some of the structural conditions for knowledge, power, and harmony that are essential to the liberative project, but which are only very incompletely sketched in the *Ethics*. From his earliest writings, Spinoza conceives of individual empowerment and perfection as bound up with collective uplift:

This, then, is the end I aim at: to acquire such a [perfect] nature, and to strive that many acquire it with me. That is, it is part of my happiness to take pains that many others may understand as I understand, so that their intellect and desire agree entirely with my intellect and desire. To do this it is necessary, first to understand as much of Nature as suffices for acquiring such a nature; next, to form a society of the kind that is desirable, so that as many as possible may attain it as easily and surely as possible (TdIE Section 14).

Spinoza never abandoned this goal of harmony and collective perfection. The political writings constitute his crowning analysis of how this is to be achieved.

1   Metaphysical Psychology and *Ingenia* Formation

> Philosophers conceive the affects by which we're torn as vices, which men
> fall into by their own fault. That's why they usually laugh at them, weep over
> them, censure them, or (if they want to seem particularly holy) curse them.
> They believe they perform a godly act and reach the pinnacle of wisdom when
> they've learned how to praise in many ways a human nature which doesn't
> exist anywhere, and how to bewail the way men really are. They conceive
> men not as they are, but as they want them to be. That's why for the most part
> they've written Satire instead of Ethics, and why they've never conceived a
> Politics which could be put to any practical application, but only one which
> would be thought a Fantasy, possible only in Utopia, or in the golden age of
> the Poets, where there'd be absolutely no need for it.
>   – Spinoza, *Political Treatise* 1/1.

Spinoza is a political realist. By this I mean that he endorses the following two
claims: (1) political theory aims to guide institution-design, legislation, and
other forms of political action; and (2) in order for political theory to guide
political action effectively, it must be grounded in an understanding of human
beings as they are *actually constituted*, not as they are conceived abstractly or
in some ideal condition. Because realism entails that psychology is prior, in the
order of analysis, to normative political theory, a full appreciation of the latter
requires an acquaintance with the former. I shall begin this study, then, with a
brief examination of some of the salient features of Spinoza's psychology that
inform his normative political theorizing.

This chapter will be divided into three sections. First (Section 1.1), I offer
an interpretation of Spinoza's account of the metaphysics of moral motivation.
I show that, on his elegant account, the way that one's essence is constituted
fixes what one desires, what one judges to be good, and, ultimately, what one
does. Here I introduce the concept of an *ingenium* (plural: *ingenia*), which, for
Spinoza, signifies the way in which one's essence is constituted – one's total
affective condition. Next, I consider how *ingenia* are formed, focusing particularly on social influences (Section 1.2). Initially and for the most part *ingenia*
are determined by features of one's environment over which one has no direct
control. The analysis in this section helps to show how a civic ethos or shared

ingenium can be formed and it reveals the extent to which one's striving is determined by one's social environment. This sets up the final section of this chapter, in which I argue that, on Spinoza's account, the state bears the primary responsibility for the affective make-up of its citizens (Section 1.3).

1.1   The Metaphysics of Motivation

Spinoza's philosophy is remarkably systematic. His political philosophy grows out of his ethics and psychology, and his ethics and psychology are rooted in his metaphysics. This systematicity can be seen in Spinoza's account of motivation, where his analysis of desire turns on his understanding of essences. For Spinoza, all singular things have essences. These essences – which, like everything else, must be conceived through and caused by God (1p25) – ground a thing's properties.[1] Unfortunately, Spinoza's account of the essences of singular things is somewhat confusing in a couple of respects. First, it is unclear whether they may be shared or if they must be particular – there are texts that seem to point in both directions. I will return to this later in the chapter. Second, Spinoza writes of a thing's "formal essence" [*formalis essentia*] as well as its "actual essence" [*actualis essentia*] without fully explaining how these two concepts relate. In terms of this second interpretative problem, I think we can offer a plausible gloss of this relationship that advances our understanding of Spinozistic motivation, while setting the stage for the analysis of the eternity of the mind that I will explore later (Chapter 8).

Formal essences are the essences of things insofar as they are contained in God's eternal attributes (2p8; 2p8c),[2] a form of existence that does not have a determinate duration (2p8c; 5p23d). Essences exist eternally in God's attributes as a kind of archetype or blueprint. One's actual essence is this blueprint insofar as it has been realized concretely in time, such that its bearer stands in dynamic causal relations with other determinate things. The actual essence of any singular thing is its striving, or *conatus*. The *conatus* doctrine states: "Each thing, as far as it can by its own power [*quantum in se est*], strives [*conatur*] to persevere in its being [*in suo esse*]" (3p6). In the subsequent proposition, we learn that this striving "is nothing but the actual essence of the thing" (3p7). The demonstration of the *conatus* doctrine reads:

For singular things are modes by which God's attributes are expressed in a certain and determinate way (by IP25C), that is (by IP34), things that express, in a certain and determinate way, God's power, by which God is and acts. And no thing has anything in itself by which it can be destroyed, *or* which takes its existence away (by P4). On

---

[1] For a compelling study that emphasizes the causal or explanatory role of essences in Spinoza's metaphysics, see Viljanen 2011. See also D. Garrett 2002 and Lin 2006a.

[2] See D. Garrett 2009, pp. 285–92. See also Section 8.1.

the contrary, it is opposed to everything which can take its existence away (by P5). Therefore, as far as it can, and it lies in itself [*quantum in se est*], it strives to persevere in its being, q.e.d. (3p6d).

Spinoza moves briskly here from a claim about what singular things *are* to a set of claims about what singular things, insofar as they are in themselves, *do*. This is understandable since for Spinoza what a thing *is* is inextricably linked to what it *does* – to exist is to exert causal power. For expository purposes it will be helpful to analyze these two features separately; but in fact the distinction is merely aspectual.[3]

Particular things (*res particulares*) are "modes by which God's attributes are expressed in a certain and determinate way" (1p25c). To say that a particular thing is certain and determinate is to say that it exists in time and can be affected or limited by other determinate things. The structure of particular things considered under the attribute of extension is most thoroughly explicated in the so-called Physical Digression between 2p13 and 2p14, where Spinoza characterizes "individual" in the following way:

When a number of bodies, whether of the same or of different size, are so constrained by other bodies that they lie upon one another, or if they so move, whether with the same degree or different degrees of speed, that they communicate their motions to each other in a certain fixed manner, we shall say that those bodies are united with one another and that they all together compose one body *or* [*sive*] individual, which is distinguished from the others by this union of bodies (II/99–II/100).

In the lemmas that follow this definition, Spinoza indicates that this account of individuals as collections of bodies that "communicate their motions to each other in a certain fixed manner" is an account of the nature (*natura*) or form (*forma*) of a thing, considered under the attribute of extension (see L4–L7 and demonstration, cf. 4p39d). Since Spinoza uses *natura* and *essentia* interchangeably (see e.g., 3p56d, 3p57d), the claim here is that the essence of an individual, considered under the attribute of extension, is its fixed ratio of motion and rest.[4] The essence of an individual considered structurally consists in a certain patterned relationship between its parts.[5]

---

[3] Michael LeBuffe points out that we seem to have two distinct candidates for what counts as the actual essence of a singular thing: a thing's causal power and its structural integrity (LeBuffe 2009, p. 206). While we can conceptually separate out the formal and the functional features of a thing, this distinction is, on my reading, purely notional. For analyses of the formal and functional striving that accord with my reading, see Viljanen 2011, pp. 74ff and D. Garrett 1994, p. 97.

[4] For a thorough treatment of Spinoza on individuation see D. Garrett 1994.

[5] Jonathan Bennett suggests that the level of abstraction here might have been deliberate, with "ratio of motion and rest" serving as "a placeholder for a detailed biological theory that still lay in the future" (Bennett 1984, p. 107).

The *conatus* doctrine tells us not what things are structurally, but what they (essentially) do. All things express God's essential power in a certain and determinate way, producing effects from their natures (1p36; 1p36d). To exist as a unified singular thing whose parts communicate a fixed ratio of motion and rest is to produce unified effects. This explains why Spinoza defines things not only structurally, but also functionally, as in 2p7: "if a number of individuals so concur in one action that together they are all the cause of one effect, I consider them all, to that extent, as one singular thing" (2d7).

3p4 and 3p5 begin to tell us more about the effects that are produced through a thing's essence alone. 3p4d states that essences posit their bearers (2D2). So, when we attend to the definition, or essence, of a thing alone, we find only what affirms its being and the properties or effects that follow therefrom. For this reason, "no thing can be destroyed except through an external cause" (3p4). Insofar as one is in oneself (*in se*) one tends to remain in oneself and to produce the effects that necessarily follow therefrom.

However, things that "actually" exist – i.e., exist determinately, in time – are not fully in themselves; they are impinged upon by external forces. 3p5 (as invoked in 3p6d) indicates how a thing's essential activity of self-positing is expressed insofar as it stands in causal relationships with things with contrary natures, natures that diminish or restrain one's own being (3p5; 4p30d). To the extent that Y's nature is contrary to X's, X's nature will posit X *and* oppose Y, for to posit X is to posit ~~X. As Valtteri Viljanen has stressed, this is not a merely logical form of exclusion: affirming one's own nature and opposing things of a contrary nature is just the way that particular things express God's power in the face of oppositional forces.[6]

The *conatus* doctrine is supposed to explain not only why we resist opposing forces, but also of why we strive to increase our power of acting (3p12ff.).[7] I think we can understand the inference from resisting oppositional forces to increasing one's power of acting by appealing again to the distinction between formal and actual essences. When we attend to the essences of things only insofar as they are contained in God's attributes – that is, insofar as they exist formally – we find that they straightway entail certain properties or effects of which they are adequate causes (3D1 and 3D2). However, when these essences are realized in time, they are subject to, and determined by, countervailing forces. Rather than simply producing effects from their natures – thereby "acting" in Spinoza's technical sense (3D2) – actually existing things have variable powers of acting (*potentia agendi*) that are constrained and affected by the essences of external things. If we understand striving to consist in positing

---

[6] Viljanen 2011, p. 101.
[7] This inference has given rise to a great deal of scholarly consternation. See Bennett 1984, Ch. 9; Carriero 2005; D. Garrett 2002; Viljanen 2011, Ch. 5; Della Rocca 2008a, Ch. 4.

one's essence and everything that follows from it as far as possible within a domain that includes contrary natures, then we can understand the striving to increase one's power of acting as a special case of opposing destructive forces: to increase one's power of acting is to diminish the power of those forces that prevent one from acting, or fully realizing one's essence, and everything that follows from it.[8] We thus have an essential tendency not only to resist opposing forces, but also to increase our power of acting.

We see from the preceding how the *conatus* doctrine grounds Spinoza's theory of motivation. But this doctrine only reveals a very general motive tendency; it does not tell us how human beings in concrete conditions will act. For a more precise account of motivation, we must turn to Spinoza's analysis of affection.

Affection, Desire, and the Constitution of Essences

Metaphysically speaking, human affections are ways in which the human essence, or striving, is constituted: "by an affection of the human essence we understand *any constitution of that essence*, whether it is innate [NS: or has come from outside]" (3 Appendix, *Definitions of the Affects*; II/190). Elsewhere, Spinoza identifies "affect" (*affectum*) with "the constitution of the body" (3p18d), affects being "affections (*affectiones*) of the body by which the body's power of acting is increased or diminished, aided or restrained, and at the same time, the ideas of these affections" (3d3). This view of affects or affections[9] as ways in which essences are constituted is also apparent in his definition of desire (*cupiditas*) as:

the very essence, *or* nature, of each [man] insofar as it is conceived to be determined, by *whatever constitution* [constitutione] *he has*, to do something (see P9S). Therefore, as each [man] is affected by external causes with this or that species of joy, sadness, love, hate, and so on, *that is, as his nature is constituted in one way or the other*, so his desires vary and the nature of one desire must differ from the nature of the other as much as the affects from which each arises differ from one another (3p56d – my emphasis).[10]

Affections are ways in which one's essence is constituted, and desire is one's essence, or striving, insofar as it is determined by these affections.

---

[8] I fully endorse Garrett's characterization of the *conatus* doctrine as the tendency to realize one's essence and all that follows from it (D. Garrett 2002). Cf. Viljanen 2011, p. 132.
[9] Spinoza is not always especially careful to distinguish "affects" from "affections." Sometimes he treats the two concepts interchangeably, but 3D3 suggests that they differ in a couple of ways. First, "affects" include the ideas of these affections, and so they may be understood as the mental correlates to one's physical affections. Second, "affects" are a mere subset of "affections," since affects involve changes in one's power of acting, but not all affections involve such changes (3 post. 1).
[10] A nearly identical definition of desire is offered in the "Definitions of the Affects" at the end of *Ethics* 3, with the term "constitution" replaced with "affection" [*affectio*] (3 DA; II/190).

Some clarification is in order here, though. For, how can desire be determined by affections, if desire is *itself*, along with joy (*laetitia*) and sadness (*tristitia*), one of the three primary affects, from which all other species of affects are derived (3p11s)? If desire is a "primary," non-derived, affect, in what sense can it be "determined" by species of joy and sadness (which I will here refer to as "emotions," so as to distinguish them from affects that are desires)? This is just one of several puzzles that haunts Spinoza's conception of desire.[11]

Rather than understanding the "determination" relationship between desire and emotions as one of causal priority, which would run contrary to the claim that desire is a primary affect, I propose that – as I've argued elsewhere[12] – we understand emotions and desire as distinct aspects of one and the same essential constitution. Emotions give specific orientation to one's striving, and this specific orientation just *is* desire.[13] So, while it might seem as though the formation of the emotion and the orientation of one's striving are successive moments in a process, in fact the orientation, the desire, is just the way in which forms of joy or sadness modify one's striving. While one can conceptually separate the emotion from the desire, emotions and particular desires are formed together since emotions give specific orientation to one's striving. Relying once again on the distinction between the structural and the functional aspects of our essence, we may say that emotions are the structural manifestation of a change to our essential constitution, while desire is the functional manifestation of this change.

A simple reflection on the general character of striving reveals why it would be a mistake to think of particular emotions and desires as distinct, successively formed modes. Since our striving, as our essence, must necessarily be expressed in all of our affections, it is not something that needs to be added to the affections. Rather there must be a conative side to any emotion, and this conative side is the desire.[14] Emotions inform and direct our striving by registering changes in our power of acting and representing sources of this change.[15]

---

[11] Another concerns the categorizing of desire as an affect, since, contrary to the very definition of an affect (see 3D3 and 3 General Definition of the Affects) desires do not themselves consist in changes in one's power of acting. For a thorough discussion of this point, see LeBuffe 2009.

[12] See J. Steinberg 2016.

[13] In his comments on an earlier draft, Andrew Youpa stressed that one's striving already has an inherent structure and orientation independently of emotions. I agree that there is an inherent structure to one's striving both in the sense that striving individuals have an intrinsic ratio or patterned relation of parts and in the sense that there is a general orientation or directionality to its activity, namely, the tendency to act in self-positing ways. My point here is that the *specific* orientation of one's striving – the particular objects that a thing pursues and the particular acts that a thing performs – will be fixed by its affections, whether these affections are innate or adventitious.

[14] Cf. D. Garrett 1996, p. 296.

[15] Viljanen 2011, pp. 137ff.

When we consider the registration of these changes in isolation from the way they modify one's overall striving, we conceive of them as emotions. When we conceive of these changes against the backdrop of our overall striving, that is, as specific orientations of this striving, we conceive of them as desires. For instance, if I am enjoying lazing around in bed in the morning, this joy does not generate a distinct mental state that is the desire to stay in bed. The desire to stay in bed just is the motivational side of the joy itself; it is the form that my striving takes when I am affected with this particular kind of joy.[16]

This conceptual distinction between emotion and desire may be illustrated the following way. Imagine a trumpet through which air is always blowing. The ceaseless force of wind represents one's striving. If a valve is then pressed down, this act may be conceived in isolation from the sound produced, as a kind of structural change to the instrument. That would be equivalent to the emotion. However, we can also conceive of the depression of the valve *in light of the wind* being forced through trumpet, as a change in the sound produced. That would be equivalent to the desire – the way in which one's striving is constituted. The changing of the note (i.e., desire) just is what the pressing of the valve (i.e., emotion) does to the wind that is being forced through it.

This account of desire as the conative aspect of emotions is quite remarkable. It implies that there is no gap whatsoever between one's affections and one's motivation. Not only does Spinoza deny that there is a free will (2p48–9), he denies altogether the ontological distinction between one's emotional experience and its motivational expression – there is no moment of conative "uptake" during which one might resist one's emotional response. If one's emotional experience is not expressed in one's striving, it can only be because a more powerful contrary emotional experience or desire has overwhelmed it. How we are affected directly fixes how we strive: there is no further explanatory work to be done.

At this point it will be useful to introduce a concept that I will rely on throughout the study, namely, the concept of an *ingenium*.[17] The Latin term *ingenium* (plural: *ingenia*) is difficult to translate, in part because it can mean

---

[16] Cf. LeBuffe 2009, p. 210.

[17] The concept of an *ingenium* goes back to classical Roman authors like Cicero and Livy. However, it took on a new prominence in sixteenth-century humanist Juan Luis Vives's study of mind, *de Anima et Vita*, a work with which we know Descartes was familiar and which might also have influenced Spinoza (see Noreña 1989, p. 110). Like Spinoza after him, Vives sought to understand the variety of *ingenia* and how they are formed (Book 2, 6–9) so that we can better understand how they might be *re*-formed. But whereas Vives relies heavily on a (Galenic) humoral physiological model to account for the varieties of temperament (Noreña 1989, p. 110), Spinoza thinks that one's *ingenium* is formed largely through one's experiences. Pierre-François Moreau's analysis of Spinoza's account of *ingenium* is the most comprehensive to date that I am aware of; he calls attention to the use of the concept in Renaissance humanist texts, including the work of Vives (Moreau 1994, pp. 396–7).

different things in different contexts. Spinoza himself uses the term in disparate ways, but in most contexts, he uses *ingenium* to refer to something like one's general cast of mind.[18] For instance, he construes one's striving to make others love and hate what one loves and hates as the striving to have others live according to one's *ingenium* (3p31c; cf. 5p4s; 4p70s). I propose that we understand *ingenium* as one's overall affective make-up – that is, the way in which one's essence or striving is constituted. This concept figures prominently in Spinoza's psychological analysis as a shorthand way of referring to one's overall mentality. As there is no single English term that adequately captures this idea, and because I rely on this concept throughout, I leave it untranslated, as all suitable English locutions ("general cast of mind," "total affective condition," "affective make-up") appear clumsy after repeated use. With this concept in place, we may say that on Spinoza's view, one's striving will simply be a reflection of one's *ingenium*.[19]

Affects and Judgments

Some may worry that the reading that I've offered – according to which emotions fix desires – fails to account for the motivating role of reason. Andrew Youpa, for instance, offers an interpretation of Spinoza's account of motivation, according to which rational moral judgments can play a distinct role in shaping desires. The main point of contestation here concerns how exactly we understand the relationship between affects – taken here to encompass emotion and desire[20] – and evaluative judgments. Spinoza claims in *Ethics* 3 that desires are prior to evaluative judgments: "we neither strive for, nor will, neither want, nor desire anything because we judge it to be good; on the contrary, we judge something to be good because we strive for it, will it, want it, and desire it" (3p9s).[21] However, the nature and scope of this priority is not clear from this passage alone.

Youpa does not take it to be a claim about evaluative judgments as such; rather, he thinks that 3p9s simply describes how most (unenlightened) people form evaluative judgments – namely, on the basis of their desires.[22] He

---

[18] Edwin Curley 2015 generally translates this sense of *ingenium* as "temperament" in the first volume of *The Collected Works of Spinoza*, and as "mentality" in the second volume. He includes a lengthy note on the difficulty of translating this term in the glossary of volume two (pp. 642–3).

[19] In the *Ethics*, *ingenium* generally refers to an individual's affective condition, while in the political treatises, he also writes of the *ingenia* of a people. For a fuller analysis of the concept, see Moreau 1994, pp. 395ff.

[20] Since emotions and desires are ultimately just two distinct ways of conceiving of the same modification of one's striving, we may revert back to the umbrella concept.

[21] Cf. Hobbes: "whatsoever is the object of any man's Appetite or Desire; that is it, which he for his part calleth *Good*: And the object of his Hate, and Aversion, *Evill*" (*Lev.* 1.6, p. 39).

[22] Youpa 2007, p. 383. See also Youpa 2010. Della Rocca seems to agree that such passages tell us only how people "typically" or "ordinarily" evaluate things (Della Rocca 2008a, p. 176).

suggests that elsewhere in the *Ethics* Spinoza reverses the priority claim, maintaining that rational agents are moved by tenacity (*animositas*) and nobility (*generositas*), desires that arise "solely from the dictate of reason" (*ex solo Rationis dictamine*) (cf. 4p61; 5p7). He reads 4p19 – "From the laws of his own nature, everyone necessarily wants, or is repelled by, what he judges to be good or evil" – as entailing that desire can arise from judging something to be good, rather than the other way around. To support his interpretation of 4p19, Youpa points to its role in 4p59 alt. dem.: "Any action is called evil insofar as it arises from the fact that we have been affected with Hate or with some evil affect (see P45C1). But no action, considered in itself, is good or evil (as we have shown in the Preface of this Part); instead, one and the same action is now good, now evil. *Therefore, to the same action which is now evil, or which arises from some evil affect, we can (by P19) be led by reason.*" Youpa takes this to be a reversal of the priority of 3p9s: rational evaluative judgments can, on their own, give rise to desire, rather than being rooted in an antecedent desire.

While Youpa's interpretation is resourceful and original, it forces one to interpolate a scope restriction on the account of motivation offered in 3p9s for which there is no direct textual evidence, and it saddles Spinoza with an inexplicably dualistic account of motivation. *Pace* Youpa, I think that we can render the remarks on motivation in *Ethics* 4 consistent with 3p9s once we get a better handle on the precise nature of the dependency relationship between affects and evaluative judgments. My proposal is that we understand Spinoza as claiming that evaluative judgments are *constituted by* desires, and that this constitution relation is strict. I will call this view – according to which, to form an evaluative judgment *just is* to be affected in one way or another and to represent some thing as the cause of this affect – the Constitution Thesis.[23] According to this interpretation, there is nothing more to evaluative judgments than the affects that constitute them.

One indication that Spinoza embraces something like the Constitution Thesis comes from 3p39s:

For we have shown above (in P9S) that we desire nothing because we judge it to be good, but on the contrary, we call it good because we desire it. Consequently, what we are averse to we call evil. So each one, *from his own affect*, judges, or evaluates, what is good and what is bad, what is better and what is worse, and finally, what is best and what is worst (my emphasis).

The claim that "each one, from his own affect [*ex suo affectu*] judges, or evaluates, what is good and what is bad" (3p39s) on its own is rather ambiguous. If we understand "from" here as indicating some temporal priority of affects,

---

[23] This label is owed in part to Youpa, who considers, and ultimately rejects, this possibility.

it would seem to support the distinction between judgments and affects. However, my proposal is that we understand "from" here as flagging explanatory priority: from the very fact that one has the affects one does, it follows that one judges such-and-such. The subsequent illustration – "So the greedy man judges an abundance of money best, and poverty worst" (ibid.) – suggests that there is such a close relationship between affects and judgments that one can, as it were, read off the judgment from the affect. The covariation of judgments and affects is suggested by a later invocation of the passage: "because each one judges from his own affect what is good and what is bad, what is better and what worse (see P39S) it follows that men can vary as much in judgment as in affect" (3p51s). The Constitution Thesis can explain the covariation of affects and judgments as well as the priority of the former over the latter in ways that alternative interpretations cannot.

We find even stronger support for the Constitution Thesis in 4p8, which states: "The knowledge [*cognitio*] of good and evil is nothing but an affect of joy or sadness, insofar as we are conscious of it" (4p8). The first thing to note here is that it is a claim about what constitutes a representation of good or evil; it is not a claim about knowledge in the sense of normative epistemology. The demonstration of 4p8 makes this clear, since the cognition in question is that of mere perception. And further support for this can be found in the demonstration of 4p64, which explicitly draws on 4p8 ("knowledge of evil [by P8] is sadness itself, insofar as we are conscious of it") in order to show that "*cognitio* of evil is an inadequate *cognitio*." 4p8 thus does not purport to be a claim about the *knowledge* of good and evil in our sense (which Spinoza calls *true* knowledge of good and evil), but about any representation of good and evil. Since to represent something *as* good or evil is just to evaluate it, this is an account of the nature of evaluative judgments. Drawing on the reduction of "good" and "evil" to joy or sadness in 3p39s, Spinoza argues here – albeit dubiously[24] – that a representation of good and evil is nothing other than the very affect of joy or sadness itself, and our idea of this affect.

In response to the evidence that Youpa cites against the Constitution Thesis, the first thing to note is that 4p19 itself does not in any way compel us to reverse the priority claim of 3p9s. The claim that "from the laws of his own

---

[24] The demonstration itself is muddy, at best. Leaving aside the last clause ("insofar as we are conscious of it"), which is treated separately (see J. Steinberg 2016), the main argument runs something like this: good and evil are nothing but changes in one's power of acting, which are themselves forms of joy and sadness. Consequently, good and evil are nothing but forms joy or sadness. So, to represent something as good or evil is just to represent it as the source of joy or sadness. This last step is highly questionable, since it assumes that we can substitute coextensive terms in an intensional context, *salva veritate*. Without trying to vindicate what looks like unsuccessful demonstration, I will simply note that Spinoza might not actually regard this as an intensional context. To see this, one must look at his multi-layered theory of representation (see J. Steinberg 2013).

nature, everyone necessarily wants, or is repelled by, what he judges to be good or evil" is perfectly consistent with the Constitution Thesis: there is a desire or aversion whenever there is a judgment of good or evil (and vice versa) because judgments of good or evil are *nothing but* the desires or aversions themselves.[25] Indeed, the demonstration relies directly on the Constitution Thesis, which, like 3p9s, posits the explanatory priority of affects. Here is the proof in full:

> Knowledge [*cognitio*] of good and evil (by P8) is itself an affect of joy or sadness, insofar as we are conscious of it. And therefore (by IIIP28), everyone necessarily wants what he judges to be good, and conversely, is repelled by what he judges to be evil. But this appetite is nothing but the very essence, *or* nature, of man (by the definition of appetite; see IIIP9s and Def. Aff. I). Therefore, everyone, from the laws of his own nature, necessarily, wants or is repelled by, and so on, q.e.d. (4p19d).

I want to focus on the first two steps of this argument. The first is just a restatement of 4p8, according to which evaluative judgments are nothing but emotions themselves. The second step appeals to 3p28, which shows that we desire (the furtherance of) whatever we represent as conducive to joy, that is, whatever we love. The argument, thus, can be encapsulated as follows: Because to judge something to be good is just to love it [from the Constitution Thesis and the definition of "love"], and because one necessarily desires whatever one loves [co-formation of emotions and desires above], one will necessarily desire what one judges to be good.

The apparent priority of evaluative judgments to desires is really just another case of the apparent priority of emotions to desires. And, as we saw above, there is no real priority here: emotions and desires are co-formed, because they are two expressions of the same mode. 4p19d does not contradict the Constitution Thesis; it depends upon it.

The reduction of evaluative judgments to affects is an expression of Spinoza's explanatory rationalism.[26] He seeks to answer the question "what is it in virtue of which one can (truly) be said to judge that x is better than y?" What is it in virtue of which, for instance, one's utterance, "I really should go to the gym right now," constitutes one's judgment rather than idle words or *half-beliefs*, in H.H. Price's sense?[27] Spinoza's answer is simple: evaluative judgments are constituted by one's affective-desiderative condition. In this way, Spinoza toes the judgment-internalist line by insisting that one who does not desire x more than y does not *really* judge x to be better than y.[28] But whereas this can smack

---

[25] Matthew Kisner makes this point effectively in Kisner 2010, pp. 101–2.
[26] See Bennett 1984, pp. 29ff; Della Rocca 2008a, b.
[27] Price 1964.
[28] See Davidson 1980, p. 27.

of stipulative or question-begging line-holding, Spinoza grounds it in the very metaphysics of moral judgment.[29]

In reducing evaluative judgments to affects, though, Spinoza is *not* endorsing moral expressivism. Affects, considered under the attribute of thought, are not raw feels; they are representational. Indeed, they are doubly representational: they directly represent a change in one's power of acting, while also representing some object associated with the production of this change (2A3). Put simply, affects are valenced (positive, negative) modes of thought that are directed at some particular object. Through their intentional content they orient one's striving. The point that I wish to stress here is that, for Spinoza, *perception, emotional response*, and *evaluative judgment* are not discrete acts of cognition. Rather, we perceive the world in a valenced, affective, and ultimately evaluative way.[30]

We can see from this analysis that Spinoza's contention that "everyone judges according to his own *ingenium* what is good" (4p70d) is in fact conceptually true: one's evaluative judgments are determined by, and encoded in, one's affective make-up, one's *ingenium*.[31] While our evaluative judgments are often to some degree informed by reason, it is a mistake to suppose that reason has some *additional* motivational force independent of its motivating power *qua* affect. This is the key point: moral motivation is fixed entirely by one's affective make-up, or *ingenium*.

---

[29] Admittedly, there are some ostensibly implausible implications of this view, for it would seem that even if evaluative judgments are rooted in desires, one could recognize that in a particular instance one's occurrent affects-desires reflect cognitive distortions (e.g., the tendency to hyperbolically discount the future), in which case one might sincerely judge that one ought to do something other than what one most desires now. For instance, I might recognize that my aversion to going to the gym is based on the saliency of the sound of the whipping wind, which leads me to exaggerate the badness of the walk to the gym and impairs my ability to represent the distal goods that follow physical exercise. And so I correct for this in my judgment, even if my affects don't follow suit. Spinoza's response would be to admit that the more time-neutral an evaluation is, the more rational it is (4p62). However, it is one thing to *have* a rational idea, and it is quite another thing to have one's judgment strongly informed by, or dominated, by this rational idea. If I am not very moved by rational considerations, it must be because my rational ideas only weakly inform my judgment, and that my irrational ideas, such as my intense appraisal "outside, BAD," exert a far greater influence on my judgment, even if I do not identify with these ideas, and even if they harmonize less well with other ideas and appetites that I might have.

[30] The error that some cognitivists commit is not in thinking that we make genuine evaluative judgments or that we act from them – we assuredly do. The mistake is to think that evaluative judgments are a thing apart from, and perhaps the ground of, our affects. For versions of this view, see Galen's report that the Stoics "do not take the soul's [evaluative] judgements themselves to be its passions, but identify these with the *results* of the [evaluative] judgements" (*HP*, §65K, p. 414); see also Descartes *Passions of the Soul* §2.56–57 in CSM. Nussbaum 2001, p. 19.

[31] Compare also the claim that "for each one governs everything from his affects [*unusquisque ex suo affectu omnia moderatu*]" (3p2s; cf. TTP 16, iii.192).

Let me conclude this section by highlighting some implications of Spinoza's account of moral motivation. While it has, reasonably enough, been accused of being too reductive, of failing to account for the different textures and dimensions to axiological judgment,[32] these limitations are to some degree offset by its virtues. It very neatly makes sense of the motivating power of evaluative judgments; it helps to explain why judgments of value are so stubbornly resistant to revision, even when the conscious idea is revised; and it accounts for the prevalent and profound dissonance between avowed and revealed judgments of value, since we are often confused about precisely what we are reporting. In other words, Spinoza can well account for the experience of feeling estranged from one's own implicit assessments. An important lesson, then, of Spinoza's theory of evaluative judgment might be that if we are to remedy this situation – if we are to reduce the dissonance between who we are and who we would like to be – we must come to grips with the perhaps uncomfortable fact that our affects, however passively or automatically formed, reveal our valuations, our values.[33]

1.2   *Ingenia* Formation

In order to see how *ingenia* are formed, and may be re-formed, we must examine in more depth Spinoza's conception of affects, which divide into two subclasses: actions and passions. The mind is composed of a great many ideas, some of which are adequate and follow from the nature of the mind alone, others of which are inadequate and reflect the influence of other things (see 3p3d; 2p11c). To the extent that one's ideas are adequate, one acts (in Spinoza's technical sense), since from them one produces effects that can be understood through one's nature or essence alone (3p1; 3D2). But to the extent that one's ideas are inadequate, one is passive, or bound to the passions (see 3p1c).

Among the things that I hope to show in this section are: (1) the passions, which initially and for the most part dominate our minds, orient one's striving in confused and unstable ways; (2) there is a profoundly interpersonal dimension to the formation of affects that is rooted in the imitation of affects; and (3) the imitation of affects can produce both harmonious and disharmonious effects. This analysis will reveal how dependent our *ingenia* are on social environments, preparing the way for the final section on the central role of the state in constituting human essences.

---

[32] Moses Mendelssohn objects to Spinoza's collapsing of feelings, emotions, and judgments, as it leaves unexplained "the difference between good and evil, desirable and undesirable, pleasure and pain" (Mendelssohn 2012, p. 96).

[33] Here I mean how one is actually constituted as a concrete, historical being.

Metaphysical Psychology and *Ingenia* Formation
25

Actions or Active Affects

Even granting that adequate ideas follow from the nature of the mind alone (3p3d; 2p11c) and that we act from adequate ideas, one might reasonably wonder what all this has to do with *affects* as ordinarily conceived? The answer is that adequate ideas have an affective aspect. This enables Spinoza at once to transcend the reason–emotion dichotomy and to account for the motivational power of reason without appealing to an untenable account of mind–body interaction (see 5 Preface): reason can limit the passions because reason is itself affective.

It is not immediately clear, though, why adequate ideas *must* be affective. The most explicit explanation for this comes in 3p58, where Spinoza introduces the notion of active affects: "Apart from the joy and desire which are passions, there are other affects of joy and desire which are related to us insofar as we act." The demonstration of why we rejoice when we have adequate ideas is quite compressed:

When the Mind conceives itself and its power of acting, it rejoices (by P53). But the Mind necessarily considers itself when it conceives a true, *or* adequate, idea (by IIP43). But the Mind conceives some adequate ideas (by IIP40S2). Therefore, it also rejoices insofar as it conceives adequate ideas, i.e. (by P1), insofar as it acts (3p58s).

One who understands something adequately also knows that she or he grasps it adequately (2p43s) and will experience joy, or an increase of power, upon reflecting on this knowledge (3p53).

One limitation of the account from 3p58 is that it suggests that joy arises only from the reflective (second-order) idea of one's activity, rather than showing that there is an affective dimension to the first-order adequate idea. This, however, isn't a problem, since, according to Spinoza, strange though it may seem, first- and second-order ideas are "one and the same thing" (2p21s). More importantly, though, Spinoza has the resources for defending the view that having first-order adequate ideas *is* joyful. To conceive of things adequately is to realize one's essence to a greater degree. And to realize one's essence to a greater degree is to exhibit a greater power of acting. The affective side of this transition to a greater state of power or perfection is joy. Put simply, to know is to increase one's power, and to increase one's power is to rejoice.

Active joys and desires are, presumably, the "innate" (*innata*) affections to which Spinoza refers in the definitions of the affects (3 Appendix, *Definitions of the Affects*; II.190). They direct one to act in ways that not only serve one's own power, but also "to aid other men and join them to him in friendship" (3p59s); so that the more rational we are, the more we act in ways that are empowering to ourselves and others.[34] But while these active affects inform our *ingenia* to

---

[34] See J. Steinberg "Spinoza on Bodies Politic and Civil Agreement" (J. Steinberg, forthcoming).

some degree and direct us toward individually and collectively empowering behavior, these affects are often not overtly expressed in one's striving, since, relative to the power or intensity of the passions (more in Sections 8.3–8.4), active affects are typically quite weak. Initially[35] and for the most part *ingenia* are dominated by the passions.

Passions or Passive Affects

Passions are ideas of the imagination, or instances of the first kind of knowledge or cognition ([*cognitio*]) (2p40s2). According to Spinoza, "the object of the idea constituting the human mind is the body" (2p13), and "whatever happens in the object of the idea constituting the human mind must be perceived in the human mind" (2p12). So, the mind will represent any affection of the body.[36] And when one's body is acted on, or affected, by an external body, one will have an idea that involves or implicates the nature of one's own body as well as the nature of the affecting body (2p16d). This idea will necessarily be inadequate and confused, since it does not distinctly represent its object or its *ideatum*. For instance, when taking a sip of the coffee in my mug, I do not represent the coffee distinctly, as it is in itself; rather, I represent the way that it affects and modifies my taste buds. And whenever an affection that was formed through sensation is elicited, one will represent as present the external things that are implicated in their formation (2p17). This is what the imagination does: it represents external bodies as present to us (2p17s).[37] If these ideas are unopposed, we will continue to posit the present existence of the thing, even when it is no longer present or no longer exists (2p17s).

The capacity for misrepresentation deepens through the association of ideas. Ideas are associated when they arise at the same time (2p18) or share a likeness (3p16).[38] Whole constellations of images and corresponding ideas are built on the basis of these associative relations. Through these associations, the boundaries between affections or images get blurred (2p40s1), and "composite images,"[39] or clusters of images that represent multiple objects, are formed.

---

[35] "[B]efore men can know the true principle of living and acquire a virtuous disposition, much of their life has passed, even if they have been well brought up" (TTP 16.7, iii.190).

[36] See J. Steinberg 2013.

[37] On this account, memory is a special case of non-veridical imaginings. While this characterization might sound odd, we must bear in mind that non-veridical imaginings are not necessarily errors, which occur only when the mind "is considered to lack an idea which excludes the existence of those things which it imagines to be present to it" (2p17s). A memory typically includes both the non-veridical imagining and the *stronger* idea that the thing that one is imagining is not in fact now occurring (see 3 DA xxxii exp.).

[38] Matthew Kisner points out that the demonstration of 3p16 is rather obscure, relying on a dubious attempt to ground resemblance in temporal associations (Kisner 2011, p. 182).

[39] This term comes from Michael Della Rocca (1996a, p. 60), who draws on Francis Haserot (1973, p. 52). Bennett describes this as a "piling up of images" (Bennett 1984, p. 39).

Spinoza's account of affection and association reveals not only how we form confused ideas, but also how deep and idiosyncratic this confusion can be. The contents of an idea of "horse," for instance, will vary between individuals according to their personal histories and happenstance encounters (2p18s; 2p40s1). So, while all rational people are alike, all confused individuals are confused in their own way.

As ideas of the imagination, passions direct our striving haphazardly. They keep us attached to ephemeral, unstable sources of happiness, leaving us ever vulnerable to fortune and superstition (Section 6.2). And since when we are guided by the imagination "any thing can be the accidental cause of joy, sadness, or desire" (3p15), we are driven to pursue things that are only good *per accidens*, or good by association (composite images), and to avoid those things that are evil *per accidens*. We judge objects in ways that are too coarse-grained to track the actual impact of these objects on our power of acting. This may take benign forms, as when listening to a record in a convivial environment leads one to overestimate the joy that the album will bring outside of that context. But it can also take more noxious forms, as when a bad experience with one person leads one to fear or hate a whole class of individuals with whom one confusedly associates this individual (3p46).

Passions also involve temporal distortions and modal confusions. Affective power varies according to the temporal proximity of the object represented (4p10). While active affects reflect the time-neutral assessment of reason (4p62),[40] passions reflect (sometimes hyperbolic) temporal discounting, such that we prefer lesser, but temporally more proximate, forms of pleasure to greater, but more distant, forms of joy. Through the imagination we also fail to grasp things as necessary, and instead often ascribe freedom to the proximate (transitive) causes of our affects. This only intensifies passions (5p5 and 5p5d; 3p49), such as the sadness that we feel when we perceive ourselves to have been injured. But when we adequately apprehend the necessity of things, we endure the effects of both good and bad fortune with equanimity (2p49s; 5p6).

So, to the extent that our *ingenia* are characterized by passions rather than active affects, we appraise things confusedly and unreliably. While passions can lead us into empowering relationships, they often do not. And even when they do, they do so only accidentally and without security. They leave us adrift, "like waves on the sea, driven by contrary winds, we toss about, not knowing our outcome and fate" (3p59s), striving on the basis of random personal encounters, idiosyncratic associations, and temporal and modal distortions.

A metaphor often invoked here is that of a waxen surface that bears two distinct, but now indistinguishable, imprints.

[40] See Lin 2006b.

Imitation, Emulation, and Conformity

While some of our passions reflect our individual histories, we are also social creatures and our *ingenia* will be profoundly shaped – for better or for worse – by our social environments. The central feature of our psychology that accounts for our sociability – as well as our unsociability, to some extent – and that militates against affective individualism is the imitation of affects. According to this doctrine, "if we imagine a thing like us, toward which we have had no affect, to be affected with some affect, we are thereby affected with a like affect" (3p27).[41] Because of the imitation of affects, others' judgments of us influence our self-judgment (3p30; see also 3p53c, 3p55c, and 3p55s). When we imagine that others approve of our actions, we feel self-esteem (*acquiescentia in se*) (3p30s; see also 3 DA xxv); when we imagine that others disapprove of our actions, we feel shame (*pudor*) (3p30s; 3 DA xxxi). To a degree, then, the imitation of affects encourages social conformity, as we seek to avoid shame and to garner esteem.

The desire for esteem plays an enormous role in our motivational economy. It enables us to act in a coordinated fashion even without the aid of reason or the iron fist of the law. This is a point that Spinoza's contemporary, and critic,[42] Lambert van Velthuysen made in moving from Hobbesian premises to more liberal, republican conclusions. Van Velthuysen claimed that the impulse for self-preservation (*conservatio sui*) naturally leads one to accommodate one's behavior to comport with mores or norms of decency of one's community. He maintained that there are many forms of behavior, such as public nudity, public urination, indecorous discourse, and so forth, which, while not contrary to natural law, are contrary to variable standards of decency,[43] and conformity to standards of decency is enjoined by the law of self-love: "Offenses against ... Decency are evil, because they are against the primary and fundamental Law of Self-preservation; for no Man can be ignorant, how much it is in his Interest not to be the object of any Man's Contempt; but those that are Impudent and Immodest, are universally scorn'd and contemn'd."[44] A sense of shame leads one to moderate one's behavior in conformity with the norms of a community.[45]

[41] I have analyzed the demonstration of this proposition in J. Steinberg 2013. Here, I will simply note that as I read him Spinoza models his analysis of the imitation of the affects on a mechanistic understanding of the transmission of motion: just as an inflamed body will, other things being equal, set ablaze an adjacent body of a like nature, and just as a billiard ball imparts its motion to another billiard ball when it strikes it, so too like beings will communicate affective states to one another.

[42] Van Velthuysen wrote a treatise that appeared in 1680, after Spinoza's death, entitled *Tractatus de Cultu Naturali, et Origine Moralitatis*, in which he announces his critical intentions on the title page: *Oppositus Tractatus Theologico-Politico* [sic] *et Operi Posthumo B.D.S.* See also Epistle 42 to Spinoza.

[43] *Dissertation*, p. 51.

[44] Ibid., p. 56.

[45] Ibid., pp. 55–6. For a more thorough discussion of this feature of Van Velthuysen's thought, see Blom 1995, pp. 120–8.

Spinoza arrives at a similar conclusion, while providing a deeper explanation of the mechanisms that govern affective regulation. For him, the reason why the impulse toward self-preservation results in sociability is that we imitate or internalize the attitudes of others.[46] While shame, as a form of sadness and a sign of impotence, is assuredly not a virtue, a "sense of shame" (*verecundiam*) (3 DA xxxi exp.) is preferable to its absence:

[L]ike pity, shame, though not a virtue, is still good insofar as it indicates, in the man who blushes with shame, a desire to live honorably. In the same way pain is said to be good insofar as it indicates that the injured part is not yet decayed. So though a man who is ashamed of some deed is really sad, he is still more perfect than one who is shameless, who has no desire to live honorably (4p58s).

Untouched by shame or concern for esteem, one would be relatively indifferent to many of the customs that help to unify a society. Consequently, "since men must sin, they ought rather to sin in that direction. If weak-minded men were all equally proud, ashamed of nothing, and afraid of nothing, how could they be united or restrained by any bonds?" (4p54s).[47]

The imitation of the affects fosters social cohesion by encouraging a desire for esteem and a sense of shame. It also tends toward the convergence of desires through emulation (*aemulatio*), which Spinoza defines as "a desire for a thing which is generated in us because we imagine that others have the same desire" (3 DA xxxiii; 3p27s). Shared affects and desires form a critical part of Spinoza's political psychology. In the *Political Treatise*, Spinoza claims that the very existence of the state depends on such common affects: "Men, we've said, are guided more by affect than by reason. So a multitude naturally agrees, and wishes to be led, as if by one mind, not because reason is guiding them, but because of some common affect. As we said in iii, 9, they have a common hope, or fear, or a common desire to avenge some harm" (TP 6/1). Alexandre Matheron leans heavily on this passage to explain the connection that Spinoza draws, but does not explain, between the formation of civil order (TP 6/1) and general indignation (TP 3/9).[48] On his reading, because of the imitation of affects, others' injuries and hatred induce a sympathetic sense of harm and resentment, leading to general indignation (3 DA xx) and desire for revenge; we are thus impelled to form a common power capable of satisfying this desire. Matheron embraces the possibility that the very affective tendency

[46] See below and Section 6.2 for the limitations of this tendency.
[47] Cf. KV II.xii. Descartes makes a similar observation in the *Passions of the Soul*: "it is not good to rid oneself entirely of these passions, as the Cynics used to do. For although the common people are very bad judges, yet because we cannot live without them and it is important for us to be an object of their esteem, we should often follow their opinions rather than our own regarding the outward appearance of our actions" (*Passions of the Soul*, 3.206 in CSM).
[48] Matheron 1990; see also Matheron 1969, pp. 307–30.

that imperils the state may also be the force that generates it: "it must be admitted that indignation produces the state in precisely the same way that it causes revolutions."[49]

Irrespective of whether or not this is a plausible interpretation, Matheron is certainly right to call attention to the role of common affects in maintaining civil life. For Spinoza, to be subject to a common law is to adopt a shared way of life (*ratio vivendi*), sustained by common affects, a popular ethos, or a shared *ingenium* (TP 3/3; TTP, Ch. 4) (more in Section 7.1).[50] And, as I will stress throughout, for a state to govern effectively, it must be mindful of this shared *ingenium*, or collective constitution, of the people.

Imitation, Ambition, and Disharmony

But while the imitation of affects can conduce to social unity, it can also undermine it.[51] Shared desires inspire competition when the sought-after object cannot be possessed equally by all parties. When others possess more of these goods, one feels envy (*invidia*) toward them and strives to dispossess them of this good (3p32). By enabling us to participate, to some degree, in the joy of others, the imitation of affects can also heighten one's sense of deprivation – or impotence – stoking further envy and resentment. Consequently, Spinoza concludes that "from the same property of human nature from which it follows that men are compassionate, it also follows that the same men are envious and ambitious" (3p32s). In the later propositions of *Ethics* 3, Spinoza extends the discussion of invidious comparisons beyond the literal possession of objects. One strives for pre-eminence over others, since one's sense of one's own virtue or power is strongly affected by one's apparent social standing: "everyone will have the greatest gladness from considering himself, when he considers something in himself which he denies concerning others" (3p55s; 3p53c; DA xxx–xxxii).

The account offered here is rather Hobbesian, or even Baconian, since Hobbes's account of honor and glory seems rooted in the writings of his one-time employer.[52] For Bacon, as for Spinoza, envy is the "the canker of

---

[49] My translation of the French, which reads: "Il faut admettre que l'indignation engendre l'Etat de la même façon, exactement, qu'elle cause le revolutions" (Matheron 1990, p. 264).

[50] Rebecca Kingston notes that on a classical account, constitution, or *politeia*, stood both for the structure of the state and the way of life of the people (Kingston 2008). The "public passions," including "the collective feeling of repentance and republican pride in self-renunciation during Savonarola's reign of influence in fifteenth-century Florence, the public fear felt by the French in the wake of 1789, the fear and anger felt by Americans in response to 9/11, and the public jubilation during the Orange Revolution in the Ukraine," were seen as playing a vital role in stabilizing or destabilizing the polity (Kingston 2008, p. 110).

[51] See Revault d'Allonnes 1999.

[52] It is telling that in his account of vainglory (in the *EL*, Ch. IX, p. 51), Hobbes makes use of the same Aesop fable that Bacon opens his essay on the same topic with ("Of Vainglory," in *MW*, p. 443).

honour."[53] The pursuit of honor and esteem entails the desire to prevail over others: "they that are glorious must needs be factious, for all bravery stands upon comparisons."[54] Hobbes develops this idea even further, defining glory itself in comparative terms: "Glory, or internal gloriation or triumph of the mind, is that passion which proceedeth from the imagination or conception of our own power, above the power of him that contendeth with us."[55] Because glory consists in "comparison and preeminence," Hobbes claims in *De Cive* that "glorying, like honour, is nothing if everybody has it."[56] This contributes to the jockeying for esteem, which breeds disputation and personal attacks: "Since all the heart's joy and pleasure lies in being able to compare oneself favourably with others and form a high opinion of oneself, a man cannot avoid sometimes showing hatred and contempt for each other, by laughter or words or a gesture or other sign."[57] So, while the pursuit of honor might seem to contribute to one's public spiritedness, Hobbes thinks that it is also apt to engender vainglorious men who are keen on dominating others and thwarting their success at all turns.[58]

For Spinoza, ambition for glory can breed civil discord if not properly regulated (see Section 6.2). His first gloss of ambition in the *Ethics* makes it appear harmless enough: "[the] striving to do something (and also to omit doing something) solely to please men ... especially when we strive so eagerly to please the people that we do or omit certain things to our own injury, or another's" (3p29s).[59] On this account, ambition is a kind of reckless pursuit of honor that Spinoza describes later as an "excessive desire for esteem" (3 DA xliv). Ambition is given an antisocial gloss just two propositions after the initial definition:

This striving to bring it about that everyone should approve his love and hate is really ambition [see 3p29s]. And so we see that each of us, by his nature, wants the others to live according to his *ingenium*; when all alike want this, they are alike an obstacle to one another, and when all wish to be praised, or loved, by all, they hate one another (3p31s; see also 5p4s).

---

[53] "Of Honour and Reputation," in *MW*, p. 445.
[54] Bacon "Of Vain-Glory," in *MW*, p. 443.
[55] *EL* IX, p. 50. For more on Hobbes and glory, see Gabriella Slomp 2000.
[56] *De Cive*, Ch. 1, §2, p. 24.
[57] Ibid., §5, pp. 26–7.
[58] Ibid., §2, p. 24.
[59] Because the imitation of affects is an ineliminable feature of human psychology, its offspring, ambition, or the desire for others to live according to one's own *ingenium*, cannot be entirely abolished: "Ambition is a desire by which all the affects are encouraged and strengthened (by P27 and P31); so this affect can hardly be overcome. For as long as a man is bound by any desire, he must at the same time be bound by this one. As Cicero says, *Every man is led by love of esteem, and the more so, the better he is. Even the philosophers who write books on how esteem is to be disdained put their names to these works*" (3 DA xliv exp.).

In Chapter 6, we will see just how destructive certain forms of ambition can be when they are encouraged by civic institutions (Section 6.2). The main point here is that, in part because of the imitation of affects, social environments play a profound role in shaping *ingenia*. Imitation can conduce to sociality; but it can also cut the other way. It is up to the state to design institutions that channel our mimetic tendency in socially salutary ways.

1.3   *Ex Uno Plures* and the State's Role in *Ingenia* Formation

We opened this chapter with the observation that Spinoza's theory of motivation is grounded in his account of essences, indicating that Spinoza is, in some sense, an essentialist. However, his essentialism differs from the pernicious forms that are rightly held in disrepute these days. Biological essentialism, for instance, attempts to account for apparent human differences in capabilities, personality traits, social roles, and so forth, by appealing to distinct natures.[60] Spinoza's metaphysical essentialism differs from such a view in at least two critical respects.

First, unlike biological essentialists who think that essences narrowly circumscribe the range of expression, Spinoza allows that essences can be constituted in radically different ways, resulting in significant diversity amongst bearers of a particular essence.[61] One's *ingenium* or constituted essence will reflect one's personal history, as shaped in part by one's social environment, allowing for variation both between peoples and individuals. Essences are plastic in the sense that the individuals who possess them may be constituted in a multitude of ways without losing this nature.

Second, he regards human nature as homogeneous.[62] Even in the TTP, where Spinoza is most disparaging toward the common people (e.g., TTP Preface 33–4, iii.12), he asserts that "with respect to intellect and virtue, [God] is equally well-disposed to all" (TTP 3.27, iii.50), claiming that Scripture confirms that "God has given the same intellect to all" (TTP 3.28, iii.50). If some are less intellectually capable than others, it is not by nature, but because superstition and prejudice "turn[s] men from rational beings into beasts"

---

[60] See Thomas Jefferson's appeal to "the real distinctions which nature has made" between the races in order to justify why blacks shouldn't be emancipated and integrated into the state (*Notes on the State of Virginia*, Query XIV). Kwame Anthony Appiah argues: "Not only, then, is race, for Jefferson, *a concept that is invoked to explain cultural and social phenomena*, it is also grounded in the physical and the psychological natures of the different races; it is, in other words, what we would call a *biological concept*" (Appiah 1996, p. 49).

[61] See Sharp 2011.

[62] Spinoza's commitment to this view is somewhat undercut by his remarks about the "natural" subordination of women in the concluding chapter of the TP. Here, he sounds like a rather execrable gender essentialist after all. I will turn to this problem in Section 7.4.

(TTP Preface 16, iii.8). And his insistence on a common human nature is even more pronounced in the TP (TP 7/27; TP 5/2).

Spinoza's appeal to a common human nature raises vexing questions about the metaphysics of essences. On the one hand, he is evidently committed to some sense of a common human essence. This is apparent not only in the politics, but also in the *Ethics*, where he relies on the notion of a shared human nature in order to make the case for why we should pursue the good of other humans (e.g., 4p35d; 4p36d; 4 Appendix IX). In various places, Spinoza seems to ground the possibility of finite things, or modes, sharing an essence in the fact that the existence of finite modes does not follow from their essence. Whereas the definition of substance "must involve necessary existence, and consequently its existence must be inferred from its definition alone" (1p8s2), in the case of finite things, like human beings, whose existence does not follow from their essence, we cannot know how many things of that nature exist, or even whether they exist, simply by attending to the definable essence:

[I]f twenty men exist in Nature (*to make the matter clearer, I assume that they exist at the same time, and that no others previously existed in Nature*), it will not be enough (i.e., *to give a reason why twenty men exist*) to show the cause of human nature in general ... whatever is of such a nature that there can be many individuals [of that nature] must, to exist, have an external cause (1p8s2 – emphasis in original).

Spinoza repeats this point about distinctly existing finite things sharing a nature in 1p17s: "a man is the cause of the existence of another man, but not of his essence, for the latter is an eternal truth. Hence, they *can agree entirely according to their essence. But in existing they must differ*" (my emphasis). A similar commitment to the shared natures of finite things is expressed in 2p10s, where, once again relying on the contrast between substance and finite things, he claims that while "there are not two substances of the same nature," there *do* exist "a number of men" of the same nature.

However, difficulties arise when we try to reconcile this with his definition of essence (2D2), which seems to indicate that essences and the things that instantiate those essences stand in a one-one relation (more on this in Section 8.1), and with his sharp critique of universals in 2p40s1, where he maintains that notions like "Man, Horse, Dog, and the like" arise only because of the confused representation of many particular things. This is no mere one-off passage. The view that universals are confused abstractions that do not exist outside of the mind pervades his early writings (TdIE, §99; KV 1.6; KV 2.16).[63]

A couple of promising avenues of reconciliation have been presented in the scholarly literature. One possibility, building on an interpretation advanced

---

[63] For a helpful survey of relevant passages, embedded within a novel and astute interpretation, see Hübner 2016. For more on Spinoza and abstraction in the early works, see Newlands 2015.

by Don Garrett, is that the formal essence that is shared by human beings is not a universal at all, but rather an infinite mode or "permanent and pervasive feature of an attribute of God."[64] This accords with Spinoza's analysis of the "essences of singular, changeable things" in the *Treatise on the Emendation of the Intellect*:

That essence is to be sought only from the fixed and eternal things, and at the same time from the laws inscribed in these things, as in their true codes, according to which all singular things come to be, and are ordered. Indeed these singular, changeable things depend so intimately, and (so to speak) essentially, on the fixed things that they can neither be nor be conceived without them. So although these fixed and eternal things are singular, nevertheless, because of their presence everywhere, and most extensive power, they will be to us like universals, or genera of the definitions of singular, changeable things, and the proximate causes of all things (*TdIE*, §101).

On this reading, distinct manifestations of a single formal essence are like multiple instantiations of a particular law of Nature. Another possibility comes from Karolina Hübner, who maintains that while only particulars and their essences have formal reality, we can nevertheless construct "well-founded," non-imaginary, general essences on the basis of shared or similar essential properties that hold between distinct individuals.[65] Leaving aside the finer details of these interpretations, the point that I want to stress is that these interpretations allow that: (1) Spinoza was indeed committed to the view that in some well-grounded sense humans share a common nature; and, (2) this view need not be seen as incompatible with his denial of the formal reality of universals. So when Spinoza refers to the shared nature of humans in the politics, he is not falling back on a confused abstraction.

Spinoza's views on the homogeneity of human nature and the plasticity of human individuals are reminiscent of view expressed by one of the Ciompi laborers in Machiavelli's *The History of Florence*:

And do not be frightened by their antiquity of blood which they shame us with, for all men, since they had one and the same beginning, are equally ancient; by nature they are all made in one way. Strip us all naked; you will see us all alike; dress us then in their clothes and they in ours; without doubt we shall seem noble and they ignoble, for only poverty and riches make us unequal (III.13, 1160).[66]

---

[64] D. Garrett 2009, p. 291. It should be noted here that Garrett himself does not commit himself to the view that formal essences may be shared, but his interpretation might help to account for shared essences.

[65] See Hübner 2014, 2016. Like Hübner, Matthew Kisner also conceives of the "agreement" that holds between human beings as rooted in shared essential properties (Kisner 2011, p. 137).

[66] Cited in Del Lucchese 2009, p. 126.

Machiavelli's account of the relationship between civic institutions and moral character suggests that he shares with the orator in this quote the view that differences between humans are largely determined by socio-political forces. It is good laws, not good blood, that make men virtuous: "men never do anything good except by necessity ... Hence it is said that hunger and poverty make men industrious, and the laws make them good."[67] And where people are vicious, bad governance is to blame.[68]

Spinoza, too, assigns primary responsibility for civic virtue and vice to the state. In the TTP, he rejects Jewish exceptionalism vis-à-vis both virtue[69] and vice. When considering "why the Hebrews so often failed to obey the law," he writes:

Perhaps someone will say that this happened because the people were stiff-necked. But this is childish. Why was this nature more stiff-necked than others? Was it by nature? Surely nature creates individuals, not nations, individuals who are distinguished into nations only by differences of *language, laws, and accepted customs* [*morum receptorum*]. Only the latter two factors, laws and customs, can lead a nation to have its particular *ingenium*, its particular character, and its particular prejudices. So if we have to grant that the Hebrews were more stiff-necked than other mortals, we must ascribe that either to a vice of the laws or to a vice of the accepted customs (TTP 17.93, iii.217).

Whenever we see differences in *ingenia*, in levels of obedience, disobedience, virtue or vice, the explanation should be sought in social and political practices, customs, laws and institutions. This point is made even more forcefully in the *Political Treatise*, where he writes: "everyone shares a common nature – we're just deceived by power and refinement [*potentia et cultu*]" (TP 7/27). Elsewhere in the work, he makes it clear that it is the power of the state in particular that bears the burden for moral variation:

[T]hat state is best where men pass their lives harmoniously and where the laws are kept without violation. For certainly we should impute rebellions, wars, and contempt for, or violation of, the laws not so much to the wickedness of the subjects as to the corruption of the state. Men aren't born civil; they become civil. Moreover, the natural affects of men are the same everywhere. If wickedness is more prevalent in one Commonwealth than in another, and more sins are committed there, this surely comes from the fact that the [more wicked] Commonwealth hasn't provided adequately for harmony, hasn't set up its laws wisely enough, and so, hasn't obtained the absolute Right of a Commonwealth (TP 5/2–5/3).

---

[67] *Discourses* 1.3, in *CWO* 1, p. 202; cf. *Discourses* 1.1, in *CWO* 1, p. 193.
[68] "The sins of the People are caused by their princes" (*Discourses*, 3.29, in *CWO* 1, p. 493). His explanation for it is that subjects mimic the behavior of their princes. He cites Lorenzo de' Medici here: "What the ruler does, afterward the many do, because on the ruler all eyes are turned" (*CWO* 1, p. 494).
[69] TTP 3.16, iii.47.

Because humans share a nature, the constitution of which significantly reflects social influences, the state is tasked with structuring the social environment in ways that promote virtue and harmony.

The claim that the state bears ultimate responsibility for the virtue or the vice of its citizens will strike many as overblown and indefensible. Perhaps it is. But I think a few observations can help us to appreciate what is most compelling about it. The first thing worth highlighting is that Spinoza seeks deep social explanations for human variation. We are, in a Heideggerian sense, thrown into the world, constituted in large part by forces that are, at least initially, beyond our control. And, as I suggested in Section 1.1, evaluative revision is particularly difficult on a Spinozistic scheme, since it requires not just changing one's judgment at a reflective level, but altering the relative power of automatically formed, and often stubborn, affects (see Chapter 8). This underscores the significance of Spinoza's insistence in the preface to *Ethics* 5 that, contrary to what Descartes and the Stoics say, we cannot have absolute control over the passions (5 Preface, II/277–8). And passages from the political works that emphasize structural explanations reveal how little faith Spinoza had in the widespread efficacy of individualist strategies for self-control in the absence of broader civic reform.[70]

But even if we agree that moral variation should be understood primarily in terms of structural forces, one might wonder why he accords so much significance to the state in particular, since people's characters would seem to be determined to a great extent by other factors, including: geography and climate; access to resources and trade routes; economic relations; institutions of civil society; geopolitical history, including the history of conquest and colonization; and so forth. It seems exceedingly and implausibly reductive for Spinoza to assign so much significance to civic structures, while ignoring these other features.

A few points can be made in Spinoza's defense. First, civic institutions have the power to influence myriad aspects of civil society. It is for good reason, then, that Althusser sees Spinoza as a source of inspiration for his concept of the ideological state apparatuses, through which the state subtly promulgates an ideology that informs the "imaginary constitution of the subject."[71]

Moreover, even while he stresses the role of the state, Spinoza could, and I think would, admit that there are many other factors that account for variation in human behavior, most of which may be subsumed under the rubric of *fortuna* (TTP, Ch. 3). Not only do we initially find ourselves oriented in the world by factors that lie beyond our control, the effects of fortune persist throughout our lives. Unsurprisingly, then, Spinoza suggests that, no matter

[70] See Huebner 2009.
[71] See Balibar 2014, pp. xvi–ii.

how effectively a state is governed, it is ineluctably subject to the influence of factors beyond its control.

Still, as we will see in more detail later (Chapter 5), a vigilant state can do much to mitigate the effects of fortune. The state has the capacity to accommodate its institutions and laws to suit the *ingenia* of its people, and, to some extent, reorient their striving. This accounts for the unique power of the state: it is dynamic and can thus respond to and redirect behavior in light of these other sources of influence. To cite one example that is central to Spinoza's analysis in the TTP, it is to Moses' great credit that he adapts his leadership to suit the Hebrew people, whose *ingenia* reflected the scarring effects of slavery and oppression. He was able to effectively govern the people because he was a realist, acknowledging the actual constitutions of his subjects and adopting prudent means of guiding them in light of these conditions. Because it has the power to adapt and respond to other forces, the state bears a unique responsibility for the ethical welfare of their subjects.

Conclusion

We see from all of this how Spinoza's plastic essentialism supports his analysis of the role of the state in shaping one's *ingenia*. The *plasticity* of plastic essentialism enables civil institutions to play a prominent role in shaping and reconstituting human natures. But the *essentialism* of plastic essentialism places constraints on the method and scope of remediation. Humans aren't amorphous lumps of matter to be shaped however one pleases.[72] Essences can be effectively reconstituted only by understanding and accommodating actual *ingenia*. Only by taking people as they are, not as we would like them to be, can we hope to influence them in intended ways. I will examine Spinoza's political method in more detail in Chapter 5. First, though, I will make the case that the aim of politics is continuous with the aim of ethics and that the fundamental purpose of the state is to reconstitute essences or reorient *ingenia* so as to promote liberty, power, and hope (Chapters 2–4).

---

[72] Because Spinoza did not think that humanity is "infinitely malleable" he cannot be said to have "provided the intellectual inspiration for attempts by totalitarian states to eradicate every trace of individuality from their subjects" (James Schmidt, *What is Enlightenment?*, p. 1, cited in Israel 2011, p. 1).

2   Eliminating Juridical Constraints and Naturalizing Right

> Resolve to serve no more, and you are at once freed. I do not ask that you place hands upon the tyrant to topple him over, but simply that you support him no longer; then you will behold him, like a great Colossus whose pedestal has been pulled away, fall of his own weight and break in pieces.
>   – Étienne de la Boétie, *The Discourse of Voluntary Servitude*[1]

In his monumental work *The Machiavellian Moment*, John Pocock traces the history of what he calls the "Machiavellian paradigm" of civic humanism from its inception in fifteenth-century Florence to its adoption and transfiguration in early-modern England and the United States. Glaringly omitted from this narrative are the works of Dutch republicans, most notably the De la Court brothers and Spinoza.[2] In a follow-up piece entitled "Spinoza and Harrington: An Exercise in Comparison," Pocock aims to justify the exclusion of these Dutch republicans from this paradigm, offering several reasons for sharply distinguishing Spinoza's political theory from James Harrington's Machiavellian approach.[3] He maintains that Spinoza and Harrington differ in their views on method, on the relationship between economic institutions and civic commitment, and on the composition of state power. But the primary reason why Pocock thinks that Spinoza's *Political Treatise* and Harrington's *The Commonwealth of Oceania* belong to entirely different genres is that they adopt distinct linguistic and conceptual frameworks. Harrington adopts the language of humanism, with its emphasis on virtue and civic engagement, while "Spinoza was a philosopher of natural jurisprudence,"[4] constructing a

---

[1] De la Boétie 1942.
[2] E. H. Kossmann has observed that: "the greatest republic of the seventeenth and part of the eighteenth century, the Dutch Republic, is totally absent [from Pocock's narrative]. Did it not belong to the Atlantic tradition, did it not conform to the Machiavellian paradigm?" (Kossmann 2000, p. 173). Several studies since the publication of *The Machiavellian Moment* have reconsidered the place of Dutch republican thought within this "common" heritage. See, for instance, Haitsma Mulier 1980; van Gelderen 1992, 1993; Scott 2002; and Velema 2002. For a helpful overview of some of the scholarly literature on Dutch Republicanism, see Prokhovnik 2004.
[3] Pocock 1987.
[4] Pocock 1987, p. 448.

system of justice for the "adjudication of conflicting claims based in natural right."[5]

Pocock is not alone in thinking that Spinoza's political thought belongs to the jurisprudential tradition. Many Spinoza scholars – including Gail Belaief, Errol Harris, Matthew Kisner, and Jon Miller[6] – have maintained that, in some sense, Spinoza is a natural lawyer. And it is easy to see why: "*ius*," "*lex*," and "*imperium*" are vital terms in Spinoza's political lexicon. However, I shall argue that Spinoza is no friend to the juridical tradition. He adopts a juridical vocabulary in part to drain it of its normative significance.[7] By replacing normative conceptions of right and law with naturalistic proxies he eliminates juridical side-constraints on action, paving the way for an interest-based, psychologically attuned analysis of civic organization.

2.1   The Carneadean Challenge to Natural Law

Given the great diversity among so-called natural law texts – dating from the ancient world to the present day – it would be foolhardy to suggest that there is a single, monolithic natural law tradition. Among early-modern natural law theorists, one finds schisms that seem less like sibling rivalries and more like tribal feuds.[8] Rather than positing the existence of a single tradition, I simply want to suggest that, however exactly one wishes to carve up the territory, there is a common commitment among the sundry late-medieval and early-modern juridical texts to a natural normative order that implies the existence of obligations that are not rooted in mere perceived utility.

The great foil for many early modern theorists of natural justice, from Hugo Grotius on, was Carneades.[9] Carneades was the head of the Academy

---

[5] Pocock 1987, p. 439; see also p. 442.

[6] Belaief 1971; Harris 1984; Kisner 2011; and Miller 2003; 2012.

[7] Others who have suggested that we read Spinoza primarily as a critic of natural law theory include Curley 1991 and Wernham 1958. One might also cite, somewhat more equivocally, Balibar 1998; A. Garrett 2003; and Rutherford 2010. For references to anti-juridical readings of Spinoza in French scholarship, see Balibar 1989, p. 115n9.

[8] Compare Santos Campos 2012, p. 5ff.

[9] There is some dispute concerning whether Grotius was the first natural lawyer to seriously engage the skeptic. Richard Tuck sees Grotius's engagement with Carneadean skepticism as "unprecedented," as part of what separates his "modern" account of natural law from medieval predecessors (Tuck 1987). See also Darwall 2012, p. 296–325. Terence Irwin, however, suggests that Grotius is following other natural lawyers like Gabriel Vásquez (Irwin 2009, p. 94). One thing that is clear is that after Grotius, Carneades functioned as a skeptical adversary of natural law theory, one whose interest-based alternative to universal justice was taken up as a legitimate challenge. See, for instance, Leibniz's letter to Hermann Conring (A II-I (2), 47; 124 – cited in Lærke 2010. Provided that we are talking about post-Grotian natural law, it is not much of an exaggeration to conclude, as John Christian Laursen does, that "Natural law thinking was spawned by the response of men like Grotius and Hobbes to Carneades's critique of natural justice" (Laursen 1992, p. 59).

in Athens in the mid-second century BCE. He served as the skeptical dele-
gate when the representatives of the great Hellenistic schools brought their
philosophy to Rome in 155 BCE. In Rome, Carneades reputedly impressed
audiences by defending natural justice on one day, only to persuasively refute
his own position the following day.[10] While Carneades' primary aim seems
to have been to show that one could present equally compelling arguments
for and against natural justice, he was portrayed in the early-modern period
as the great critic of natural justice. Grotius presents the Carneadean in the
following way:

Laws (says he) were instituted by Men for the sake of Interest; and hence it is that
they are different, not only in different Countries, according to the Diversity of their
Manners, but often in the same Country, according to the Times. As to that which is
called NATURAL RIGHT, it is a mere Chimera. Nature prompts all Men, and in general all Animals, to seek their own particular Advantage" (*De Iure Belli*, prolegomena
Section 5).

On the Carneadean view, interest (*utilitas*) alone is the measure of right (*ius*) or
law (*lex*); because utility varies according to place and time, we must renounce
any universal conception of rights or law. The Carneadean utility-based account
of right and law was thus seen as fundamentally destructive to the very notion
of natural law since it denied both the universality and the obligatoriness of
noninterest-based rules of reason. In the late Renaissance and Modern periods,
this view came to be associated with skeptics like Michel de Montaigne and
Pierre Charron, the latter of whom wrote:

If we must say what the laws thereof are, and how many they are, we are much hin-
dered. The ensign and mark of a natural law is the universality of approbation: for that
which Nature shall have truly ordained for us, we with a common consent shall follow
without doubting; and not only every nature, but every particular person. Now there is
not any thing in the world which is not denied and contradicted, not by one nation, but
by diverse: and there is not any thing so strange and unnatural in the opinion of diverse,
which is not approved and authorized in many places by common use.[11]

Machiavelli, too, was sometimes regarded as a Carneadean opponent of natural law since he denies the existence of real, noninterest-based, obligations,

---

[10] Reported by Lactantius in Divine Institutes 5.14.3–5 and Epitome 50.8, in *HP*, p. 442.
[11] Charron 1971, pp. 261–2. Barbeyrac, in his annotations of Pufendorf, *The Law of Nature and
Nations*, cites Charron, alone with Montaigne and Bayle, as a modern proponent of the skeptical
(Carneadean) challenge to natural law (Barbeyrac, *An Historical and Critical Account of the Sci-
ence of Morality*, pp. 5–8, appended to Samuel Pufendorf, *The Law of Nature and Nations*, ed.
Jean Barbeyrac, trans. Basil Kennet [London, 1749]; cited in Tuck 1987, p. 108).

maintaining, like Carneades (Lactantius, *Divine Institutes*, 5.16), that it is the height of foolishness to sacrifice life and limb for justice.[12]

Despite his adoption of a juridical vocabulary, I think that Spinoza belongs to this group of critics of natural law since he too denies the existence of a conception of justice independent of (perceived) utility. In order to appreciate the force of his critique, we must consider some of the models of natural law that function as its target.

2.2   Natural Law and Obligation

Natural Law and the Divine Will

Standard accounts of natural law maintain that there are universal moral principles, apprehensible by right reason, that bind intelligent agents independently of considerations of utility. Built into the very notion of law is the idea of obligation, which separates laws from mere instructive precepts. As Aquinas puts it, "'law' [*lex*] is derived from 'binding' [*ligando*], because it obliges us to act."[13] One question that all defenders of natural justice had to answer was whence the binding force of real, or non-prudential, obligations derived.

The answer was, of course, the will of God. However, this left open ample space for dispute regarding God's precise relationship to the right-making and binding features of law. Disputes between intellectualists and voluntarists centered on the relationship between God's will and the right-making, or moral, features of law. But even intellectualists, who maintained that the right-making features of law do not depend on God's will, conceded that such dictates would not have the binding status of law had they not been issued by the will of a commander. For instance, Aquinas claims that right reason (*recta ratio*) grasps *ius*, but that *ius* only becomes *lex* when it is promulgated by an authorized legislator.[14] The binding force of natural law depends on imposition from a higher authority.

Francisco Suárez, who lent clarity and moderation to the intellectualist position, distinguished between the indicative and prescriptive components of natural law, claiming that precepts of right reason alone cannot have prescriptive force unless they are imposed by a superior.[15] And even more extreme intellectualists, like Gregory of Rimini and Gabriel Biel, whom Suárez takes to deny the prescriptive function of law,[16] actually stopped short of saying that

---

[12] See Irwin 2009, pp. 93–4. Grotius and Hobbes turn the tables on such a view, casting the utility-calculator as the fool.
[13] *Summa Theologiae* IaIIae 90 in Aquinas 2008, p. 77.
[14] See for instance *Summa Theologiae* IIaIIae57a1 in Aquinas 2008, p. 160.
[15] *De Legibus*, II.6.4, Trans. Alfred J. Freddoso. Available at: www3.nd.edu/~afreddos/courses/301/suarezdelegii6.htm.
[16] *De Legibus*, II.6.3.

the dictates of right reason would be *obligatory* independently of God, holding only that sin and moral evil (*peccatum*) are determined independently of God's will.[17] For medieval natural lawyers, laws, as binding rules, require a legislator (civil or divine).

Grotius on Natural Justice

Grotius was a pivotal figure in the development of modern natural law theory. He sought to save the notions of morality and rights from skeptical and anti-nomian challenges by advancing a somewhat attenuated conception of right, grounded in principles that "no member of any sect of philosophers, when embarking upon a discussion of the ends [of good and evil], has ever failed to lay down."[18] For instance, he lays down as the first law of nature in *De Iure Praedae Commentarius* – a posthumously published work that was written in 1604 to legitimate the Dutch East India Company's seizure of a Portuguese ship – the right to self-defense, based on the impulse for self-preservation that is acknowledged by Stoics, Epicureans, Peripatetics, and even Academic Skeptics.[19]

Grotius sought to demonstrate that from innocuous and widely held principles one could arrive at a theory of natural law that does not reduce to mere self-interest. In his influential account of natural law from 1625, *The Rights of War and Peace* (*De Jure Belli ac Pacis*), he directly confronts the skeptical, interest-based views that he attributes to Carneades and Horace.[20] On his account, we have a strong natural impulse for sociability (*DJB, Prolegomena*, Section 6) and are endowed with a faculty of reason for discerning what is required for peace and society: "whatsoever is contrary to such a Judgment is likewise understood to be contrary to Natural Right, that is, the Laws of our Nature."[21] He concludes that it is not utility that is the "Mother of Natural Law," but "human Nature itself," from which the impulse for both self-preservation and sociability spring.[22] While rules of prudence and natural law will converge in most instances, the point here is that even if one's interest could be best advanced through the violation of the natural law, one would still remain bound by the law.

By maintaining that human nature alone supplies the warrant for natural law, Grotius is doing something rather new – or perhaps something rather old, since

---

[17] See Haakonssen 1998, p. 1322.
[18] Grotius *CLPB*, II.10–11.
[19] *CLPB* II.10–11.
[20] *DJB*, Prolegomena, Section 17.
[21] *DJB*, Prolegomena, Section 9; cf. *DJB*, I.10.
[22] *DJB*, Prolegomena, Section 17.

it is reminiscent of the older Stoic approach to natural law.[23] This is apparent in the famous *etiam si* passage, where he insists we would still be bound by natural law "though we should even grant, what without the greatest Wickedness cannot be granted, that there is no God, or that he takes no Care of human Affairs."[24] Unlike divine positive law, which makes things obligatory or unlawful solely on the basis of God's command, Grotius claims that, according to natural law, things are "in themselves, or in their own Nature, Obligatory and Unlawful."[25] It is worth underscoring here that, even though Grotius is quick to assure the reader that these laws should be seen as proceeding from a divine legislator, they have the force of law independently of a legislator.[26] This distinguishes Grotius's position even from medieval intellectualists.

Human nature – which is the ground of our instinct for self-preservation, our impulse for sociability, and our capacity to recognize what is essential to each – anchors Grotius's concept of right (*ius*) as a moral power. This conception of right, the second of his famous three fold analysis of right, can be taken to signify "a moral Quality annexed to the Person, enabling him to have, or do, something justly."[27] Rights in this subjective sense have "moral effects," most notably the effect of placing others under obligations.[28] Grotius conceives of this sense of right as a kind of alienable possession, a *dominium*, which enables him to advance a contract-based account of sovereign authority, from which a scheme of civil rights, laws, and duties follows.[29] And, as with natural law, the duties incurred through the transference of alienable rights are binding irrespective of utility or profit.[30] By insisting on genuine moral rights and obligations that are rooted in human nature, Grotius seeks to find a way between the Scylla of skepticism and the Charybdis of overblown theological accounts of natural law.

Hobbes on Natural Justice

Hobbes's theory of natural law – marked by some significant shifts between his early political treatises (*Elements of Law* [1640], *De Cive* [1642]) and his masterwork, *Leviathan* (1651) – admits of a range of interpretations. I will canvass some of the more plausible readings, noting some of the

---

[23] For the influence of Stoicism on Grotius's thought, see Blom and Winkel 2004. As Jon Miller points out, even for the Stoics, natural laws were genuinely obligatory: "the 'ought' here is not merely prudential" (Miller 2012, p. 204).

[24] *DJB*, Prolegomena, Section 11.

[25] *DJB*, 1.10.2, 153.

[26] *DJB*, Prolegomena, Sections 12–13; *DJB*, 1.10.1–2, 151.

[27] *DJB*, I.i.4.

[28] *DJB*, Prolegomena, Section 21. Cf. *DJB*, 3.24, 223.

[29] See *DJB*, 1.10.4, 154.

[30] *DJB*, Prolegomena, Sections 19–21.

complications associated with each.[31] At the core of Hobbes's political philosophy is a vexed conception of right. In *Leviathan*, right appears, at first blush, to be devoid of moral force. He defines Right of Nature as "the Liberty each man hath, to use his own power, as he will himself, for the preservation of his own Nature; and consequently, of doing any thing, which in his own Judgement, and Reason, he shall conceive to be the aptest means thereunto" (*Leviathan*, Ch. 14, 91). This accords with his claim in *De Cive* that "Nature has given each man a right to all things" (*De Cive*, 1.10). Indeed, in this earlier work, Hobbes seems to directly embrace the Carneadean skeptical position concerning natural justice: "in the state of nature the Measure of *right* [*ius*] is Interest [*Utilitas*]" (*De Cive*, 1.10).

His position, however, is rather more complicated than these passages might suggest. In *De Cive*, he maintains that in order to act by right, one's liberty must be exercised "in *accordance with right reason*" (1.7, p. 27). In other words, one's right extends only to actions that are in conformity with natural law, which is itself defined as "certain *right reason*" concerning "what should be done or not done for the longest possible preservation of life and limb" (*De Cive* 2.1, 33). And he claims that one acts without right when one performs wantonly cruel and destructive acts.[32] This belies the view of the state of nature as a moral vacuum. But if there are juridical limits on what we may do, what grounds them?

One possibility is that Hobbes follows Grotius in claiming that there is a moral order inscribed in nature itself. Nature supplies obligations irrespective of a legislative will. In some passages Hobbes does suggest that natural law could be seen as intrinsically binding, even in the absence of a legislator.[33] But the preponderance of the textual evidence indicates that Hobbes rejects the view that there could be binding natural laws without a legislator. He refers to laws of nature as "precepts"[34] or "theorems"[35] that tend toward peace, indicating that such "laws" are prudential rules of thumb that play a merely *advisory* role, but do not, on their own, restrain one's liberty or right.[36] And he explicitly endorses the more familiar, anti-Grotian view that precepts are obligatory only if they are imposed by some authorized will: "These dictates of Reason, men used to call by the name of Lawes, but improperly: for they are but Conclusions, or Theoremes concerning what conduceth to the

---

[31] For a sharp analysis of the many ways in which Hobbes's account of natural law might be understood, see Gauthier 2001.

[32] See *De Cive* 3.27, p. 54; *De Cive* 1.10n, p. 29. A. G. Wernham puts it, on Hobbes's view, man's natural right "covers only some of his actions" (Wernham 1958, p. 14)

[33] Natural law obligates *in foro interno* "always and everywhere" (*De Cive*, 3.27, 54; cf. *Lev.*, Ch. 15, p. 110).

[34] *Lev.*, Ch. 14, p. 91.

[35] *Lev.*, Ch. 15, p. 111; exchange with Bramhall, *EW* IV, pp. 284–5.

[36] *De Cive*, Ch. III, p. 56.

conservation and defence of themselves; whereas *Law, properly is the word of him, that by right hath command over others*" (*Leviathan*, Ch. 15, 111 – my emphasis).

Perhaps, then, we should read Hobbes as a more traditional natural lawyer, for whom the obligatoriness of natural law derives from the will of God (*Leviathan*, Ch. 15, 111). This interpretation is encouraged by his claim that "properly speaking, the natural laws are not laws, in so far as they proceed from nature. But in so far as the same laws have been legislated by God in the holy scriptures ... they are very properly called by the name of laws" (*De Cive*, Ch. III, 56). However, there is reason to doubt that Hobbes thinks that the "precepts" of natural law are binding on account of their divine origin. Even leaving aside questions about the sincerity of Hobbes's religious beliefs,[37] it would seem that God's will cannot underwrite the obligatoriness of natural laws, since insofar as we know these precepts only through reason, we do not conceive of them *as* commands of God; it is only through the independent support of Scripture, i.e., revealed law, that we could see these laws as divine commands.[38] And because "Scripture is made law only by the authority of the commonwealth," in the state of nature, where there is no ultimate interpreter or arbiter of Scripture, such precepts cannot constitute laws and so cannot be obligatory.

This last point – concerning the role of the civil authority for determining divine law – suggests another way in which these theorems might become laws, namely, through the will of a civil sovereign. On this account, one's obligation to the natural law is parasitic on one's obligation to the civil authority. Hobbes's account of how we incur an obligation to the sovereign is familiar, if somewhat conceptually muddy. The commonwealth is created by a covenant, through which one transfers one's natural right to defend oneself to a common sovereign body, which is authorized to determine how peace and order are to be secured. The content of one's obligations is made determinate through the legislative will of the sovereign, whose will is an expression of the wills of subjects.[39] In the act of covenanting, one lays down one's right and takes on obligations (*Leviathan*, Ch. 14, 92). By presenting the civil legislator as the source of the obligatory force of law, Hobbes would seem to provide an alternative to the traditional medieval view, which roots obligation in God's will, and to Grotius, who grounds it in nature as such.

However, this secular voluntarist account of the origin of obligation is unstable. For instance, it would appear that, in claiming that there is "no Obligation on any man, which ariseth not from some Act of his own" (*Leviathan*, Ch. 21, 150),

---

[37] See e.g., Curley 1992.
[38] *De Cive*, Ch. IV. This point is stressed in Gauthier 2001, p. 272.
[39] *De Cive*, Ch. XIV, p. 165.

Hobbes is arguing that moral effects are introduced into the world *ex nihilo*. This leaves Hobbes susceptible to Cudworth's critique of voluntarism:

> [I]f we well consider it, we shall find that even in positive commands themselves, mere will doth not make the thing commanded just or obligatory, or beget and create any obligation to obedience ... [morality cannot be] the product of the mere will if the commander ... For if they were obliged before, then this law would be in vain, and to no purpose; and if they were not before obliged, then they could not be obliged by any positive law, because they were not previously bound to obey such a person's commands.[40]

An obligation to follow the orders of a commander cannot originate from an act of one's own will unless one is antecedently obligated to keep one's will or honor one's promises. Put somewhat differently, if one's natural right did not put others under obligations in the state of nature, why would its transference to another bind one's own will? Making obligation a consequence of agreement would be putting the cart before the horse.

In light of the instability of the secular voluntarist account of obligation, it is tempting to take another tack altogether, namely to deny that Hobbes allows for noninterest-based obligations. David Gauthier, for instance, proposes that we read Hobbes in this way, since it provides "the most coherent reading of his overall position."[41] However, there is a deep problem with this interpretation, which is that if Hobbes is simply a long-term prudentialist, the very apparatus of the contract is otiose in the production of obligation. This would render normatively irrelevant the distinction that Hobbes insists upon between commonwealths formed by institution and those formed by acquisition.[42] His account of the irreversible transfer of right would have to be read as a massive smokescreen, a subterfuge designed to engender in his readers a false sense of non-prudential obligation. Hobbes's abiding commitment to the significance of the contract in generating obligation suggests that, minimally, the onus is on the defender of such an esoteric reading to justify it. Hobbes himself certainly did not wish to be perceived as embracing a purely prudentialist position. And, as we shall see, in the eyes of many late seventeenth century political theorists, it was Spinoza, not Hobbes, who represented the modern Carneadean opponent of natural justice.

2.3   Spinoza's Critique of Natural Law

Spinoza's Critique of Divine Legislator

Spinoza upends the very basis of most accounts of natural law. On his view, there is only one substance – God, or Nature (*Deus, sive Natura*) – and

---

[40] Concerning Eternal and Immutable Morality, 1.ii.3, in Raphael 1991, pp. 108–9.
[41] Gauthier 2001, p. 283.
[42] E.g., *Lev.*, Ch. 17, p. 121; cf. *Lev.*, Ch. 20.

everything that exists is causally determined by God's nature and the laws that follow therefrom. These laws of nature are themselves necessary and unchanging, as there is no "nature" outside of Nature that could alter or oppose them. To conceive of God as a legislator is to conceive of a being with a will distinct from its intellect, a creative power distinct from its nature, which is to ascribe to God a power outside of his power, or a nature outside of Nature – this is patently at odds with monism (see *Ethics* 1p33d; 1p33s2). Spinoza makes this point forcefully in the *Ethics* – as, for instance, in 2p3s, where he inveighs against those who "confuse God's power with the human power or right of kings" – and in his critique of miracles in the TTP, where he lambastes those who "imagine powers numerically distinct from one another, the power of God and the power of natural things ... But what do they understand by these two powers, and by God and nature? They don't know, of course, except that they imagine God's power as the rule of a certain Royal majesty" (TTP 6.2, iii.81).[43] The idea of an anthropomorphic, legislative God is, according to Spinoza, the very fount of the prejudices that hamper the understanding: "All the prejudices I here undertake to expose depend on this one: that men commonly suppose that all natural things act, as men do, on account of an end; indeed, they maintain as certain that God himself directs all things to some certain end, for they say that God has made all things for man, and man that he might worship God" (*E*1 Appendix, II/78; cf. 2p3s).

Rather than conceiving of laws as violable edicts of a superior potentate, Spinoza defines law (*lex*) "taken without qualification" to be "that according to which each individual, or all or some members of the same species, act in one and the same fixed and determinate way" (TTP 4.1, iii.57). At their core, laws are those features of Nature that determine things to act in fixed and determinate ways. God does not issue laws through an act of will; rather, the laws of nature are just the operations of Nature itself (TP 2/4). Anything one does, one does in accordance with these very laws, which are "eternal and can't be violated" (TP 2/18), and which "[prohibit] nothing except what no one can do" (TP 2/18; cf. TP 2/8; TP 2/4).

The notion of a natural law as a violable command of God can, then, only be a product of misapprehension and confusion. This point is vividly illustrated in Spinoza's interpretation of the parable of Adam. Spinoza thinks that it is absurd to suppose that Adam actually acted contrary to God's command not to eat the forbidden fruit, because nothing can act contrary to God's laws. Rather, on Spinoza's quite idiosyncratic rendering, what was "revealed" to Adam was a necessary law that Adam, in his ignorance, construes as a command. Spinoza

---

[43] See also Ep. 56, where Spinoza claims that those who "consider God's will to be different from his essence and from his intellect ... fall from one absurdity to another" (Ep. 56; cf. 1p33d; 1p33s2; 2p49s; 2p3s).

expressed these same ideas roughly a half-decade before the publication of the TTP in a letter to Willem van Blyenbergh in which he sought to disabuse his interlocutor both of the view that evil is a positive feature of the world and of the conception of God as a divine legislator:

For because [will] does not differ from [God's] intellect, it is as impossible for something to happen contrary to his will as it would be for something to happen contrary to his intellect. I.e., what would happen contrary to his will must be of such a nature that it conflicts with his intellect, like a square circle ... in this way the prophets wrote a whole parable. First, because god had revealed the means to salvation and destruction, and was the cause of them, they represented him as a king and lawgiver. The means, which are nothing but causes, they called laws and wrote in the manner of laws. *Salvation and destruction, which are nothing but effects which follow from the means, they represented as reward and punishment.* They have ordered all their words more according to this parable than according to the truth. Throughout they have represented god as a man, now angry, now merciful, now longing for the future, now seized by jealousy and suspicion, indeed even deceived by the devil ... *The prohibition to Adam, then, consisted only in this: god revealed to Adam that eating of that tree caused death, just as he also reveals to us through the natural intellect that poison is deadly to us.* (Ep. 19, 5 January, 1665 – my emphasis)

God's "decrees" are nothing but the necessary, inviolable laws of Nature.

By exposing the absurdity of the conception of God as a divine legislator who issues violable commands, Spinoza defangs natural law, rejecting one of its central premises, namely that God has a will distinct from his intellect,[44] and even ruling out the kind of double order of nature assumed by Grotius. Susan James captures well-striking theological implications of Spinoza's account:

By entirely extinguishing any conception of God as a legislator who imposes commands on human beings, Spinoza not only abandons the assumptions of moderate Calvinism, but simultaneously undercuts the theological outlooks of a number of other denominations as well. In a sequence of concentrated arguments, he reshapes the framework of natural law within which Christian commentators had traditionally positioned the moral laws imposed by God. Divine laws, he argues, are either necessary and eternal, so that they cannot be disobeyed, or else they are made by human beings. God does not issue commands, and our salvation or blessedness cannot therefore depend on obeying them. (*Spinoza on Philosophy, Religion, and Politics*, 84)

While James expresses Spinoza's position quite well here, I think that she somewhat undersells his subversiveness: by denying that God issues binding but violable laws, Spinoza does not so much "reshape" natural law as destroy it.

---

[44] Intellectualists are particularly confused, since "they seem to place something outside God, which does not depend on God, to which God attends, as a model, in what he does, and at which he aims, as at a certain goal" (1p33s2).

Spinoza's Critique of Natural Right

In a well-known letter to his friend Jarig Jelles, Spinoza sets his views apart from Hobbes's: "As far as Politics is concerned, the difference you ask about, between Hobbes and me, is this: I always preserve natural Right unimpaired [*ego naturale jus semper sartum tectum conservo*] and I maintain that in each State the Supreme Magistrate has no more right over its subjects than it has greater power over them" (Ep. 50). This is no trivial difference. By explicitly embracing the view that one's right extends as far and only as far as one's power, Spinoza rejects the view that right is an alienable moral title, which supports both Grotian and Hobbesian conceptions of authority and civil obligation. The argument for the co-extensiveness of right and power is advanced at the outset of Chapter 16 of the TTP:

> For it's certain that nature, considered absolutely, has the supreme right to do everything it can, i.e., that the right of nature extends as far as its power does. For the power of nature is the power of God itself, and he has the supreme right over all things. But the universal power of the whole of nature is nothing but the power of all individuals together. From this it follows that each individual has a supreme right to do everything it can, or that right of each thing extends as far as its determinate power does (TTP 16.3, iii.189).[45]

Roughly the same argument – divested of the apparent fallacy of division and supplemented by a better account of the relationship between God and singular things[46] – appears in the TP (2/2–2/4), and may be reconstructed in the following way:

P1 Everything that a singular thing does, it does from God's power (TP 2/2).
P2 Everything done from God's power is done by right (TP 2/3).
∴. Therefore, everything that a singular thing does, it does by right (TP 2/4).

Not all of his readers would accept the premises on which the conclusion rests. Spinoza's political allies, the Arminians, who believed in an absolutely free will, might have balked at the first premise on the grounds that God's omniscience does not entail total causal efficacy. Ironically, though, Spinoza's political opponents, orthodox Calvinists, would have embraced it. As for P2, while it is hard to imagine any of Spinoza's contemporaries denying the premise outright, there would have been plenty of room for dispute over its meaning. Spinoza's position would have been most closely aligned with voluntarists

---

[45] Cf. TP 2/3, TTP 4/49.
[46] The claim in the TTP version that "the universal power of the whole of nature is nothing but the power of all individual things together" would only apply to *Natura Naturata*, not *Natura Naturans* – or substance as conceived through itself, considered as a free cause (1p29s) – which is causally and conceptually prior to the collective power of modes or singular things.

who deny that there is any moral constraint on the exercise of God's power (1p33s2): to say that "everything done from God's power is done by right" is just to say that there is no normative restriction on what God may do, no standard of right *other* than God's power. What is peculiar about Spinoza's position, though, is that he does not intend to provide a positive account of right in terms of power. Rather, his aim is thoroughly critical: there is no independent standard of justice from which we may declare an action just or unjust, legitimate or illegitimate.[47] For this reason, it is somewhat misleading when scholars ascribe to Spinoza the view that "might makes right."[48] This is an instance of Spinoza adopting conventional language – in this case, the language of right – only to purge it of its conventional significance.[49]

Spinoza's skepticism about moral rights leads him also to reject the account of obligation found in Hobbes. Whereas Hobbes suggests that we incur binding obligations through the transference of right, Spinoza baldly asserts that "a contract can have no force [*vim*] except by reason of its utility [*utilitatis*]. If the utility is taken away, the contract is taken away with it, and remains null and void" (TTP 16.20, iii.192; cf. TP 2/12). In the TP, he puts this in the language of right, arguing that any time one breaks a pledge because of the perceived advantage of doing so, one does so by right (TP 2/12). By treating natural right as coextensive with power, Spinoza denies the alienability of right, and consequently rejects the very division between nature and artifice on which Hobbes's account of obligation depends. Instead, Spinoza embraces the Carneadean position: there is no right or duty distinct from desire or perceived utility.

Spinoza's denial of real (non-prudential) obligations relies on his theory of moral motivation (Section 1.1) and reflects his psychological realism. In the TTP, he asserts that "it's a universal law of human nature that no one neglects to pursue what he judges to be good, unless he hopes for a greater good, or fears a greater harm ... Between two goods, each person chooses the one he judges to be greater, between two evils, the one which seems to him lesser" (TTP 16, iii.191–2). This claim is grounded in the Constitution Thesis, according to which judgments of goodness are nothing but affects or desires (Section 1.1). Since judgments of relative goodness necessarily covary with strength of desire, and since strength of desire dictates choice, one will necessarily choose that which one perceives to be best.[50] To demand that people act contrary to

[47] See Curley 1996, p. 322. See also Strauss 1965, p. 233.
[48] Barbone and Rice 2000, p. 19; cf. McShea 1968, p. 139; Balibar 1998, p. 59.
[49] Spinoza's philosophy is full of examples of terms deployed in startlingly new ways. This vexed critics like Christoph Wittich who objected that Spinoza has "given himself the right to remove the words from their usual and received signification in order to arbitrarily give them a different one that nobody has agreed to" (Wittich, *Anti-Spinoza sive Examen Ethices Benedicti de Spinoza et commentaries de Deo*, Amsterdam: Joannem Wolters 1690, 17; cited in Lærke 2014).
[50] J. Steinberg 2018a.

perceived utility is to demand the impossible. And, of course, it is absurd to suppose that anything impossible could be obligatory. The argument here is relatively straightforward:

P1 It is an immutable law of nature that one will act on the basis of perceived utility, thereby choosing the perceived greater of two goods or perceived lesser of two evils (see TTP 16, 198; iii.192).

P2 No obligation can contravene an immutable law of nature.

∴   There can be no obligation to act contrary to perceived utility.

Interestingly enough, Hobbes seems to embrace each the premises of this argument.[51] Indeed, in a single passage in *De Cive* in which he explains why we cannot covenant not to resist the penalty of death Hobbes puts forth *the entire argument*: "an obligation not to resist is an obligation to choose what will seem the greater of two present evils. For certain death is a greater evil than fighting. But it is impossible not to choose the lesser of two evils. Hence by such an agreement we would be obligated to the impossible, and that is contrary to the nature of agreements."[52] In *Leviathan* he repeats the point that agreements that contravene psychological laws are invalid; consequently "a Covenant not to defend my selfe from force, by force, is always voyd" (*Leviathan*, 98).[53]

But while Hobbes seems at some points to accept the preceding argument, he does not fully pursue its implications. To do so would be to concede that one cannot alienate one's right to judge what conduces to one's welfare, since this is psychologically impossible. This would undermine the very foundation on which Hobbes's account of obligation is built. In this respect, Hobbes is a less consistent realist than Spinoza.[54]

By strictly adhering to naturalism, Spinoza not only repudiates natural rights as Grotian moral faculties, he also renders incoherent any noninterest-based account of obligation. Spinoza was thus not so much offering a radical version of natural law theory as hacking away at the stilts on which this juridical nonsense stood. Pocock couldn't be more wrong, then, when he concludes that "the nature of politics to Spinoza rested on artifice and alienation."[55]

---

[51] He explicitly embraces the first premise: "all men, by a *necessity of nature*, choose that which to them appears to be the less evil" (*De Cive*, II.18, p. 40; compare *De Cive*, VI.4, p. 78). And the second premise expresses an extremely minimal version of realism that Hobbes would surely accept.

[52] *De Cive*, II.18, p. 40. Hobbes surely means the *perceived* lesser of two evils here.

[53] Howard Warrender makes the case that among the "validating conditions" of obligation to which Hobbes is committed is that one "must be capable of having a sufficient motive to perform the action which it prescribes" (Warrender 2000, p. 23; cf. pp. 87–97).

[54] For more on this, see Matheron 1986.

[55] Pocock 1987, p. 448.

2.4   Critical Reception of Spinoza's Account of Natural Law

The destructive implications of Spinoza's analysis of natural law were not lost on his early critics. Spinoza's TTP was attacked not only by anti-Socinian crusaders like Johannes Musaeus, who thought that Spinoza undermined natural law by reducing justice to utility,[56] but also by relatively liberal Hobbists like Lambert van Velthuysen and Samuel von Pufendorf, who regarded Spinoza's treatment of law and right as a perversion or a farce. In a letter to Spinoza in which he roundly condemns the TTP, Velthuysen cites the rejection of a divine author of law as one of the most scandalous features of the work:

[Spinoza] maintains that, for those who consider things correctly, there's no place for [divine] precepts and commands, but that human ignorance has brought in terms of this kind ... So precepts and decrees exist for the same reason, and agree in this: men's lack of sophistication and ignorance have moved God to provide that there should be some use for them among those who cannot form more perfect thoughts about God, and who require wretched aids of this kind to excite in them zeal for virtue and hatred of vices (Ep. 42).

Because divine commandments are treated as mere props for the ignorant, Velthuysen concludes that there is no real sense of natural justice in Spinoza's system.

Samuel Pufendorf registers a similar complaint. Like Velthuysen, Pufendorf was generally sympathetic to Hobbes's approach to natural law. What he found in Spinoza's account in the TTP was not someone who advanced a Hobbesian account of law, but one who sought to obliterate the very concepts of natural law and right. As he puts it, "just as it is speaking improperly to use the term law of nature when you mean that according to which each thing acts in a certain and determinate way, so it is improper when the power and way of acting found in beings not endowed with reason is called by the name of right. For properly we speak of a right to act only in connection with beings who act according to the guidance of reason."[57] And genuine rights must have "moral effects," putting others under obligations: "it must be recognized that not every natural faculty to do something is properly a right, but only that which concerns some moral effect ... it is absurd to try to designate as a right that faculty which all other men have an equal right to prevent one from exercising."[58] According to Pufendorf, it is Spinoza, not Hobbes, who assails the moral conceptions of right and law.[59]

---

[56] *Spinosismus*, p. 82 ff., as cited in Israel 2010b, p. 91.
[57] Samuel Pufendorf, *The Law of Nature and of Nation* (*De Jure Natura et Gentium Libri Octo*, 2 vols., Volume 2: *Translation*, C. H. Oldfather and W. A. Oldfather Oxford, Clarendon Press, 1934, 2.2.3 (3.4.4), cited with altered translation in Curley 1995.
[58] *DJN* III.v.3, 391.
[59] See Curley 1995.

Leibniz and his early professor Jakob Thomasius, too, regarded Spinoza's views as more "pestilential" than Hobbes's. Thomasius reserved particular scorn for Spinoza, composing an entire refutation of the TTP: *Adversus Anonymum, de Libertate Philosophandi*. And Mogens Lærke has shown that while Leibniz evidently regarded Spinoza's TTP as deeply influenced by Hobbes,[60] he treated the two thinkers differently.[61] While Leibniz strongly opposed Hobbes's political philosophy, he nevertheless saw it is as worthy of engagement, finding within it salvageable – if overblown – insights.[62] By contrast, he viewed Spinoza's political philosophy as irredeemably confused on account of its unstinting naturalism. While Hobbes's conception of natural law was at least compatible with the notion of a divine legislator, Spinoza's was not.[63]

The early reception of Spinoza's TTP lends further support to what we have already shown, namely, that Spinoza is doing something quite unlike what others who adopted juridical vocabularies were doing.[64] Even those who were sympathetic to Hobbes saw Spinoza as dismantling the normative framework from which rights and real obligations could spring.

2.5   Naturalizing Authority and Obligation

Before concluding that Spinoza decisively broke with the juridical tradition, we must confront some apparently countervailing evidence. In both of his political treatises, Spinoza claims that because, in the state, one has ceded one's right to one's sovereign, one is bound to new standard of justice. This gives the impression that, like Hobbes, Spinoza decouples right and power and introduces violable laws and real obligations, forsaking his radical naturalism.

There are differences between Spinoza's accounts of the origin of the commonwealth in his two treatises.[65] In the earlier *TTP*, Spinoza sounds rather Hobbesian. Because the state of nature is a state of misery,[66] men are compelled to join forces:

[T]o live, not only securely, but very well, men had to agree in having one purpose. So they brought it about that they would have collectively the natural right

[60] See Leibniz's 1670 letter to Thomasius (A II-12, 106), analyzed in Curley 1990a.
[61] Lærke 2010.
[62] See Lærke 2010, pp. 121–5.
[63] Lærke 2010, p. 125.
[64] The critical response to Spinoza's work by contemporaneous natural lawyers, gives one reason to question Jon Miller's assertion that the reception of Spinoza leaves us at an "impasse" on the question of whether or not Spinoza is rightly regarded as a natural lawyer (Miller 2012, p. 202).
[65] There is considerable scholarly debate concerning whether this marks a substantive or a merely rhetorical difference. For an overview of the dispute, see Barbone and Rice 2000, pp. 20–4.
[66] It is worth noting, however, that Spinoza does not construe the state of nature as a *bellum omnium contra omnes*, but as a state of insufficiency and helplessness. And in the TP, Spinoza even goes so far as to accept the Aristotelian characterization of man as a social animal (TP 2/15).

each one had to all things. It would no longer be determined according to the force and appetite of each one, but according to the power and will of everyone together. Nevertheless, they would have tried this in vain if they wanted to follow only what appetite urges. For according to the laws of appetite each person is drawn in a different direction. So they had to make a very firm resolution and contract [*pacisci*] to direct everything only according to the dictate of reason. (TTP 16.13–14, iii.191)

Through this agreement they have "transferred to the supreme power all their power to defend themselves, i.e., all their right" (TTP 16.26, iii.193). Spinoza goes on to illustrate this through his historical account of the Hebrew state, in which "everyone surrendered his right equally, as in a Democracy, and they cried out in one voice 'whatever God says' (without any explicit mediator) 'we will do'" (TTP 17.33, iii.206). In the *Political Treatise*, however, Spinoza dispenses with the apparatus of the contract, claiming instead to "deduce" (*deducere*) the formation of the state from human nature as it actually is (TP 1/4).[67]

We need not worry too much about the differences between the TTP and the TP on the origin of the commonwealth, since Spinoza does not think that sovereign right depends on any particular provenance: "[f]or us to recognize [sovereign] right, it's not necessary now to know what their origin is or how they often arise" (TTP 16.37, iii.195). Irrespective of what induces one to cede one's right to the sovereign, in doing so one binds oneself to a new standard of right and wrong, a new standard of justice. By authorizing a sovereign, whose power reflects the collective right of the citizenry, one subjects oneself to a common standard of justice and right. In the state, any act that is contrary to the legislative deliverances of the sovereign is an act of injustice (TTP 16.44, iii.196), an injury (TTP 16.41, iii.196), or a sin (TP 2/19; 2/23; 4p37s2). And a distinctive form of right – namely, *civil right* – is introduced, delimiting the realm of *permissible* action as determined by the sovereign (TTP 16.39ff, iii.195–6; TP 2/19).

Two non-naturalistic consequences would appear to fall out from this account of right-transference: (1) one can now act without right, contrary to the coextensivity thesis; (2) one now stands under obligations that do not depend on perceived utility. As Spinoza writes in the preface to the TTP: "those who have the sovereignty have the right to do whatever they can do ... they alone are the defenders of right and freedom, and ... everyone else ought always to act [*omnia agere debere*] according to their decree alone" (TTP Preface 30, iii.11). The language of obligation is at least as prominent in the TP, where he claims that the citizen "has no right over nature beyond what the common right grants him. For the rest, whatever he's commanded to do according to the common

[67] Still, he does refer to the "contract [*contractus*], or the laws by which a multitude transfers its right to a Council or a man" in TP 4/6.

agreement, he's bound [*teneri exequi*] to carry out" (TP 2/16). Spinoza thus seems to smuggle back into his account of the state much of the very normative juridical flotsam and jetsam that he had previously expelled.

There is a genuine tension here that needs resolution. His commitment to naturalism and his commitment to apparently normative juridical language are both too pervasive to dismiss either as insincere. I will now try to explain how I think Spinoza seeks to account for authority and obligation within his naturalism, while maintaining a critical stance toward the juridical tradition.

Authority Naturalized

In order to understand how one can cede one's right, and thereby authorize another, without thereby alienating this very right, we must probe deeper into what it means to be a subject (*subditus*) or to stand under the right or power of another, i.e., to be *in alieni juris* or *sub potestate alterius*. Spinoza operates with two senses of right (*ius*), corresponding to the two concepts that are translated into English as "power": *potentia* and *potestas*.[68] To be subject to another is to stand under their power, to be *sub potestate*. To the extent that one's actions follow from one's own authority, one is *sui iuris*; to the extent that one's actions reflect the authority of another, one is *sub potestate alterius*.[69] Spinoza indicates that are many ways of standing under the power of another:

One person has another in his power [a] if he has him tied up, or [b] if he has taken away his arms and means of defending himself or escaping, or [c] if he has instilled fear in him, or [d] if he has so bound him to himself by a benefit [*beneficium*] that the other person would rather conduct himself according to his benefactor's wishes than according to his own, and wants to live according to his benefactor's opinion, not according to his own (TP 2/10; cf. TTP 17.5–6, iii.202).

The final example, of one who would "rather conduct himself according to his benefactor's wishes than according to his own" because of some benefit rendered or promised, is at once the most revealing and the most opaque. How can one be guided by the judgment of another rather than one's own, if "whoever has resolved to obey all the commands of a Commonwealth, whether because he feared its power or because he loves peace, is surely *looking out for his own security and his own advantage, according to his own* ingenium" (TP 3/3 – my

---

[68] See J. Steinberg 2008. Cf. Negri 1991.

[69] Barbone and Rice propose that we understand "*potestas*" as "permission, authorization, or privilege that is conferred upon the individual. *Potestas* represents a power that is not essential to the individual, but a capacity that is super-added" (Barbone and Rice 2000, p. 17). Hans Blom recommends rendering *potestas* as "coercive power" (Blom 1993, p. 341).

emphasis)? If whenever one decides to do something, one acts from one's own judgment, it would seem to be impossible to act from the judgment of another. Spinoza confronts this quandary in a rich passage from the TTP:

To understand rightly how far the right and power of the state extend, we must note that its power is not limited to what it can compel men to do from fear, but extends to absolutely everything it can bring men to do in compliance with its commands. It's obedience which makes the subject, not the reason for the obedience. *For whatever reason a man resolves to carry out the commands of the supreme power,* whether because he fears punishment, or because he hopes for something from it, or because he loves his Country, or because he has been impelled by any other affect whatever, *he still forms his resolution according to his own judgment, notwithstanding that he acts in accordance with the command of the supreme power. So we must not infer simply from the fact that a man does something by his own judgment, that he does it by his own right, and not by the right of the state.* For since he always acts by his own judgment and decision – both when he is bound by love and when he is compelled by fear to avoid some evil – if there is to be a state and a right over subjects, political authority must extend to everything which can bring men to decide to yield to it. So whatever a subject does which answers to the commands of the supreme power – whether he's been bound by love, or compelled by fear, or (as indeed is more frequent) by hope and fear together, whether he acts from reverence (a passion composed of fear and wonder) or is led by any reason whatever – he acts by the right of the state, not his own right [*ex jure imperii, non autem suo agit*] (TTP 17.5–7, iii.201–2—my emphasis).

If sovereignty required the alienation of one's power to judge, there could be no sovereignty.[70] However, there is another way to conceive of being under the right of another, which depends on the way that the judgments and actions of others impinge upon one's own. One can act both from one's own judgment *and* from the right of another, since one's own judgment may reflect the intervention or imposition of another's judgment. One's actions can be dependent on the judgment of another in a counterfactual sense: If P didn't believe that she were satisfying some demand, request, or desire of Q, P would not have acted as she did.

This notion of transference of right is perfectly consistent with naturalism. The transfer of right is not the product of an irreversible contract through which a normative title is given away. Rather, it consists in maintaining an ongoing pattern of psycho-physical commitment.[71] This allows Spinoza to declare that one can retain one's right (as *potentia*), while subjecting oneself to the authority (*potestas*) of another. The *potestas* of the sovereign, then, depends on its ability to keep people in its thrall. Spinoza directly connects authority with the judgmental dependency in the concluding chapter of the TTP: "I confess that someone can get prior control of another person's judgment in many ways, some of them almost incredible. So though that person does not directly command the other person's judgment, *it can still depend so much on what he says that we can rightly say that to that extent it is subject to his control*" (TTP 20.4, iii.239; cf. TTP 17.8, iii.202; TP 2/9–10). Authority is constituted by psychological dependence or deference. Alternatively, as the twentieth-century legal theorist Hermann Heller glosses Spinoza's position, obedience makes the ruler.[72]

This way of naturalizing civic authority is not without historical precedent. Marsilius of Padua advances a naturalistic account of political authority in *Defensor Pacis* (1324), claiming, like Spinoza, that *potestas* is rooted in actual configurations of power, or *potentia*, specifically, the power of the people. And a century before Spinoza, Montaigne's dear friend Étienne de La Boétie wrote, in *Discourse on Voluntary Servitude* (first published posthumously in 1576), that sovereignty depends entirely upon the will of subjects, so that if the subjects were to cease to recognize the authority of tyrants, the authority itself would dissipate. Hobbes, too, flirted with such an account, claiming in his history of the English Civil War, *Behemoth* – which, while composed by 1668, prior to the publication of either of Spinoza's political treatises, was only published posthumously in 1681 – that "the power of the mighty hath no foundation but in the opinion and belief of the people" (EW VI, 184, 237).[73] However, the consistency and thoroughgoingness of Spinoza's naturalizing program far exceeds that of any of his predecessors. And, by treating authority as a kind of sociological phenomenon, Spinoza not only preempts spurious appeals to right and obligation, he also shows how sovereign authority is continuous with other forms of dependency (including, for instance, filial dependency or the mutual dependency of friendships) and how such authority might be conceived without fixed hierarchical relationships.

Obligation Naturalized

The preceding account helps to us to see how the coextensivity of right and power (*potentia*) can be reconciled with authority and subjection and, to some extent, how the ostensible contractualism of the TTP can be reconciled with

---

[72] This was brought to my attention by David Dyzenhaus. Heller attributes the expression "*oboedientia facit imperantem*" to Spinoza, though he never actually uses this phrase. Spinoza does, however, state that *obtemperantia subditum facit* (TTP 17.5; iii.202; cf. TP 2/9–2/10) and, given the reciprocity between the conditions of subjection and authority, we may infer that for Spinoza obedience makes both subjects and rulers.

[73] Cited in Curley 1996, p. 326.

the "spontaneous" account of the commonwealth in the TP.[74] Still, it does not yet show how one can act contrary to right, or how one can violate a civil obligation, since it seems like one is subject to laws only to the extent that one actually has an interest in complying with them. On such a reading, any act of noncompliance would simultaneously de-authorize, in which case one would no longer be subject to the law. This would fit neatly with the coextensivity thesis, but it would render Spinoza's treatment of civil right and law unintelligible.

To see how one can be subject to laws with which one does not always comply, or how one can lack the right to do something that one has the power to do, I propose that we distinguish between compliance and obedience, taking compliance to consist in conformity to particular laws in particular instances and obedience to consist in general disposition to comply with a particular commanding body. Since obedience entails deference to the will of a legislating body, it also entails *general* compliance; but, in any particular instance, one may fail to comply, while remaining subject to the right of the other.

Something like this distinction seems to underlie Spinoza's contrast between a criminal, even treasonous, subject and an enemy of the state (*hostis imperii*). Only subjects, who have exhibited obedience, or patterned dependence, can commit acts of treason (TTP 16.48, iii.197). By contrast, an enemy of the state is one who does not recognize the state's sovereignty at all (TTP 16.47, iii.197; TP 3/8). The difference between noncompliant subjects and enemies of the state turns on their level of dependence on, and obedience to, the apparatus of the state.

On this picture, there are violable legal obligations, but these obligations are conditional, hinging as they do on ongoing patterns of deference and dependency. The commands of a ruler are binding on an individual to the extent and only to the extent that the individual *acknowledges* the authority of the commanding body through general obedience.[75] Laws "depend on a human decision" (*ex humano placito pendet*) not only in that they are the issuances of a legislative body, but also in that it is only through the (widespread) obedience

---

[74] According to Alexandre Matheron, the spontaneity account of the TP could only have been conceived once Spinoza had fully developed his account of the imitation of the affects, which he had not yet done when he published the TTP in 1670 (Matheron 1969, pp. 307–330; 1990). Even if Matheron is right about this, the issue of the origin of the state is orthogonal to the question of right and obligation for Spinoza.

[75] We find an interesting illustration of self-binding in Spinoza's analysis of why we cannot underestimate our powers in the appendix to *Ethics* 3. Here he claims: "[N]o one thinks less highly of himself than is just, insofar as he imagines that he cannot do this or that. For whatever man imagines he cannot do, he necessarily imagines; and he is so disposed by this imagination that he really cannot do what he imagines he cannot. For so long as he imagines that he cannot do this or that, he is not determined to do it, and consequently it is impossible for him to do it" (3 DA xxviii exp.; ii.198). To believe that one lacks a capacity is effectively to incapacitate oneself. This is reminiscent of a dictum commonly ascribed to Alice Walker that "the most common way people give up their power is by thinking they don't have any."

of subjects that these issuances become genuine laws at all.[76] To fully appreciate this point, we must turn once again to Spinoza's conception of law. He opens TTP 4 by defining law in the absolute sense as "that according to which each individual, or all or some members of the same species, act in one and the same fixed and determinate way" (TTP 4.1, iii.57). Laws govern the activity of some set of individuals. Spinoza proceeds to distinguish between laws that "follow from the very nature or definition of a thing" and those that "depend on human decisions" (ibid.), defining civil law – which is obviously a form of the latter – as a "*ratio vivendi* man prescribes to himself or to others for some end" [*finem*] (TTP 4.5, iii.58). As subjects, we exhibit a literal *ratio*, or pattern of behavior, without which a "law" would not really be a law at all.[77]

These laws may be somewhat irregular, depending as they do on the decisions of individuals to "bind themselves [*adstringant*] to a fixed way of living" (TTP 4.2–3, iii.58); and these decisions are, as we've seen, rooted in the more basic psychological law of acting in accordance with perceived utility (TTP 16, iii.191–2), for "no one makes a contract or is bound to stand by a contract, except out of hope of some good, or anxiety about some evil" (TTP 16.44, iii.196). One's obligation to the laws is thus conditional: one is bound by laws so far, and only so far, as one "decides" to remain a subject. Spinoza himself makes the conditionality of obligation explicit when he writes that we are bound to carry out the commands of the sovereign, "unless we want to be enemies of the state, and act contrary to reason" (TTP 16.27, iii.193–4).

In treating civil laws as conditional laws that are realized only to the extent that subjection remains in the perceived interest of individuals, I don't wish to deny that they have a certain normative force. As Spinoza sees it, it really is in our long-term interest to comply with laws, even when we regard them as irrational (TP 3/6). However, fools and madmen who cannot be compelled to comply are not violating nature as such, as "nature is not restrained by the laws of human reason [alone] ... the ignorant and weak-minded are no more bound by the Law of nature to organize their lives wisely than a sick man is bound to have a sound body" (TP 2/8, 2/18; cf. TTP 16.17, g iii.190).[78]

---

[76] See Rutherford 2010.

[77] In order for an issuance of law ("law") to be a genuine *ratio vivendi*, a certain threshold of compliance must be met. Spinoza indicates something like a minimal threshold when he notes that if only a few people disregard the laws they remain valid, since "most of the citizens are restrained by them" (TP 3/8) – the suggestion being that if most citizens were not compliant, there would cease to be laws.

[78] There is a sense in which even fools and madmen may be acting without right, which is that they lack the compossible right to disobey the law and retain their long-term power. They lack long-term right, as on their own their power is negligible. This sense of lacking the right to do something that one *may* do is explicitly invoked in the concluding chapter of the TTP, where Spinoza claims that even if rulers can, in the short-term, terrorize and needlessly harass their subjects, "because [they] can't do these things without great danger to the whole state, we can also deny that they have the absolute power [*absolutam potentiam*] to do such things. So we can

Divine Law and Obligation

Still, there are some interpreters who think that for Spinoza citizens are obligated to normative laws irrespective of perceived utility. They point to his account of "divine law" in TTP 4. Unlike civil law, divine law is comprised of moral precepts that are "universal, or common to all men" (TTP 4.18, iii.61). Also, unlike civil law, divine law looks not to one's temporal, material welfare, but rather "aims only at the supreme good, i.e., the true knowledge and love of God" (TTP 4.9, iii.59).[79] Spinoza's characterization of these eternal moral truths as laws has led commentators like Jon Miller and Matthew Kisner to emphasize Spinoza's affinity with the natural law tradition. For instance, Kisner claims:

> Spinoza's practical laws look a great deal like natural laws, as they were conceived by the tradition running from the Stoics, through Aquinas, Suarez, Grotius and Hobbes. Where there is much variety among these accounts, they tend to agree on certain fundamental claims about natural laws, that they are universal, divine commands revealed by reason and binding independently of political enforcement.[80]

While Kisner concedes that "Spinoza's divine laws are not divine decrees in any literal sense,"[81] he thinks that Spinoza's willingness to using the language of law here indicates that he is congenial to the natural law tradition. Jon Miller agrees that divine laws are genuinely moral and genuinely binding: "divine laws are natural in the sense that they exist independent of any human action. Moreover, they issue obligations since they reveal the true path to happiness."[82]

While I agree that divine laws are in fact moral precepts, I disagree with the suggestion that they are normatively binding. We saw (Section 2.3) that Spinoza takes pains to undercut the view that Nature is bound by the laws of reason. When Spinoza denies that the ignorant violate the law of nature (TP 2/5–6; cf. TTP 16.7, iii.190), he is quite evidently denying the Grotian view of natural justice and natural obligations.[83] He announces his critical intent when he asserts that "the Law of nature prohibits nothing [*nihil absolute naturae iure prohibetur*] except what no one can do" (TP 2/18). Spinoza never wavers

---

deny also that they can do them with absolute right [*absolutum jus*]" (TTP 20.7, iii.240). Just as the sovereign lacks the absolute right or power to govern oppressively, since oppressive regimes do not last long (*violenta imperia nemo continuit diu*) (TTP 5.22, iii.74; TTP 16.29, iii.194), subjects typically lack the long-term right to disobey, since disobedience is not compatible with the long-term retention of power. See Della Rocca 1996b, pp. 207–8.

[79] Kisner rightly notes that "divine laws are the same as the dictates of reason from 4p18s" (Kisner 2011, p. 116).

[80] Kisner 2011, p. 117.

[81] Ibid.

[82] Miller 2012, p. 211.

[83] Spinoza certainly critiques Grotian moral universalism. See Hackett edition editors' notes to TP 2/8.

or walks back this claim. Divine laws are laws just in the sense that they are eternal truths (TTP 4, iii.63–5), if-then laws about what leads to our greatest happiness.[84] It is the philosophical Christ – rather than Adam or Moses – who apprehends divine law rightly as eternal truths rather than the decrees of a divine legislator, even if he too had to present these truths as divine commands because of the ignorance and obstinacy of ordinary people (TTP 4.33, iii.65).

Given that Spinoza repeatedly denies that there are normative natural laws that obligate in the absence of binding forces, why do some interpreters insist on attributing to him a belief in obligatory moral laws? Kisner thinks that divine laws bind in the "weaker sense" that "all people have reason to accept the natural law as authoritative."[85] He is certainly right that all people have a reason (relative to their striving to persevere in their power) to act in accordance with divine law; but to call divine law *binding* on this account is to fail to appreciate the full polemical aims of Spinoza's argument, which targets any conception of a binding natural moral order. Spinoza directly rebuts the claim that "everyone is equally bound by the divine command – unconditionally, whether they have the use of reason or not – to love his neighbor as himself," arguing instead that "no one knows, by nature, that he's bound to obey God" and that "no one is bound by a divine law he can't help but not know" (TTP 16.52–4, iii.198). While we undoubtedly *should* act from divine law, it is not the case that we *must*.[86] One is not bound to do what one has a perfectly good reason to do; the irrational are not obligated to do what they would do if they were rational (TTP 16.7, iii.190).

2.6   The Significance of Spinoza's Critique of Natural Law

This point about obligation might appear to be merely semantic, but Spinoza's rejection of natural obligation reveals something very important about his normative political project. Proponents of natural jurisprudence contend that there are constraints on what one may do in the pursuit of one's interests. To put it anachronistically, they contend that there is a sense of The Right that is independent from, and limits the permissible pursuit of, The Good.[87] Spinoza denies that there is an independent conception of The Right, thereby rejecting

---

[84] See Rutherford 2010. Part of which is most interesting about Spinoza's account is that he renders "law" univocal at precisely the time when "natural law" was diverging into two quite distinct concepts: (1) violable moral laws governing the actions of rational beings, and (2) inviolable, universal physical principles governing all bodies. See C. Wilson 2008b; Milton 1998. See Miller 2003 and Rutherford 2010 for two very different accounts of how Spinoza understands the relationship between these conceptions of law.

[85] Kisner 2011, p. 120.

[86] Lest we fall prey to Hobbes's criticism of those who unscrupulously "confuse law [*lex*] with advice [*consilium*]" (*De Cive*, XIV.1, p. 153).

[87] See, for instance, Sidgwick 1962; Ross 1988; Frankena 1963; Rawls 1971.

what Henry Sidgwick calls the "imperative" conception of morality.[88] In doing so, he removes juridical barriers to action.

By casting off juridical constraints, Spinoza is able to adopt a more psychologically attuned approach to politics, one that does not recognize a realm of moral powers distinct from actual capacities (a kingdom within a kingdom [*imperium in imperio*]) (E 3 Preface), one that takes the good *in situ* to be determined in light of the actual psycho-physical capacities of individuals. The significance of this power-based approach to politics may be seen from the perspective of the governors. The ruling body cannot appeal to some ethereal conception of right or obligation to justify their actions. Instead they must consider what actually produces compliance and the coordination of powers. This requires accommodating commands to the *ingenia* of their subjects (see Chapter 5). In order to maintain authority, governors must determine how – given the psychological make-up of the citizenry – loyalty will be promoted and dissent minimized.

While Spinoza does not accord to the people a proper right of revolution, he proposes a naturalistic surrogate, since the right of the state is constituted and limited by the power of the people (TP 2/17); the more indignant the people are, the less powerful the commonwealth will be (see TP 3/8–9; TP 4/4–5).[89] So, by adhering to a strict naturalism about right and obligation and maintaining that "the Supreme Magistrate has no more right over its subjects than it has greater power over them" (Ep. 50), Spinoza – unlike Hobbes – places the onus of political stability squarely on the sovereign rather than the subject.[90]

By replacing a juridical approach to politics with an interest-based one that places the burden of stability on the sovereign, Spinoza's attitude toward statecraft somewhat resembles Machiavelli's. Machiavelli, like Spinoza, thought that, at least in the case of civil principalities, the governor or governors must retain popular support,[91] for "a ruler can never protect himself from a hostile people, because there are too many of them" (*The Prince*, Ch. IX, 35). Indeed, Machiavelli seems to presage Spinoza's naturalistic account of authority when he writes that citizens can remove a ruler "either by moving against him or simply by refusing to obey him" (*The Prince*, Ch. IX, 37),[92] making it the chief priority of the sovereign to cultivate loyalty: "A shrewd ruler, therefore, must try to ensure that his citizens, whatever the situation may

[88] Sidgwick 1962, p. 105.
[89] In TP 4/4–4/5, Spinoza presents this in terms of natural laws required for a state's survival: "there are certain conditions that, if operative, entail that subjects will respect and fear their commonwealth, while the absence of these conditions entails the annulment of that fear and respect and together with this, the destruction of the commonwealth" (TP 4/4). See Sharp 2013.
[90] See TP 5/3; Wernham 1958, p. 27.
[91] "A man who becomes ruler through popular favour, then, must keep the people well disposed towards him" (*Prince*, Ch. IX, p. 36).
[92] Compare, once again, with de la Boétie, *Discourse on Voluntary Servitude* (see Epigraph)

be, will always be dependent on the government and on him; and then they will always be loyal to him."[93] This leads him to conclude, as Spinoza would later, that political measures must be accommodated to historical and psychological circumstances: "A ruler can win over the people in many ways; but because these vary so much according to the circumstances one cannot give any definite rules."[94] And, as was noted in Section 1.3, for both Machiavelli and Spinoza, when powers are not well coordinated, when there is widespread noncompliance and/or criminality, the explanation for this must be sought in the laws and institutions of the state.

We can see from this that, *pace* Pocock, there is a considerable affinity between Machiavelli's approach to political theory and Spinoza's. Both reject juridical constraints, offering instead an interest-based account of governance that puts the burden on the sovereign to accommodate the natures of the people so as to promote order. The difference in their nomenclatures can be explained by the fact that whereas Machiavelli simply eschewed the concepts of right and obligation, Spinoza sought first to drain them of their deontic core.[95] The connections between Spinoza's and Machiavelli's political methodologies will be examined in more depth in Chapter 5. Lest we assimilate their views too much, though, it is worth pointing out that Spinoza and Machiavelli adopt very different views concerning the purpose of the state. While both take liberty to be a vital political norm, Spinoza has a more robust, perfectionist conception of what political liberty – an extension of ethical liberty – consists in. I will develop his account over the course of Chapters 3 and 4.

---

[93] *Prince*, Ch. IX, p. 37. See Bonadeo 1969; Del Lucchese 2009, pp. 123–5.
[94] *Prince*, Ch. IX, p. 36.
[95] See Balibar 1998, p. 60.

3   The Continuity Thesis and the Aim of Government

> The Untouchables are in need of social liberty, more than that which is guaranteed by law. So long as you do not achieve social liberty, whatever freedom is provided by law to you is of no avail. Some persons might advise you that you have physical freedom. Of course, you can go anywhere, can speak anything you wish, subject to the restrictions imposed by law ... But what is the use of such freedom of a man whose mind is not free? The freedom of mind is the real freedom.
>
> – B.R. Ambedkar, "What Path to Salvation?"[1]

In Chapter 2, I argued that Spinoza removes juridical or deontological constraints on the promotion of the civic good. In Chapters 3 and 4, I examine the nature of the good that the state aims to promote. I will contend that the state has a single directive: to liberate or empower its citizens as far as possible. This reveals that the aim of politics is continuous with the aim of ethics and that the political treatises and the *Ethics* play complementary roles within Spinoza's unified normative program.

I defend this claim against a battery of challenges. Spinoza seems to distinguish between ethical and political aims in both of his political treatises, where he operates with a series of contrasts that apparently drive a wedge between ethics and politics: ethics is universal in scope, is concerned with the perfection of the intellect (TTP 4.9, iii.59ff), and results in eternal rewards, namely, salvation (*salus*) and beatitude (*beatitudo*); politics, by contrast, has a narrower scope, is concerned primarily with obedience rather than knowledge, and gives rise only to temporal or material rewards. After fully explicating the challenges (Section 3.1), I make the case for continuity, arguing that, for Spinoza, there is a single standard of goodness and that a state can achieve its goals of peace (*pax*) and security (*securitas*) only by empowering or liberating its citizens (Section 3.2). Finally, in Section 3.3, I begin to respond in detail to the alleged evidence for the discontinuous, anti-perfectionist readings of Spinoza's politics.

While anti-perfectionist readings introduce untenable and unmotivated divisions within Spinoza's normative project, my interpretation reveals the

---

[1] Ambedkar 1988, Section 11.

systematic coherence of Spinoza's works, showing how his political writings contribute to his liberative project.

3.1   Discontinuity and the Classical Liberal Interpretation

In the final chapter of the *Tractactus Theologico-Politicus*, in the midst of a discussion about the bounds of effective governance, Spinoza declares: "the end of the Republic is really freedom" (TTP 20.12, iii.241). While this remark obviously purports to tell us something important about Spinoza's conception of the *civitas*, it is not clear exactly what is revealed. What, after all, does "freedom" (*libertas*) mean in this context? And how does the state promote such freedom? The way that one answers these questions will, to a large extent, fix how one conceives of Spinoza's normative political project as a whole.

According to one prominent line of interpretation, "freedom" here must be understood in a distinctively political sense, denoting something weaker than the freedom of the *Ethics*. The is how Douglas Den Uyl reads Spinoza:

Since freedom is itself defined in terms of security and harmony, "freedom" and "peace" are virtually synonymous terms in Spinoza's political thought. Freedom, like reason, has a political as well as an ethical sense. In book five of the *Ethica* freedom means not being subject to the passions. Since it would be utopian to expect a social condition where men are not moved primarily by their passions, freedom takes on a more limited normative content in the politics. In the political writings "freedom" means merely peace – that is, security and harmony.[2]

On this interpretation, "freedom" ought to be understood as *mere* peace. Since it would be wildly unrealistic to suppose that the state could bring it about that men are led more by reason than by passions, some sort of deflation of the concept of freedom is in order.

This deflationary interpretation of freedom is typically invoked by those who read Spinoza as a kind of classical liberal, for whom the aim of the state is simply to provide conditions for moral development by protecting (negative) civil liberties.[3] The view is well captured by Den Uyl's claim that "in essence, Spinoza's prescriptive political philosophy amounts to little more than the recommendation that the *civitas* focus its attention on what is most fundamental to social order – namely, peace – and leave people free to pursue their own desires on all other matters."[4] Later in the same work, he writes: "Spinoza does not consider the 'final cause' of the *civitas* to be the development of individuals;

---

[2] Den Uyl 1983, p. 114.
[3] The liberal interpretation was first fully developed in Feuer 1958, but has been revived and reconfigured by several commentators. See, for instance, Smith 1997 and Den Uyl 1983.
[4] Den Uyl 1983, p. 118.

nor does he regard good citizenship as the end of personal development. Rather, he sees the *civitas* as a foundation for one's development. Spinoza does not ask the *civitas* to make men virtuous, nor does he believe the *civitas* could do so if it wanted to ... the purpose of the *civitas* is peace rather than the shaping of virtuous men."[5] Barbone and Rice, too, lump Spinoza together with Adam Smith as a "minimal state"[6] theorist, since on their reading the state is concerned primarily with the civil protections and institutions that preserve stability. But perhaps the clearest expression of this classical liberal interpretation comes from Steven B. Smith:

The *Treatise [TTP]* does not answer the question of how people who are described as naturally credulous and prone to superstition can be made rational. By what leap of faith could Spinoza maintain that men who are driven by nothing other than "desire and power" could conclude an agreement to curb their passions and "live wholeheartedly according to the guidance of reasons?" Unlike Plato or Maimonides, Spinoza does not advocate the rule of a philosopher-king or a prophet who might educate his subjects to a lofty vision of human perfection. Spinoza's politics are, by contrast, starkly anti-perfectibilian. He is not bereft of an idea of human perfection, but he does doubt that politics or law is the appropriate means by which to achieve it.[7]

According to Smith, it is a serious mistake to connect Spinoza's "anti-perfectibilian" politics to his ethics, as ethical perfection is a "deeply private matter ... for which the requirements of political rule are inappropriate."[8]

The claim of discontinuity finds *prima facie* support in Chapter 4 of the TTP, where Spinoza distinguishes between divine law and human law by appealing not only to their distinct origins, but also to their distinct aims: "By human law I understand a principle of living which serves only to protect life and the republic; by a divine law, one which aims only at the supreme good, i.e., the true knowledge and love of God" (TTP 4.9, iii.59). He proceeds to portray divine law as a "universal Ethics" (TTP 4.13, iii.60), comprised of eternal truths, whose "highest precept is to love God as the highest good" (TTP 4.15, iii.60–1). Human law, on the other hand, is comprised of a set of civil commands that are adapted to the temperament and conditions of a particular group of people, aiming at a more modest good: peace and the preservation of the state (TTP 4.9, iii.59).

Spinoza elsewhere relies on an array of distinctions that appear to reinforce the discontinuity between ethics and politics. For instance, in the TTP, he

[5] Ibid., p. 128.
[6] Barbone and Rice 2000, p. 29.
[7] Smith 1997, pp. 136–7. Elsewhere, though, Smith acknowledges to some degree the liberative potential of the state, pointing to the "political or public dimension" of virtue or *fortitudo* (Smith 1997, p. 162).
[8] Smith 1997, p. 144.

introduces the distinction between obedience and knowledge in order to show that faith and philosophy regulate distinct domains: religion aims at obedience; philosophy aims at knowledge (TTP 14). And he proceeds to interpret faith in wholly political terms, taking faith to consist in *whatever* set of beliefs is conducive to the worship of God, and showing that the civil sovereign alone has the authority to determine how one's piety is to be expressed (TTP 19) (see Section 6.4).

Of course, it does not follow that politics and philosophy have distinct ends just because faith is defined politically and *it* is distinct from philosophy. Politics could be broad enough to incorporate both religious and philosophical ends. However, Spinoza does suggest that politics is concerned primarily with outward obedience rather than the beliefs or motives of the citizens (TTP 17.5–7, iii.201–2; TP 1/6). This conception of politics figures into his defense of the freedom to philosophize, where he maintains that unlike matters of obedience, beliefs do not lie under the absolute power of the sovereign (TTP 20.8-14, iii.240–1) (Section 6.5). On one straightforward reading of Spinoza, the state aims to promote certain forms of action, while remaining indifferent to the content of the mental states that beget these actions. Philosophy, by contrast, is concerned precisely with the content of one's ideas, remaining relatively less concerned about the outward expression of these ideas (see 4p59 and 4p59s). On this view, politics has a rather limited bailiwick: it aims at preventing destructive behavior rather than promoting the moral or intellectual perfection of subjects, which lies beyond the scope of the state.[9]

Considering matters purely under the attribute of thought, we might say that whereas philosophy aims to cultivate the intellect, the mechanisms of the state act only on the imagination. Through commands, institutional practices, and symbolic performances, the state promotes passions that secure compliance. The sharp division between the imagination and the intellect lends further support to the discontinuity of politics and ethics. There are several reasons for thinking that ideas of the imagination are utterly unlike ideas of the intellect. First of all, there is an etiological difference between these kinds of ideas: ideas of the imagination arise from external causes, whereas adequate ideas follow from the nature of one's mind. As Jonathan Bennett has noted in a slightly different context, one can no more make an inadequate idea adequate than one can "become royal by altering who [one's] parents were."[10] Moreover, ideas of the imagination take as their (direct) object the actually existing body and represent particular things *sub specie durationis* (5p29s). By contrast, when we know things adequately, we conceive of the essence of the body (5p29) and

---

[9] See Balibar 1998, pp. 25–6. See Rosenthal's claim that the purpose of the state is "physical welfare" (Rosenthal 2003a).
[10] Bennett 1984, p. 336.

Table 3.1. *Apparent discontinuity of ethics and politics*

	Scope	Primary aim	Part of mind engaged	Temporal status of rewards
Ethics (Divine Law)	Universal	Knowledge and freedom	Intellect	Eternal
Politics (Human Law)	Circumstance-specific	Obedience and peace	Imagination	Durational

we grasp things *sub specie aeternitatis* (2p44c2 and 5p29s). It would seem, then, that the imagination keeps us mired in confused, mutilated, and inadequate representations of particular things in time, rather than contributing to our knowledge of the eternal features of Nature (see Chapter 8).

Assembling all of these bits of evidence, we are left with what looks like a stark contrast between ethics and politics. Ethics is universal in scope, it consists in perfecting the intellect or gaining adequate knowledge, and its rewards are eternal (salvation [*salus*], beatitude). Politics, by contrast, is fixed to a specific time and place, it operates on the imagination, contributing to obedience rather than knowledge, and yielding only temporal rewards (security and material welfare).[11] It seems, then, that there are at least four dimensions according to which ethics may be rather strictly distinguished from politics (Table 3.1).

3.2   The Case for Continuity

Having limned the case for discontinuity, I will now begin to argue that this view is mistaken. On my reading, when Spinoza writes that the purpose of the state is freedom, he means freedom in the full, ethical sense. Moreover, Spinoza thinks that the state liberates not only by providing conditions for philosophizing, but also by aiding moral development in substantial ways. As a first step toward defending the claim of continuity, I propose that we look at Spinoza's conception of the good and consider how it relates to his idea of liberty.

Normativity and Liberation

While there is considerable scholarly debate about how exactly to characterize Spinoza's metaethics, the following two points are evident: (1) nothing is absolutely good or evil – things are good or evil only relative to some striving agent;

---

[11] The religio-political ceremonies of the Jews helped to promote material welfare, but "contribut[ed] nothing to blessedness [*beatitudinem*]" (TTP 5.31; iii.76).

and (2) what makes a thing good or evil relative to a striving agent is the way in which it affects the agent's power of acting (*potentia agendi*). He puts this latter point in terms of utility in his definition of goodness at the start of *Ethics* 4: "By good I shall understand what we certainly know to be useful [*utile*] to us" (4d1), and then proceeds to show that a thing's utility is measured by its capacity to enhance one's power of acting:

We call good, or evil, what is useful to, or harmful to, preserving our being [by D1 and D2], that is [by IIIP7], what increases or diminishes, aids or restrains, our power of acting. Therefore [by the definitions of joy and sadness in IIIP11S], insofar as we perceive that a thing affects us with joy or sadness, we call it good or evil (4p8d).

Because joy [*laetitia*] is an increase one's power of acting or one's perfection (3p11s; 3 DA ii), Spinoza infers from the definition of goodness as power-enhancement that things are good, or useful, to the extent that they are conducive to joy. This reinforces his earlier assertion that, "By good here I understand every kind of joy, and whatever leads to it" (3p39s). Goodness can thus be measured affectively.

Some have thought that the "hedonic" thesis of 3p39s differs from the perfectionism articulated in the preface to *Ethics* 4: "In what follows, therefore, I shall understand by good what we know certainly is a means by which we may approach nearer and nearer to the model of human nature we set before ourselves. By evil, what we certainly know prevents us from becoming like that model. Next, we shall say that men are more perfect or imperfect, insofar as they approach more or less near to this model" (4 Preface, ii.208).[12] However, since immediately after this passage Spinoza presents transitions in one's level of perfection in terms of changes in one's power of acting, there is a straightforward way of uniting all of these formulations. If becoming more perfect means *both* approximating the model of human nature *and* increasing one's power of acting, the model of human nature must be a model of (human) power. Consequently, things are good for us to the extent that they increase our perfection, *or* increase our power of acting, *or* bring us joy, *or* bring us closer to the model of human nature. All of these formulations are equivalent.

However, not all forms and sources of joy are equally good. Spinoza distinguishes between "cheerfulness" (*hilaritas*), a form of joy that affects the whole person, and "titillation" (*titillatio*), a form of joy that affects one part of the mind/body more than the rest (3p11s). Watching a telenovela might be more titillating than reading Pablo Neruda, and so might prompt a more intense desire, even if reading Neruda promises a more pervasive increase in one's

---

[12] See LeBuffe 2010a, Ch. 8. Kisner raises a related concern, but attempts to reconcile the perfectionist and desire-satisfaction accounts of the good, by claiming that the latter is restricted to "active desires" (Kisner 2011, Ch. 5).

power. Whereas cheerfulness is good for the whole person, titillation can actually interfere with one's general flourishing (4p43 and 4p43d). So titillating objects are not always good.

The difference between cheerfulness and titillation also plays out diachronically. Cheerfulness is always good (4p48), leaving only joy in its wake. However, forms of titillation are often followed by sadness and regret. Taking sensual pleasures as paradigmatic here, we get a sense of why Spinoza thinks that such titillating forms of joy are not categorically good in the opening of the *TdIE*: "For as far as sensual pleasure is concerned, the mind is so caught up in it, as if at peace in a [true] good, that it is quite prevented from thinking of anything else. But after the enjoyment of sensual pleasure is past, the greatest sadness follows. If this does not completely engross, still it thoroughly confuses and dulls the mind" (*TdIE*, Section 4; see 4p43).[13] Here Spinoza highlights both the "spatial"[14] and temporal limitations of titillation: by exciting part of the mind, it stultifies the rest, and often gives way to long-term sadness.

In light of the distinction between cheerfulness and titillation we may formulate Spinoza's account in the following way:

X is good relative to some thing, T, to the extent that X contributes to T's *overall* joy or empowerment. X is evil relative to some thing, T, to the extent that it contributes to T's *overall* sadness or disempowerment.[15]

Having concluded in Chapter 2 that Spinoza eradicates all juridical constraints on the promotion of the good, we are left with a single normative scale, according to which things are good or evil relative to their overall affective impact.

What makes a thing good also makes it liberating. To see this, we must consider Spinoza's account of human freedom. In *Ethics* I, Spinoza defines a free thing (*res libera*) as that "which exists from the necessity of its nature alone, and is determined to act by itself alone. But a thing is called necessary, or rather compelled, which is determined by another to exist and to produce an effect in a certain and determinate manner" (1d7). To be a free thing is to be causally self-sufficient, determined to act from its own nature alone. By this criterion, God alone is free, since God alone acts only from its own power (1p17; 1p17c2). The essences and existences of other things, including human

---

[13] Spinoza is describing why the three things that are most ardently sought – honor, wealth, and sensual pleasure – are not "true goods" (*TdIE*, Section 1). Spinoza does not oppose all pursuits of sensual pleasure, which can be restorative when pursued in moderation (4p45s).

[14] Taking "spatial" here metaphorically to refer to the *extent* of the affect with respect to the whole person.

[15] This thesis is compatible with his claim that good and evil "indicate nothing positive in things, considered in themselves [*in se*]" (*E*4 Preface), which is nothing more than the denial that things have absolute, or agent-independent, value. See TP 2/8; TTP 16.7–11.

beings, depend on God (1p16c1; 1p17s). And so no finite thing can be fully free in this strict sense of self-sufficiency.

But even if finite things like us can't be entirely causally self-sufficient, we necessarily possess a certain degree of causal power (1p36), producing some effects through our natures alone. To the extent that we adequately understand things, we produce effects that are explicable through our natures alone (see 3p1; 3p3), and we steel ourselves against things that "diminish or restrain our power of acting" (4p30d; 5p1–20). So, even if the scope of human power is necessarily limited, we nevertheless possess a certain power of acting and can do things that further increase this power.

Rather than conceiving of "being free" as a binary predicate, Spinoza operates with a scalar conception of freedom, corresponding to a thing's *degree* of power of acting.[16] In the very title of *Ethics* 5, Spinoza identifies "human liberty" with the "power of the intellect,"[17] and he proceeds to delineate how enhancing the power of the intellect liberates us from the bondage of the passions and promotes blessedness. He links freedom to causal power in precisely the same way in the TP, maintaining that:

[B]ecause we ought to reckon human power not so much by the strength of the Body as by the strength of the Mind, it follows that people are most their own masters when they can exert the most power with their reason, and are most guided by reason. So I call a man completely free *just insofar* as he is guided by reason, because *to that extent* he is determined to action by causes which can be understood adequately through his own nature alone, even though they determine him to act necessarily. (TP 2/11, my emphasis)

Anything that increases one's power of thinking – or one's power of acting considered under the attribute of thought – such that one is more capable of exercising reason or forming adequate ideas, liberates one to that very degree, and vice versa.[18] Combining this analysis with Spinoza's account of normativity, we may conclude things are good to the extent and only to the extent that they are liberating, or empowering, or joy-producing.

Since external things can be good, they can also liberate. As Michael Della Rocca points out, "external causes can make an object more or less dependent on external causes when it comes to bringing about that thing's destruction."[19] So, external aids, like a copy of the *Ethics*, an inspiring setting, or a curious and intelligent interlocutor, may prompt one to think more clearly or more adequately and thereby to become freer, more powerful, and more joyful.

---

[16] Spinoza indicates that freedom is something that one can have more or less of in TP 2/7 and 4p73s. See Della Rocca 1998, p. 1231; Kisner 2011, p. 32.
[17] *De Potentia Intellectus, Seu de Libertate Humana.*
[18] See McShea 1969, p. 142.
[19] Della Rocca 1996b, p. 212.

Table 3.2. *Free man vs. slave*

	Is reliably able to grasp the dictates of reason	Is reliably able to act in accordance with the dictates of reason
Free man	Yes	Yes
Slave	No	No

Since the function of the state is unquestionably to empower its citizens *in some way*, those who argue that the aims of the state are fundamentally discontinuous with the aims of the *Ethics* are mistaken. But even if civil mechanisms and philosophical teachings produce effects on a single scale, if their effects occur at wholly distinct registers of this scale, one might be justified in claiming that civil mechanisms do not contribute to the level of perfection that one seeks ethically. As a first step in narrowing the gap between politics and ethics, let us turn now to consider Spinoza's conception of the citizen.

The Citizen-Subject

In the *Ethics*, Spinoza sets out a contrast between the free man, who "complies with no one's wishes but his own, and does only those things he knows to be the most important in life" (4p66s), and the slave, who "does those things he is most ignorant of" (4p66s). While a free, rational person serves his own advantage, striving effectively (E4p20), and obeying himself alone (TP 2/20; TP 2/22), the slave "is drawn by his own pleasure, and can neither see nor do anything useful to himself" (TTP 16.32, iii.194). The distinction between the freedom and the slave is captured in Table 3.2 (above). The free man and the slave are paradigms, models of human power and impotence, respectively.[20]

In reality, all humans fall somewhere in between these extremes. Spinoza's political writings help to flesh out other regions of this spectrum. We see this in his analysis of the citizen-subject. The main difference between the

---

[20] In referring to Spinoza's notion of the "slave" as a paradigm of human imperfection I don't mean to diminish the suffering of *actual* slaves or oppressed people in Spinoza's time. The point is that Spinoza's categories in 4p66s function as poles between which all genuine human beings fall. We are all free to some degree and all enslaved to some degree. Thanks to Hasana Sharp for encouraging this clarification.

citizen-subject and the slave hinges on the *cui bono* question, i.e., the question
of whose interests are served:

An action done on a command – obedience – does, in some measure, take away freedom.
But that isn't what makes the slave. It's the reason for the action. If the end of the action
is not the advantage of the agent himself, but of the person who issues the command, then
the agent is a slave, useless to himself. But in a Republic, and a state where the supreme
law is the well- being of the whole people, not that of the ruler [*salus totius populi, non
imperantis, summa lex est*], someone who obeys the supreme power in everything should
not be called a slave, useless to himself, but a subject (TTP 16.33, iii.194–5).

What Spinoza calls a "subject" here in the TTP is replaced by the designation "citizen" in the TP, which Spinoza defines as one who enjoys "all the advantages of a
Commonwealth" (TP 3/1) – hence my designation "citizen-subject."[21] The citizen-
subject of a well-organized state will reliably act in accordance with his own real
interests, whether or not he is rational. The citizen-subject in a well-organized
commonwealth will resemble the free man in that he will "live according to the
prescription of reason [*ex rationis praescripto vivere*]" (TP 6/3), meaning that he
will do what is in the interest of the welfare of the people as a whole, which is in
turn to do what is in his own interest (TP 3/3). The laws of a good state conduce to
the power or welfare of all citizens, and so function as surrogates of reason. Yet the
very existence of the *civitas* depends upon the defectiveness of human reason; its
laws are correctives that check or harness the passionate, myopic, grasping nature
of most people and replace would-be destructive behavior with power-promoting
behavior (TP 6/3; cf. Section 5.3). Humans, in general, must be compelled to act
in accordance with their own real interests. This is part of what Spinoza means
when he writes: "Men aren't born civil; they become civil" (TP 5/2).[22]

But even if good laws lead citizens to "live according to the prescription
of reason," this does not mean that such laws enable citizens to act *from* the
dictates of reason.[23] To act from the dictates of reason is to have adequate ideas
and to apprehend why certain things promote one's power. Acting in accordance with reason simply requires doing the very things that reason dictates.
The citizen-subject, or one who merely acts in accordance with reason, occu-
pies a middle position between the free man and the slave (Table 3.3).

Unlike the free man, the citizen-subject may not himself be wise; his power
depends on the rationality of the laws. But, unlike the slave, he is nevertheless able to act in empowering ways. For this reason, Spinoza maintains that
heeding the laws is an exercise of freedom (TP 4/5). I now want to extend this

---

[21] Citizenship does not expressly include participatory rights, but they might be taken to be
implied by the phrase "enjoy[ing]...*all* the advantages of a Commonwealth."
[22] Cf. Hobbes, *De Cive*, I, 2n1.
[23] See Den Uyl 1983, p. 64.

Table 3.3. *The middle position of the citizen-subject*

	Is reliably able to grasp the dictates of reason	Is reliably able to act in accordance with the dictates of reason
Free man	Yes	Yes
Citizen-subject	No	Yes
Slave	No	No

analysis further, showing that the state can liberate by altering not only the behavior, but also the affective make-up, or *ingenia*, of its citizens.

Peace, Sociability, and Virtue

The deflationary interpretation of Spinoza's account of political freedom (Section 3.1), which supports the case for discontinuity, misrepresents Spinoza's intent in identifying liberty and peace as the chief aims of the state. Rather than operating with a deflated notion of liberty, he is adopting an inflated conception of peace. Peace signifies a flourishing civil condition, wherein the members of a state are committed, to some degree, to the common good, guided by socially harmonious affects. Spinoza straightforwardly rejects Hobbes's definition of peace as the mere absence of war,[24] claiming instead:

A Commonwealth whose subjects, terrified by fear, don't take up arms should be said to be without war, but not at peace. Peace isn't the privation of war, but a virtue which arises from strength of mind. For [by ii, 19] it's obedience, a constant will to do what must be done in accordance with the common decree of the Commonwealth. When the peace of a Commonwealth depends on its subjects' lack of spirit – so that they're led like sheep, and know only how to be slaves – it would be more properly called a wasteland than a Commonwealth. When we say, then, that the best state is one where men pass their lives harmoniously, I mean that they pass a human life, one defined not merely by the circulation of the blood, and other things common to all animals, but mostly by reason, the true virtue and life of the Mind (TP 5/4–5/5).

Mere stability is not the same thing as peace. The latter requires positive harmony, or the agreement of minds and bodies. Spinoza illustrates this point by appealing to the putative peace of "the Turks":

No state has stood so long without notable change as that of the Turks... Still, if slavery, barbarism, and being without protection are to be called peace, nothing is more

---

[24] *De Cive*, I, xii.

wretched for men than peace. No doubt there are more, and more bitter, quarrels between parents and children than between masters and slaves. Nevertheless, it doesn't make for the orderly management of a household to change paternal Right into mastery, and treat children like slaves. To transfer all power to one man makes for bondage, not peace. As we've said, peace does not consist in the privation of war, but in a union or harmony of minds (TP 6/4).[25]

The *ingenia* of its citizens distinguish a peaceful state from a merely strife-less one. The mere absence of war is characterized by conformity to the law through fear. In this condition, men do not really agree with one another; rather, they are made not to disagree with one another. By contrast, peace is said to arise "from strength of mind [*animi fortitudine*]" (TP 5/4) and indicates a genuine agreement or harmony of minds.

Because the purpose of the state is peace or the harmony of minds, and since this arises through *fortitudo* – which Spinoza defines in the *Ethics* as a class of active affects "related to the mind insofar as it understands" (3p59s; see Section 1.2) – it would seem that peace requires the rationality or virtue of its citizens (see TP 5/5). One might worry at this point that the ideal of peace is at odds with Spinoza's realism. He seems to be committed to following three theses, which jointly entail that peace is an unreasonable civil ideal:

T1 Peace is a civil condition wherein citizens act primarily from strength of mind (*fortitudo*) (TP 5/4).
T2 To act from strength of mind is to act from reason (3p59s).
T3 It is unrealistic to expect most people to act from reason (TP 1/5; TP 6/1).

How could Spinoza, who opens the TP by castigating utopians, himself embrace a wholly unrealistic political ideal?

The short answer is that he does not. Perfect peace or perfect harmony may not be attainable, but close approximations can be achieved if citizens are guided primarily by affects that are rooted in joy and love, rather than by affects that are rooted in sadness and hatred. The liberative superiority of affects like hope, trust, and confidence (*securitas*) – will be the subject of Chapter 4. Here it is sufficient to note that Spinoza takes very seriously the goal of fostering a robust harmony among its citizenry. A good state will not only ensure that citizens don't act in outwardly destructive ways, it will also act as a bulwark against resentment, fear, and other stultifying passions, promoting instead the formation of joyful *ingenia*. The upshot of all of this is that, contrary to the anti-perfectionist interpretation, Spinoza is firmly

---

[25] This nicely illustrates the sharp contrast with Hobbes, who claims that there is every bit as much liberty in Constantinople as there is in the Republic of Lucca (*Lev.*, xxi).

committed to view that the state plays a powerful role in the moral development or liberation of its citizens. The putatively minimal ends of peace and
security (*securitas*) are achieved only when citizens are flourishing.

3.3   Debunking Discontinuity

If, as I've argued, the aim of politics is continuous with the aim of ethics, what are
we to make of the differences between ethics and politics identified above (See
Table 3.1)? While a full response will depend on analysis from later chapters –
especially Chapter 8 – I will begin to address here the apparent differences in
the scopes and aims of ethical and political injunctions.

Difference of Scope

While ethics (divine law) is portrayed as universal in scope, and human law is
indexed to a particular time and place, this in no way implies that they are discontinuous. One way of understanding the relationship between divine and human
law is that the latter is an application of universal moral principles to particular
circumstances. As I have argued elsewhere, there are strong reasons to think
that rational moral laws are, on their own, too general to provide useful prescriptive guidance.[26] To determine what is good in a particular situation – what
I should do *here* and *now* – one must attend to things as they actually are, rather
than acting as we would if we were all fully rational. On this reading, human
laws may be concrete expressions of divine law, attempts to accommodate the
teachings of the moral law to suit the *ingenia* of a particular set of people (see
Section 5.3).

This conception of how civil law and moral (divine) law relate would hardly
have been unique to Spinoza. Samuel von Pufendorf, writing just a few years
after Spinoza, uses an analogy with pedagogy to illustrate how natural law, a
universal law, might be variably expressed according to the condition of the
affected individuals:

Two boys of very different character have been entrusted to someone for their education. One is modest, scrupulous and afire with the love of letters; the other is dissolute
and saucy, more in love with lewd desires than with books. *The sum of their duty is
the same for both, to learn letters; but the particular precepts will be different.* For the
former it is enough to give him a schedule and a plan of studies to follow. The other,
however, besides this, must be admonished with the direst threats not to run around, not
to gamble, not to sell his books, not to plagiarize other students' work, not to carouse,
not to run after prostitutes.[27]

---

[26] J. Steinberg 2014.
[27] *DO*, p. 13 – my emphasis.

Later in the same work, Pufendorf directly claims that civil law makes determinate what is left unspecified in natural law: "Many of the precepts of natural law are indefinite, and their application is left to each man's own discretion. In its concern for the dignity and peace of the community the civil law normally prescribes time, manner, place and persons for actions of this kind... The civil law has also the function of clarifying whatever is obscure in natural law."[28] While I showed in Chapter 2 that Spinoza and Pufendorf held very different conceptions of law, this doesn't affect the central point here, which is that it is perfectly consistent to maintain that civil laws are more limited in application than ethical laws *and* that civil laws are themselves determinate expressions of ethical law. Moreover, I will argue in Section 5.4 that ordinary ethical injunctions themselves must be accommodated to concrete conditions in order to effectively guide action, thereby further eroding the putative scope distinction between ethics and politics.

Difference of Aim

What about the apparent difference in the aims of human and divine law? As noted above, Spinoza appears to distinguish the aim of human law, which is "to protect life and the republic," from the aim of divine law, which "looks only at the supreme good, i.e., the true knowledge and love of God" in TTP 4 (TTP 4.9, iii.59). Human law looks only to coordinate actions so as to preserve the state, remaining relatively indifferent about the cognitive-affective states that conduce to this end (TTP 17.5, iii.201–2; TP 1/6). Ethics, by contrast, aims at increasing one's knowledge and love of God or Nature, focusing primarily on emending the content of one's beliefs, while remaining relatively indifferent about what actions follow from one's beliefs (4p59s). Politics aims at obedience; ethics at knowledge.

The first thing to note in dispelling the appearance of discontinuity here is that Spinoza's distinction between ethics and politics is *not* in fact a distinction between private judgments and public deeds. It is tempting to project onto Spinoza's account some version of the distinction between one's conscience and one's actions, given his defense of toleration and his broad political alignment with Arminian liberals, who invoked this distinction in order to counter the arguments for persecution from theocratically-minded orthodox Calvinists (Section 6.1).[29] But Spinoza's metaphysics precludes a sharp distinction between the public body and the private mind (see Section 6.5). Those features of human life that are public and fall under the power of the state must have a mental, as well as a physical, manifestation.

---

[28] *DO*, p. 156. Van Velthuysen advances a similar view in *A Dissertation*.
[29] See Nadler 1999, p. 12.

78   Spinoza's Political Psychology

Consider the concept of "obedience" (*obedientia*). While this might appear to depend only on the outward performance of some act, Spinoza claims that obedience is actually an "internal action of the soul" (TTP 17.8, iii.202), a fixed intention to follow the decrees of another (TP 2/19–20). In order to secure obedience, the state must influence the *minds* of its citizens. Spinoza makes this point when he qualifies his claim that one person's mind cannot be under another's absolute control, admitting that "some can get prior control of another person's judgment in many ways, some of them almost incredible" (TTP 20.4, iii.239). Indeed, as we saw in Section 2.5, authority depends precisely on the ability of the state to compel another's judgment: "So that person is most under another's control who resolves wholeheartedly to obey all the other's commands ... that ruler has the greatest authority who reigns over the hearts of his subjects" (TTP 17.8, iii.202).

There are, however, a couple of important differences between the way that the state aims to influence judgment and the way that philosophy does. First, the state influences the "hearts and minds" of citizens by way of the passions and the imagination, whereas philosophy seeks to move the intellect. And, whereas philosophy is primarily concerned with the content of one's motivating judgments, obedience to the state does not depend on the epistemic status of the judgments (TTP 17.6, iii.202; TP 1/6). I will return to the first point in Section 8.4. Here, I will simply make a couple of clarificatory notes about the state's apparent motive-neutrality.

First, the point about motive-neutrality must be understood in light of the fact that "men are mostly guided by appetite without reason" (TP 2/18). Given this suboptimal condition, we must allow that expedient motivators will vary with *ingenia*. Patriotic myths or calls for solidarity might contribute to the obedience of some, while only fear of punishment will motivate others.[30] The state must work with this motivational pluralism: "to establish things so that everyone, whatever his *ingenium*, prefers the public right to private advantage, this is the task, this is our concern" (TTP 17.16, iii.204). Base-level obedience can be achieved without total motivational uniformity.

The second observation is that motive-neutrality, as a practical principle, is not the same thing as motive-indifference. While it is true that, for Spinoza, the *fact* of obedience does not depend on any particular motive, as we noted above (Section 3.2), not all motive types are equally conducive to a peaceful state. As Spinoza points out, it is one thing to act by right, it is another to act in the best way (TP 5/1): a state that compels compliance from *whatever* motivation acts by right, but in order to produce genuine peace, citizens must be guided by

---

[30] Susan James highlights Spinoza's pluralism concerning reasons for obedience, calling particular attention to the role of "particular narratives" in coordinating action (James 2010).

the right kinds of motives.[31] Spinoza's political writings allow for a distinction between socially conducive and antisocial passions, the former being rooted in joy and love, the latter in sadness and hatred. As we shall see in Chapter 4, Spinoza thinks a peaceful state arises only when *securitas* prevails over fear.

Conclusion

In this chapter, I have argued that for Spinoza a thing is good to the extent and only to the extent that it increases one's power of acting or freedom. Civil goods are on the same scale as other goods. I have also raised and responded to some of the alleged reasons for thinking that ethics and politics are discontinuous. We can see now that the difference in scope between divine law and human law need not entail a difference in purpose, and while Spinoza does uphold some form of distinction between knowledge and obedience, this distinction does not indicate a sharp disjunction between politics and ethics. Even if the operations of the state must allow for antecedent irrationality, the function of the state is to reorient the *ingenia* of its subjects so that they are as rational and as joyful as possible. The question of precisely *how* civil mechanisms – which operate (primarily) on the imagination – can contribute to liberty or blessedness, remains to be worked out later in this study (especially in Chapters 6 and 7). And the full case for continuity will not be complete until the end of this book. But this chapter takes a major step in the direction of establishing the liberating and empowering function of the state. Chapter 4 will further delineate Spinoza's perfectionism by showing precisely why affects like hope and trust render us so much more powerful than affects like fear and indignation.

[31] See Blom 1995, p. 205.

4   The Politics of Hope and Fear

> Fear is the main source of superstition, and one of the main sources of cruelty. To conquer fear is the beginning of wisdom, in the pursuit of truth as in the endeavour after a worthy manner of life ... Under the influence of great fear, almost everybody becomes superstitious ... Fear generates impulses of cruelty, and therefore promotes such superstitious beliefs as seem to justify cruelty. Neither a man nor a crowd nor a nation can be trusted to act humanely or to think sanely under the influence of a great fear.
> – Bertrand Russell, "An Outline of Intellectual Rubbish"[1]

Fear is often regarded as indispensable to governance. This was certainly the view of two of Spinoza's chief political influences, Machiavelli and Hobbes, who regarded fear as the very tissue that binds together the body politic. Machiavelli infamously maintains in *The Prince* that, while it is best to be *both* loved and feared, "if one of them has to be lacking, it is much safer to be feared than loved."[2] And Hobbes writes that "the origin of large and lasting societies lay not in mutual human benevolence but in men's mutual fear,"[3] claiming also that "of all the passions, that which inclineth men least to break the laws is fear...excepting some generous natures, it is the only thing [when there is appearance of profit or pleasure by breaking the laws] that makes men keep them."[4] On Hobbes's account, the state aims to replace the pervasive and diffuse anxiety of the state of nature with a more limited and less debilitating form of fear, namely, fear of sovereign power.[5]

---

[1] B. Russell 2009, pp. 68–70.

[2] *Prince*, Ch. XVII, p. 59.

[3] *De Cive*, 1.3, p. 24.

[4] *Lev.*, Ch. 29, p. 206.

[5] In describing the diffuse fear of the state of nature, Hobbes writes: "I mean by [fear] any anticipation of future evil. In my view, not only flight, but also distrust, suspicion, precaution and provision against fear are all characteristic of men who are afraid" (*De Cive*, 1.2 note, p. 25). Collective fear of a common power helps to check mutual suspicion: "men's natural Disposition is such that if they are not restrained by fear of a common power, they will distrust and fear each other" (*De Cive*, preface to the readers, p. 10). Jan Blits has argued that civil fear replaces the "indeterminate or objectless fear" that "precedes all experience and underlies all particular fears" (Blits 1989, pp. 424–5). Profound, unfocused existential fear is supplanted by a more concrete,

While Spinoza acknowledges that the commonwealth must "preserve the causes that foster fear and respect"[6] (TP 4/4; cf. 4p37s2), he seeks to diminish the role of fear in civic affairs, tellingly breaking with Machiavelli and Hobbes. Against Machiavelli, he commends the decidedly more moralistic, Ciceronian approach of governing "more by benefits than by fear [*beneficiis magis quam metu*]" (TP 9/14).[7] Indeed, he claims that part of the very purpose of the state is to liberate people from fear:

From the foundations of the Republic explained above it follows most clearly that *its ultimate end is not to dominate, restraining men by fear, and making them subject to another's control, but on the contrary to free each person from fear, so that he can live securely* [secure], *as far as possible,* i.e., so that he retains to the utmost his natural right to exist and operate without harm to himself or anyone else. The end of the Republic, I say, is not to change men from rational beings into beasts or automata, but to enable their minds and bodies to perform their functions safely, to enable them to use their reason freely, and not to clash with one another in hatred, anger or deception, or deal inequitably with one another. *So the end of the Republic is really freedom.* (TTP 20.11–12, iii.240–1 – my emphasis)

In this passage, Spinoza revealingly links freedom and the maximization of power or right with the diminution of fear and the establishment of security. The language here, I submit, is quite deliberate: security (*securitas*) is a form of hope bereft of fear (3p18s2). The suggestion is that to the extent that the state can promote *securitas,* it empowers its citizens, liberating them from fear. We should not be surprised, then, to find Spinoza taking the establishment of *securitas* to be a principal aim of the state (TP 1/6; TP 5/2). *Securitas* is just an expression of the other ends that Spinoza cites: peace and freedom.

Spinoza does not wish simply to replace one form of fear (*metus*) with another, he wants to promote hope (*spes*) and devotion (*devotio*) to the state in place of fear. He even suggests that this affective distinction separates a free from an oppressed people: "a free multitude is guided by hope more than by fear, whereas a multitude which has been subjugated is guided more by fear than by hope. The first want to cultivate life; the second care only to avoid death. The first are eager to live for themselves; the second are forced to belong to the victor. So we say that the second are slaves, and the first free" (TP 5/6). While the reasoning here is not exactly pellucid, a close analysis of the text

---

circumscribed fear of sovereign power. For a reading of Hobbes as somewhat less fear-driven, see C. Wilson 2008a, esp. p. 192.

[6] I take the language here to be significant: it is the preservation of the scheme of punishments and deterrents that give rise to fear that must be preserved, not the affect itself. The importance of this distinction will be clear by the end of this chapter.

[7] Cicero writes: "there is nothing at all more suited to protecting and retaining influence than to be loved, and nothing less suited than to be feared" (Cicero 1991, II, 23, pp. 70–1).

suggests that Spinoza is claiming that fear is part of what constitutes the latter's subjugation or unfreedom, while hope (joyful, affirmative motivation) is part of what constitutes the former's freedom.[8]

This account dovetails with Spinoza's treatment of hopeful obedience to the state as willing or voluntary and fearful obedience as compelled by force (*vim*) or constraint (*coactus*). The hopeful person is presented in Spinoza's political treatises as "eager to live for themselves" (TP 5/6), while one who lives from fear is said to be "compelled [*coactus*] by evil, acts like a slave, and lives under the command of another [*sub imperio alterius*]" (TTP 4.38, iii.66).[9] Spinoza relies on the same conceptual pairs of fear-constraint and hope-willingness in the subsequent chapter, where he maintains that "in each state the laws must be so instituted that men are checked not so much by fear as by the hope of some good they desire very much. For in this way everyone will do his duty eagerly [*cupide*]" (TTP 5.24, iii.74). This leads him to praise Moses for taking "the greatest care that the people should do their duty, not so much from fear, as voluntarily [*sponte*]" (TTP 5.28, iii.75) citing his deployment of religion to bind the people "with benefits [*beneficiis*]," or perceived future rewards – that is, by hope (TTP 5.29, iii.75).

The connection between hope and willingness is no less evident in the TP, where Spinoza claims that legislators should "take special care that the subjects do their duty voluntarily [*sponte*] rather than because the law compels them to" (TP 10/7) and that "men must be so led that they seem to themselves not to be led, but to live according to their own *ingenium* and from their free decision [*libero decreto*]" (TP 10/8), treating "hope" as a species of willing motives (ibid.). He celebrates willing compliance not only because it contributes to a more stable state, but also because freeing people from fear enables them to act from virtue (TP 10/8). The privileging of hope over fear is thus absolutely critical to Spinoza's normative political thought,

---

[8] We can reproduce the main skeins of the argument by working backwards from the conclusion: "So [*unde*] we say that the second are slaves, and the first free." Spinoza distinguishes between two people (or types of person), one of whom, A, is a slave; the other, B, is free. Spinoza concludes that A is a slave because she is "forced to belong to the victor," seeking "only to avoid death." A's servitude is thus inferred in part from her motivational state; and this motivation – that acting so as to avoid death – is a form of fear that Spinoza calls "timidity" (*timor*) (more in Section 4.4). The suggestion then is not merely that a subjugated people *tend* to be more fearful; rather, fear is part of what constitutes her subjugation or unfreedom. A similar analysis can be provided in the case of B. We are justified in calling her free because she "want[s] to cultivate life" and is "eager to live" for herself – in other words, she acts more from hope than from fear. Joyful, affirmative motivation is part of what constitutes freedom.

[9] Elsewhere, Spinoza indicates that all citizens act from the command of another irrespective of motive (TTP 17.5–7; TP 2/10). In the early chapters of the TTP (Chs. 4–5), though, Spinoza seems to have allowed for the possibility of remaining fully *sui iuris* in a republic. The incompatibility of these passages with claims from the later part of the work (Ch. 17) suggests that these chapters may have been composed at rather different times in the five-year stretch (1665–1670) when he was composing the TTP. For more, see Section 7.2.

as hopeful citizens not only preserve the state more effectively than fearful citizens, they are also freer, less constrained, and more willing than their fearful counterparts.

But despite Spinoza's evident preference of hope-driven over fear-driven governance and its importance for grounding his political advice, this preference has garnered relatively little attention by scholars.[10] Perhaps this is because this privileging looks unsupportable on Spinozistic grounds. We'll begin this chapter by considering several reasons why Spinoza's promotion of hope over fear looks untenable.

4.1   Three Challenges to Spinoza's Privileging of Hope over Fear

Inseparable Counterparts Challenge

One obvious reason for thinking that Spinoza isn't entitled to drive a normative wedge between hope and fear comes from his very definition of these affects in the *Ethics*. Hope is defined as "inconstant joy, born of the idea of a future or past thing whose outcome we to some extent doubt" (3 DA 12); and fear is defined as "an inconstant sadness" born of the same kind of idea. Following these definitions, Spinoza concludes that "there is neither hope without fear, nor fear without hope" (3 DA 13, exp.); the uncertainty that hope involves is fear (namely, fear that the desired thing won't come to be), and vice versa.[11] Hope and fear are presented as inseparable counterparts, containing all of the same components. The inextricable connection between these unstable affects explains why Spinoza claims in the preface to the TTP that people mired in uncertainty "vacillate wretchedly between hope and fear" (TTP Preface.1, iii.5). If "hope and fear are more or less interchangeable," as one scholar maintains,[12] then Spinoza's normative privileging looks unjustifiable. We may refer to this as the *Inseparable Counterparts Challenge*.

---

[10] There are some notable exceptions here. Hasana Sharp stresses the extent to which Spinoza attempts to overcome fear-driven politics, though she does not emphasize the superiority of hope and *securitas* (Sharp 2005). Étienne Balibar acknowledges the distinction between hope and fear, but does not put as much stock in the normative privileging as I do (Balibar 1989). Matheron's observations, which stress the entanglement of hope and fear, come closest to my own: "l'Etat peut gouverner en utilisant comme principal stimulant (principal seulement, car aucune des deux méthodes n'est jamais entièrement négligée), soit l'espoir de récompenses lié à la crainte de ne pas en être reconnu digne, soit la crainte de châtiments liée à l'espoir de ne pas les mériter; et le premier système est bien préférable au second, car il suscite l'amour et non la haine" (Matheron 1969, pp. 129–30).

[11] Cf. Descartes's definition of fear as an "insecure hope" (*Passions of the Soul* III, 165).

[12] Verbeek 2003, p. 27.

Passions as Equal Constraints Challenge

The second challenge concerns whether or not Spinoza is entitled to the specific claim that fearful actions as more constrained than hopeful action. Spinoza's treatment of *coactus* in the *Ethics* and in his correspondence seems to preclude any division between hope and fear on these grounds. Spinoza opposes constraint or compulsion (*coactus*) to free action in his definition of a free thing (*res libera*): "that thing is called free which exists from the necessity of its nature alone, and is determined to act by itself alone. But a thing is called necessary, or rather compelled [*coacta*], which is determined by another to exist and to produce an effect in a certain and determinate manner" (1D7). Spinoza provides a similar gloss in a letter to his friend Georg Schuller: "I say that a thing is free if it exists and acts solely from the necessity of its own nature, and compelled [*coactam*] if it is determined by something else to exist and produce effects in a fixed and determinate way" (Ep. 58).[13] The distinction between free action and compelled action is rather straightforward in these passages: the former follow from one's nature alone; the latter follow in part from the nature of an external cause.

This distinction maps directly onto the distinction between adequate and partial causation introduced in 3D2. In the subsequent analysis, passions are defined as partially caused – that is, compelled – affects. Not only are the passions themselves compelled, anything that we do from these passions will also be compelled, reflecting the influence of external causes. On this strict view, it looks like hope, fear, and whatever follows from these passions are compelled. Since our aim is liberation from passivity, constraint, and bondage, we should seek to transcend both hope and fear: "the more we strive to live according to the guidance of reason, the more we strive to depend less on hope, to free ourselves from fear, to conquer fortune as much as we can, and to direct our actions by the certain counsel of reason" (4p47s). Based on the account of *coactus* in the *Ethics*, it isn't clear what could justify treating hopeful action as less constrained than fearful action. We may call this the *Passions as Equal Constraints Challenge*.

Equal Willingness Challenge

Finally, it is unclear how, given his conception of volition, Spinoza could defend the specific claim that hopeful actions are more *willing* than fearful

---

[13] See also his response to Hugo Boxel's version of the tiresome charge that if everything is necessitated there is no such thing as freedom. Spinoza accuses his interlocutor of making "no distinction between coercion [*coactio*], or force [*vim*], and necessity [*necessitatem*]" (Ep. 56, 1674). We learn very little about how Spinoza understands "coercion" (*coactio*) here. But his remarks indicate that when we have adequate ideas, we are necessitated, but unconstrained: "That a man wants to live, to love, etc., is not a coerced action. But it is necessary. Much more does God will to be, to know and to act [freely, but necessarily]."

ones. If Spinoza's strict account of constraint seems to entail that all passionate behavior is (equally) constrained, his conception of volition seems to imply that all passionate behavior is equally willing. To appreciate this, consider his conception of the will. He denies, of course, the existence of an "absolute, or free, will" (2p48; see also 1p29, 1p33). Rather, all ideas *qua* ideas involve "singular volitions" (2p49d), that is, affirmations (or negations). And anything whatsoever that we do, from *either* adequate or inadequate ideas, follows from our striving (3p9), which, insofar as it "is related only to the mind," is called the will (*voluntas*) (3p9s).[14]

By conceiving of will in terms of striving, Spinoza's conception of will somewhat resembles Hobbes's. Hobbes famously claims that the will is just the "last appetite" of deliberation (which is itself just the succession of appetites).[15] On the basis of this account, he rejects the Aristotelian category of mixed actions, claiming that "when man throweth his goods into the Sea for *feare* the ship should sink, he doth it nevert_helesse very willingly, and may refuse to doe it if he will: It is therefore the action, of one that was *free*."[16] The key implication here is that "Feare, and Liberty are consistent."[17] This provides support for Hobbes's claim that "Covenants entered into by fear...are obligatory."[18]

Spinoza of course rejects Hobbes's conception of liberty as the absence of external impediments. In doing so, he severs the connection between free action and physically unhindered voluntary action, since not all unhindered voluntary acts are adequately caused. But once voluntariness is cut loose from freedom, it is difficult to see how Spinoza can claim that actions performed out of fear could be said to be less *willing* than actions performed out of hope, given his broadly Hobbesian, naturalistic, account of voluntariness. And, in the passage where Spinoza attempts to ground the concepts of subjection and authority in the TTP (see Section 2.5), he indicates that fearful and hopeful

---

[14] It is difficult to see how this definition of will is to be squared with his earlier formulation "by will I understand a faculty of affirming and denying, and *not desire*" (2p48s – my emphasis). One possibility is that affirmation is just a special case of striving – the striving of an idea.

[15] *Lev.*, 1.6.

[16] *Lev.*, p. 146; Cf. Aristotle's *Nicomachean Ethics*, 3.1

[17] *Lev.*, p. 146.

[18] Ibid., p. 97. See also "It is a question often moved, whether such covenants oblige, as are extorted from men by fear. As for example: whether, if a man for fear of death, hath promised to give a thief an hundred pounds the next day, and not discover him, whether such covenant be obligatory or not. And though in some cases such covenant may be void, yet it is not therefore void, because extorted by fear. For there appeareth no reason, why that which we do upon fear, should be less than that which we do for covetousness. For both the one and the other maketh the action voluntary" (*EL*, p. 86; cf. *De Cive* 2.16). Contrary to what he says elsewhere, though, in his *Treatise "Of Liberty and Necessity,"* Hobbes admits that terror or compulsion can limit freedom: "the distinction of free into free from compulsion and free from necessitation I acknowledge. For to be free from compulsion is to do a thing so as terror be not the cause of his will to do it" (*HBLN*, p. 30).

compliance with the law are at once voluntary *and* performed by the right of another:

> For whatever reason a man resolves to carry out the commands of the supreme power, *whether because he fears punishment, or because he hopes for something from it,* or because he loves his Country, or because he has been impelled by any other affect whatever, *he still forms his resolution according to his own judgment* [*ex proprio suo consilio deliberat*] notwithstanding that he acts in accordance with the command of the supreme power. (TTP 17.6, iii.202 – my emphasis)

If hopeful and fearful compliance are equally voluntary, how can Spinoza be justified treating the former as more willing than the latter? Let us call this the *Equal Willingness Challenge.*

There are, thus, several Spinozistic reasons to doubt whether he can justify strongly privileging hope over fear: hope and fear are inseparable counterparts; to the extent that we are in the grips of any passion whatsoever, our behavior is constrained, passive, and unfree; and, finally, hopeful and fearful actions reflect our striving or will to the same extent. One might also question the independent plausibility of thinking that the motivational or affective state of an agent is relevant to matters of freedom and constraint. It is sometimes proposed, not altogether implausibly, that the question of whether or not one is constrained is determined by objective material and social conditions that do not depend on one's desires or on one's perception of the condition.[19] Spinoza's claim that hopeful citizens are freer, less constrained, and more willing than fearful citizens thus faces a host of challenges.

4.2   Fear and Disempowerment

Fear as Destabilizing

As a first step toward vindicating Spinoza's disparate treatment of hope and fear, let's briefly consider some of the debilitating effects of fear. One of the main reasons why Spinoza thinks that fear is so disempowering is that it contributes to civil disintegration. Whereas Machiavelli allows that the right sort of fear – something like awe – promotes not only compliance, but also reverence for the leader, Spinoza thinks that intense and pervasive fear tends to degenerate into to indignation (*indignatio*),[20] which is the source of civil dissolution. Consider his analysis of the natural limits of state power in TP 3/9:

> [T]hings most people resent are less within a Commonwealth's Right. For certainly men are guided by nature to unite in one aim, either because of a common [hope

---

[19] Kramer 2003.
[20] See Matheron on the place of *indignatio* in defining, and circumscribing the limits of, state power (Matheron 1969, 1994).

or] a common fear, or because they long to avenge some common loss. Because the Commonwealth's Right is defined by the common power of a multitude, it's certain that its power and Right are diminished to the extent that it provides many people with reasons to conspire against it. Certainly the Commonwealth has some things it must fear for itself. Like each individual citizen, or like a man in the state of nature, the greater the reason for fear it has, the less it is its own master (TP 3/9).

The argument here is fairly straightforward: civic fear naturally gives way to indignation and, ultimately, conspiracy and revolt.[21] As Étienne Balibar points out, the "fear of the masses" in the subjective sense (i.e., the fear *experienced* by the masses) gives rise to the "fear of the masses" in the objective sense – the fearful multitude becomes an object of fear for the sovereign.[22] Consequently, to the extent that a state generates pervasive fear, it undermines its own power, as the more reason one has to fear others, the less power or right one has (TP 2/15).

We get further insight into why fear weakens the state in TTP 5, where, after endorsing Seneca's dictum that violent or tyrannical governments never last long,[23] Spinoza writes:

For as long as men act only from fear, they act very unwillingly, and don't recognize the advantage, even the necessity, of doing what they're doing. All they care about is saving their necks, and avoiding punishment. They can only rejoice whenever some evil or harm happens to their ruler, however much evil it may bring them; they can't help wanting all sorts of bad things to happen to him; when they can, they help to bring them about (TTP 5.22, iii.74).

We will want to bear in mind the suggestion here that those who act from fear alone "act very unwillingly, and don't recognize the advantage...of doing what they're doing" when we return to Spinoza's treatment of willingness at the end of this chapter. The key point for now is that those who are guided by fear regard the sovereign as a hostile force and will only reluctantly uphold its laws and institutions. And those who comply only grudgingly, from fear alone, will celebrate the toppling of an oppressive governor and will look for opportunities to depose their oppressor. This supports the connection between fear and conspiracy drawn in TP 3/9.

In both of his political treatises, then, Spinoza maintains that fear contributes to political instability and weakness, and that one who promotes general

---

[21] It should not be surprising that widespread fear often transforms into indignation, since to the extent that something provokes pervasive public fear, it will come to be hated as the source of disempowerment. Indignation for Spinoza is hatred (in part) on behalf of others (3 DA xx) – a kind of Strawsonian vicarious reactive attitude. A sovereign that provokes fear can avoid indignation only to the extent that it can offset this sense of hatred with a stronger promise of benefits (3 DA xix).

[22] Balibar 1989, esp. p. 107.

[23] See also TTP 16.29, iii.194.

fear will reap what he or she sows.[24] While some degree of stability might be wrought by fear, it cannot be relied upon to maintain loyalty. As Spinoza puts it in the *Ethics*, "Harmony [*concordia*] is...commonly produced by fear, but then it is untrustworthy" (4 Cap XVI; cf. TP 7/2).

One might perhaps think that Spinoza is overstating his case here. Surely, there are instances where fear seems to have played the primary role in producing stability. Spinoza himself seems to acknowledge this in his discussion of the Ottoman Empire ("the Turks") (see TP 6/4; TTP, preface, Section 6–7). But, as we saw in Section 3.2, Spinoza distinguishes peace from mere stability, claiming that "A commonwealth whose subjects, terrified by fear, don't take up arms should be said to be without war, but not at peace" (TP 5/4). A similar point is made in Spinoza's discussion of the Israelites after the election of the Levite priests in TTP 17. These angry and rebellious people were subdued only after being "worn out by a great calamity or plague...in such a way that they all preferred death to life" (TTP 17.104, iii.219). Spinoza claims that this should be described as an end of rebellion rather than as a period of harmony (ibid.).

So, even when fear is effective in eliminating strife, the absence of strife must not be confused with genuine peace. Here, as elsewhere, fearful action is portrayed as slavish,[25] and slavish compliance gives rise to a languid, lifeless body politic: "When the peace of a Commonwealth depends on its subjects' lack of spirit – so that they're led like sheep, and know only how to be slaves – it would be more properly called a wasteland than a Commonwealth" (TP 5/4). Citizen-subjects of a fear-driven state will themselves, in turn, be rather weak and unfree, as they will live in a condition of distrust and suspicion, lacking the many comforts and aids that come with living in a genuinely harmonious state.

The Incapacitating Effects of Fear

Spinoza belongs to a long and distinguished line of thinkers who regard fear as epistemically impairing. Cicero, for instance, in his analysis of the "perturbations" (*perturbationes*) of the soul, identifies a range of forms of fear, many of which are disruptive of judgment.[26] The Stoics were said by Andronicus to have regarded fear as an "irrational shrinking" of the soul.[27] And the Epicureans, of course, took as their main goal the liberation of men from fear and anguish,

---

[24] Rebellion is "without doubt a natural thing" (TP 3/9). See Sharp 2013.
[25] Spinoza repeatedly claims that those who comply with divine law only out of fear of punishment act as slaves, in a manner wholly unfitting of those who know and love God. See again his response to van Velthuysen's critique of the TTP in Ep. 43 to Jacob Ostens; See also Epistle 76 to Burgh.
[26] *Tusculan Disputations*, esp. 4.viii.
[27] *HP*, p. 411.

especially fear of eternal suffering.[28] Closer to Spinoza's time, Montaigne, Vives, and Bacon all offer variations on these ancient themes.[29]

Spinoza's most sustained treatment of the way in which fear evacuates judgment can be found in the preface to the TTP, where he singles fear out as "the reason...why superstition arises, lasts, and increases" (Preface.5, iii.6). Spinoza repeats his view that fear, specifically fear of hell,[30] is the wellspring of superstition in an irritated response to Albert Burgh who wrote to Spinoza to try to convert him to Catholicism. Spinoza replies by claiming that Burgh has "become a slave of this Church...guided not so much by the love of God as by fear of hell, the only cause of superstition" (Ep. 76). Spinoza's primary explanation of why fear leads to superstition is that it renders men desperate and credulous (TTP Preface, Section 4), as a consequence of which people recklessly place their trust in unreliable systems of belief (see Section 6.2).

Spinoza provides us with an object lesson in TP 10, where he attributes the fall of the Roman republic to a fear-driven and calamitously stupid concession of nearly unlimited dictatorial powers to a hero-savior.[31] The point here is that "in the greatest crises of the state, when everyone is seized by panic, as often happens, then everyone approves only what the present fear urges, without giving any consideration to the future or to the laws" (TP 10/10).

What emerges from Spinoza's treatment of fear and superstition is that they stand in a mutually reinforcing relationship. Superstition is enabled by fear; and fear is often encouraged by superstition. Because superstitious teachings will not be able to sustain credence on their own merits, they must be propped up by emotional inducements and internal policing:

The superstitious know how to reproach people for their vices better than they know how to teach them virtues, and they strive, not to guide men by reason, but to restrain them by fear, so that they flee the evil rather than love virtues. Such people aim only to make others as wretched as they themselves are, so it is no wonder that they are generally burdensome and hateful to men (4p63s1).

The result is a vicious circle: fear breeds superstition and superstition keeps people in fear.

[28] "[T]hat fear of Acheron [must] be sent packing which troubles the life of man from its deepest depths, suffuses all with the blackness of the death, and leaves no delight clean and pure" (Lucretius 2006, 3.36–8.
[29] Montaigne, "Of Fear" (in Montaigne 1958, esp. p. 53). Bacon, "Of Death" in *MW*. See Noreña 1989, p. 184.
[30] The Epicurean flavor of Spinoza's thought is nowhere more evident than in his concern with diminishing fear, which runs throughout his political treatises.
[31] The editors of the Hackett edition plausibly propose that the fall of the Roman republic could be understood here as a proxy for the fall of the stadtholderless republic of the United Provinces in 1672. Spinoza analyzes the two episodes together at the end of the previous chapter.

We will explore the relationship between fear and superstition in far greater detail in Section 6.2. For now, though, it is sufficient to have shown that Spinoza thinks that fear generally impairs judgment and erodes epistemic standards, which is one reason why, even in a stable state, a fearful citizenry will be disempowered.

4.3   Hope, Security, and Empowerment

Fear is politically and personally harmful. That much is clear. But in order to see why those who are guided by hope are freer, less constrained, and more willing subjects than those who act from fear, we must consider exactly what Spinoza envisages when he commends civil hope. Spinoza often portrays the hope that typifies a good commonwealth as a hope for political power or civic standing. A deeply exclusionary or political unequal state will undermine hope and, in turn, undermine stability (see Section 7.2). Inequality and the absence of hope leads "to envy and incessant murmurings and finally to outbreaks of sedition" (TP 7/13). Only if widespread hope for civic standing, including the "hope of achieving honors," is preserved will people "seem to themselves not to be led, but to live according to their own *ingenium* and free decision" (TP 10/8).

More generally, civic hope consists in the idea that one will benefit in some way by supporting the institutions of the state. As opposed to one who defers to authority out of a fear of punishment, one who acts from hope is bound to authority because of some perceived benefit (*beneficium*) (TP 2/10; TTP 17.6, iii.202). One model of hopeful governance is the Hebrew commonwealth: "Moses did not try to convince the Israelites by reason, but was concerned only to bind them by a covenant, oaths and benefits" (TTP 14.7, iii.174). Spinoza calls the specific affect that bound the Israelites to Moses "devotion" (*devotio*), defined as love mixed with wonder (3 DA x), which he regards as the most powerful way of winning people over (TTP 17.90, iii.216–17). Moses established a state religion, which imbued him with a kind of preternatural power, to help promote devotion.

At first blush, one might be tempted to conclude, with Theo Verbeek, that devotion "does not belong to the same class of feelings as hope and fear."[32] Unlike hope, devotion is a form of love that renders one dependent on another. But while not all forms of hope entail devotion, civic hope – at least in its best form – does. The connection between hope and devotion is indicated in

---

[32] Verbeek's further claim that "devotion" is "not a passion" (Verbeek 2003, p. 28) is rather suspect. Devotion is most certainly a passionate, as opposed to a rational, form of love, since it springs from wonder, the quintessential product of the imagination (Spinoza exploits the etymological connection between *miraculum* and *admirari*).

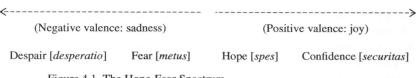

Figure 4.1. The Hope-Fear Spectrum

TTP Ch. 5, where immediately after claiming that "in each state the laws must be so instituted that men are checked not so much by fear as by the hope of some good they desire very much. For in this way everyone will do his duty eagerly" (TTP 5.24, iii.74), Spinoza approvingly relates how Moses was able to motivate compliance "not so much from fear, as voluntarily" (TTP 5.28, iii.75), indicating that devotion to Moses is an expression of the hope that characterizes a good state. This point is reinforced by the description of Moses as binding the Israelites with benefits: one is devoted to another because one regards the other as a source of benefits, a fount of hope. While secular states may be hard-pressed to inspire religious wonder in the way that Moses could, well-functioning states will try to promote a republican surrogate for religious devotion (more in Section 6.3).[33]

One's level of devotion, or commitment, to the state will vary according to the intensity of one's hope, which lies on a kind of spectrum with fear. One end of this spectrum is positively valenced (forms of joy); the other is negatively valenced (forms of sadness). At negatively valenced extreme is despair (*desperatio*), which is "a sadness borne of the idea of a future or past thing, concerning which the cause of doubting has been removed" (3 DA xv, ii.194; 3p18s2) – that is, a resignation to the coming to pass of some undesirable thing or event. At the other end of spectrum is "confidence" (*securitas*), which is "a joy born of the idea of a future or past thing concerning which the cause of doubting has been removed" (3 DA xiv; 3p18s2). Closer to the middle are garden-variety forms of fear and hope (see figure 4.1).

In the best kind of state, which serves the interests of its members and encourages their participation, citizens will be guided by a relatively stable form of joy, arising not from some faint hope, but from something more like an expectation that they will benefit from a well-functioning state. The better the state, the more it will approximate full *securitas*.

This is, in fact, precisely what Spinoza maintains in both of his political treatises. For instance, in the *Political Treatise*, he identifies peace (*pax*) and security (*securitas*) as the primary aims of the state (TP 1/6; TP 5/2). And in

---

[33] We see evidence of an ideal of "secular devotion" in the TP, where he claims that people may (voluntarily) subject themselves to authority because they love of the civil order (*statum civilem amant*) (TP 3/8).

the TTP, in the passage where he explicitly identifies liberty as the goal of the state (see opening of this chapter), he claims that the purpose of the state is to "free each person from fear, so that he may live securely [*secure*], as far as possible" (TTP 20.11, iii.240–1). Unfortunately, the significance of these passages is often missed, as readers seem to take *securitas* to indicate something more like physical safety. Safety is, no doubt, a good. But just as peace is not merely the absence of war, *securitas* is not merely the absence of violence. *Securitas* indicates both a condition of civic security and an affective or psycho-social condition, a kind of social trust, without which the civic ideal of peace, harmony, and the unity of minds is not possible (*E*4p37s2; cf. TP 6/3; TTP 17.13, iii.203).[34] Only in a state where fear has largely been vanquished, replaced by the firm hope of *securitas*, can citizens be said to truly and reliably agree with one another, since only those who live in *securitas* will love the same thing (4p34s) – namely, civic order – and function cooperatively to produce a common desired effect, namely, the preservation of the state.[35] It is a mark of a good state that in it people feel secure that they will benefit from the functioning of the state and will consequently feel a sense of devotion or civic commitment.

We can begin to see now why Spinoza thinks that a hopeful citizenry is significantly better off than a fearful people. Part of the explanation is that hope conduces to greater political stability than fear. Where hope is pervasive, the state will be more stable, creating a positive feedback loop through which hope and stability are encouraged. Hope is also intrinsically better than fear for the individual. As we saw in Section 3.2, welfare may be gauged affectively, in terms of the extent of one's overall joy. Hope, as a species of joy, is sign of increased power, while fear, a species of sadness, indicates a diminution of power. *Securitas*, as a relatively stable and pure form of joy, is a particularly empowering form of hope.

Moreover, whereas fearful citizens are epistemically incapacitated – credulous and deeply susceptible to superstitious manipulation – secure citizens are relatively well-positioned epistemically. Consider the relationship between a secure citizen and a fully rational agent. A fully rational person apprehends the link between her power and the power of the state in which she lives, steadfastly obeying the laws knowing that this will enhance the power of the state and in turn his own power. Few people are like this (TTP 4.6, iii.58–9). Nevertheless, citizens of a well-organized state will apprehend, to some extent, that the laws are for the general good, and this recognition grounds their hopefulness or *securitas*. What Spinoza is describing is not the false hope of the

---

[34] Even if confidence and trust can be achieved through timidity (4p37s2), harmony (*concordia*) wrought by fear is *sine fide*, and so only impermanent (4 Cap. xvi).

[35] See J. Steinberg, forthcoming on co-operation and *convenire*.

ignorant or the wishfulness of the vulnerable; it is a robust, experientially well-grounded hope. The secure citizen perceives the connection between his power and the power of the state in which he lives, steadfastly upholding civic laws and institutions believing correctly that this will enhance the power of the state and in turn one's own power. To use a Spinozistic turn of phrase, we may say that those who are guided by *securitas* (vis-à-vis the state) seem to grasp the goodness of the *civitas* "as if through a cloud." To live with a firm, pervasive, well-grounded sense of hope is to live joyfully, to have one's power of acting increased, even if it is not "increased to the point where he conceives himself and his actions adequately" (4p59d).

This account enables us to flesh out the model of civil liberation sketched in Section 3.2. There we saw that peace is not merely the absence of strife. Full peace, which arises from the rational fortitude of the people, looks rather unattainable. Nevertheless, we now have a vision of what a somewhat more achievable approximation might look like: a state characterized by widespread *securitas*.

4.4   Dispelling the Challenges

Response to the Inseparable Counterparts Challenge

We are now in a position to respond directly to the concerns raised in Section 4.1, beginning with the *Inseparable Counterparts Challenge*. According to this concern, it is no accident that those who are uncertain fluctuate between hope and fear, since hope and fear are unstable passions that are inextricably bound to one another. Consequently, it is difficult to see how Spinoza could be justified in sharply distinguishing between them.

A couple of observations help us to dispel this worry. First, while hope and fear may have all of the same ingredients, hope-*cum*-fear has a different character from fear-*cum*-hope, at least in the sense that these affects take different objects. There is a difference between representing a good while fearing that one will not attain it and representing an evil while hoping it doesn't come to pass.[36] Moreover, we saw that the ratio of joy to sadness may vary considerably

---

[36] Matheron rightly distinguishes between *crainte-espoir* and *espoir-crainte,* writing "même s'il n'y a ni espoir sans crainte ni crainte sans espoir, la crainte mêlée d'espoir n'est pas la même chose que l'espoir mêlé de crainte. Dans le premier cas, nous craignons une diminution future de notre puissance d'agir et espérons seulement y échapper; cet espoir, certes, augmente lui-même notre puissance d'agir, mais seulement par rapport à la diminution que l'image attristante nous avait infligée de façon anticipée: en fait, il nous ramène au *statu quo ante*. Dans de telles conditions, si la crainte peut fort bien devenir désespoir, la sécurité absolue, en revanche, n'est guère concevable...Dans le second cas, au contraire, nous espérons positivement une augmentation future de notre puissance d'agir et craignons seulement de ne pas l'obtenir; pour la même raison, dès lors, le désespoir absolu n'est guère concevable" (Matheron 1969, pp. 128–9).

between hope and fear. And the hope that Spinoza thinks typifies a good state – namely, *securitas* – is a particularly stable and joyful variant, one that is relatively free from the debilitating effects of fear. Furthermore, in elevating hope over fear, Spinoza is not merely distinguishing between fleeting, occurrent affections, he is distinguishing between affective constitutions or *ingenia*. Indeed, he often seems to have in mind the prevailing public affect of a commonwealth or nation – its ethos (Section 1.2). Citizens who are reliably confident both in relation to the state and to one another will be significantly and consistently more powerful than those who live in fear. So, while hope and fear are kindred passions, this in no way precludes sharply privileging of *securitas* over fear. So much for the *Inseparable Counterparts Challenge*.

Response to the Passions as Equal Constraints Challenge

What about the *Passions as Equal Constraints Challenge*? According to this worry, Spinoza's suggestion that fearful action is constrained (*coactus*), while hopeful action is not, is unjustified. All passions – be they forms of joy or forms of sadness – depend upon external causes and are thus, in Spinoza's strict sense, constrained or compelled; as is anything that follows from these passions.

While Spinoza's account unmistakably entails that all passionate activity is constrained (*coactus*), it does not follow that all passions are equally constraining. Here we must distinguish an affect's causal history from its consequences. Whereas active affects follow from one's nature alone, passions are, by definition, partially exogenous. And to the extent that we are affected by external causes, we are passive, and so constrained. However, it is perfectly possible for one's power of acting to be increased – or for one to be made more joyful – by external causes (Section 3.2). In light of this, we can see how Spinoza can maintain that those who act from fear, with a diminished power of acting, are more constrained on the whole than those who act from *securitas*, an elevated power of acting. One who is guided by *securitas* is both freer and less constrained on the whole than one who is guided by fear.

Response to the Equal Willingness Challenge

There is another way that one might answer the *Passions as Equal Constraints Challenge*. Since Spinoza sometimes conceives of being *coactus* not in contrast with *free* action, but in contrast with *willing* action,[37] if it could be shown that

---

[37] E.g., "whoever has transferred his power to defend himself to another, whether voluntarily [*sponte*] or because compelled by force [*vi coactus*]..." (TTP 16.11, iii.195); "it's been necessary to set it up so that everyone is compelled to live according to the prescription of reason,

Spinoza has good reasons for maintaining that fearful actions are performed less *willingly* than hopeful ones, this would give us a reason for thinking that the former are more constrained than the latter.

For this, we must respond to the third challenge, which requires more explication than the first two, as it turns on an interpretation of the concept of willingness in Spinoza. Spinoza does not, as the challenge supposes, iden- tify willingness with voluntariness. Even if everything that is done from one's desire or striving may be said to be voluntary, one needn't conclude that all actions performed from one's desire or striving are equally willing. Rather, willingness may be seen as a function of the directness with which one affirms one's actions.

We find the distinction between direct and indirect affirmation in the *Ethics*, where Spinoza contrasts fearful and rational action. Spinoza here emphasizes that rational people always act *directly for the sake of some good*, affirming their actions, rather than acting out for fear. One who is rational may flee dan- gers, but she will do so out of strength of mind, rather than out of a fear of death: "one who lives according to the dictate of reason alone, is not led by fear (by P63), but desires the good directly (by P63C)" (4p67d; cf. 4p69d). He proceeds to claim, a few propositions later, that with respect to civil laws, a rational per- son "is not led to obey [the state] by fear," but rather obeys from the knowledge that a common law facilitates agreement with others (4p73d; see 4p37s2).

The fearful person, by contrast, acts from timidity (*timor*), which Spinoza defines as that affect "by which a man is so disposed that *he does not will what he wills, and wills what he does not will* [*id quod vult nolit, vel ut id quod non vult velit*]...[it] is therefore nothing but fear insofar as a man is disposed by it to avoid an evil he judges to be future by encountering a lesser evil (see P28)" (3p39s – my emphasis; cf. 3 DA xxxi exp. 39). One who acts from fear or timidity has as her direct aim the evasion of some evil; she fails to attend to the positive good in the performance of her action. Spinoza illustrates the distinc- tion between one who directly follows the good and one who directly flees evil by analogy to a healthy and sick person: "the sick man, from timidity [*timore*] regarding death, eats what he is repelled by, whereas the healthy man enjoys his food, and in this way enjoys life better than if he feared death, and directly desired to avoid it" (4p63s2; cf. 4p63c).

A particularly striking example of timorous action that underscores the con- nection between fear and unwillingness or constraint can be found in Spinoza's analysis of suicide (4p20s). In this passage, he appeals to the *conatus* doctrine to

---

whether of his own accord, or by force, or by necessity [*sponte vel vi vel necessitate coacti*]" (TP 6/3); "Besides these [devices], in each state we can think of others which are agreeable to the nature of the place and the *ingenium* of the people, and take special care that the subjects do their duty voluntarily [*sponte*] rather than because the law compels them to [*lege coacti*]" (TP 10/7).

show that no one destroys himself "unless he is defeated by causes external, and contrary, to his nature" (4p20s). Among the ways that one might be "compelled" (*coactus*) by external, contrary forces is by being "forced by the command of a tyrant [as Seneca was] to open his veins, *that is* [*hoc est*], he desires to avoid a greater evil by [submitting to] a lesser" (ibid.). The suggestion here is that there is something distinctive about timidity – namely, that it involves willing what one does not will – that makes behavior from this passion compelled. When one acts from fear or timidity, one is acting under constraint not simply because one acts from a passion – as Spinoza's definition of *coactus* in the *Ethics* would seem to imply – but because one acts aversively, willing what one does not will.

The political writings further develop these points about fear, constraint, and unwillingness. In these works, the focus is on how one affectively relates to the laws and institutions of the state, whether one's compliance stems from an affirmation of the goodness of the *civitas* or from a fear of punishment. As we saw in the opening, Spinoza claims in TTP 4 that "he who does good from a true knowledge and love of the good acts freely and with a constant heart, whereas he who acts from fear of evil is compelled [*coatus*] by evil, acts like a slave, and lives under the command of another" (TTP 4.38, iii.66). And in the subsequent chapter, he elaborates on why the fearful are slavish and compelled: "For as long as men act only from fear, they act very unwillingly [*quod maxime nolunt*], and don't recognize the advantage, even the necessity, of doing what they're doing. All they care about is saving their necks, and avoiding punishment" (TTP 5.22, iii.74). This jibes with Spinoza's response to van Velthuysen's claim that by denying that God is a kind of supreme potentate, Spinoza cuts off the basis of morality:

I think I see what mud [Velthuysen] is stuck in. He finds nothing in virtue itself, or in understanding, which delights him, and he would prefer to live according to the impulse of his affects, if one thing did not stand in his way: he fears punishment. *So he abstains from evil actions, and obeys the divine commandments, like a slave, reluctantly and with a vacillating heart.* For this slavery he expects God to load him down with gifts far more pleasant to him than the love of God. And he expects this all the more, the more he resists the good he does and the more unwillingly [*invitus*] he does it. As a result, he believes everyone not held back by this fear lives without restraint and casts off all religion (Ep. 43 to Jacob Ostens, responding to Van Velthuysen – my emphasis).

Fearful obedience, mixed with confused hope for eternal rewards, is portrayed here as unwilling, reluctant, wavering, and slavish. This is repeated at various points in the TP, where he asserts that those who act from fear "care only to avoid death," willing what they do not will, rather than "cultivat[ing] life" and affirming their actions directly (TP 5/6).[38]

---

[38] See Matheron 1969, p. 130.

Table 4.1. *Degrees of willingness*

	Complies with laws out of perceived benefit	Adequately grasps the goodness of civil institutions/laws	Degree of willingness
Rational citizen	Yes	Yes	High
Hopeful citizen	Yes	No	Moderate
Fearful citizen	No	No	Low

Throughout Spinoza's later writings, then, we find a sharp contrast between the rational and the fearful with respect to the degree of willingness with which they perform their actions. The political writings carve out a middle position between the rational and the fearful, namely, the hopeful. Hopeful citizens resemble rational individuals in that they comply with the law out of a perceived benefit. In this sense, they directly engage in living. However, unlike one who is rational, one who is hopeful fails to conceive adequately the connection between compliance and power, and must often be enticed by extrinsic benefits, such as the promise of honor, glory, and other material or spiritual[39] rewards (TP 10/6). The hopeful affirm the rewards of compliance, but they do not fully understand the reasons why laws directly contribute to their empowerment or liberty. As fear diminishes, and citizens become more secure, they may come increasingly to see the good of civil laws and institutions, even if their understanding remains somewhat confused.

In light of this, we may say that there are two dimensions that determine the directness or willingness of one's actions. The first concerns whether or not one performs an action out of a perceived benefit rather than to evade some evil. Because hopeful people directly affirm their action while fearful people do not, the former may be said to act more willingly. But willingness is also a function of the extent to which one apprehends directly the goodness of one's action. The more directly one apprehends an action as good, the more directly she affirms this action. The rational person, who directly apprehends the connection between her good and the good of the state, thus complies more willingly than the hopeful person, who apprehends this connection only on the basis of past experience or association. These two dimensions are captured in Table 4.1.

Taken comprehensively, Spinoza's account of willingness entails that the degree to which one is willing in the performance of some action, ϕ, is, at least in part, a function of how directly one sees ϕ-ing as bound up with one's

---

[39] See Moses and the Israelites (TTP 2.47, iii.41; TTP 3.6, iii.45).

desires. The more directly one affirms ϕ-ing, the more willing one is when ϕ-ing

For Spinoza, one who lives well resolutely affirms her actions, while one who acts primarily from fear acts only grudgingly, unwillingly. The latter's actions are more constrained than the former's. And this is true even when they are subject to the same objective payoff matrix. While, in this scenario, the difference between seeing a course of action as a greater good and seeing it as a lesser evil is only notional, Spinoza seems to take this difference in how one conceives of, or frames, one's situation to be relevant to one's level of constraint.

Is it really plausible to think that one's level of constraint depends on whether or not one looks on the bright side of things? Well, perhaps. It is not especially strange to suppose that willingness depends to some extent on the directness with which one affirms an activity. Consider three distinct attitudes that one might take in relationship to jogging. A very willing jogger might take up jogging because she finds the activity itself to be invigorating and enjoyable. A somewhat less-willing jogger might take up jogging out of the hope that it will improve her health and help her to feel more energetic and alert. She embraces the activity of jogging, but only as an instrument to the satisfaction of some other set of desires. Still, the hopeful jogger is more willing than that grudging jogger, who dislikes jogging but does it anyway out of a fear that if she doesn't get more exercise she is at risk of a premature death. The hopeful and a fearful jogger might be in the very same objective condition, subject to the same objective matrix of payoffs and penalties, and yet it is perfectly natural to regard the hopeful jogger, who attends to the benefits of the action, as more willing than the fearful jogger.

This point obviously transfers to the case of compliance with the laws. Spinoza seems to conceive of civil laws and institutions as operating, at least some of the time, as what some contemporary philosophers call "throffers." There is a dual, duck–rabbit like quality to them: they may be perceived as threats or as offers. One's relationship to them depends on the features to which one attends: the benefits of serving the state or the punishments attached to noncompliance. Being able to affirm of one's compliance is a sign of strength, whereas acting aversively, is a sign that one is divided against oneself. Acting from an enticement, whereby one conceives of the external thing as improving one's condition, seems to betray a greater willingness than acting from fear of punishment, whereby one strives simply not to have one's condition diminished.[40]

---

[40] Harry Frankfurt's analysis of coercion supplies grounds for understanding why the hopeful act more willingly than the fearful. According to Frankfurt, there are two basic conditions of coerced action. One is that one is left with no reasonable alternative than to perform the action.

Conclusion

In those passages where Spinoza identifies hopeful actions with willingness and fearful actions with constraint, we find a more subtle and compelling analysis of free action and coercion than what the strict account from the *Ethics* – grounded in the distinction between adequate and partial causation – allows for. Perhaps because in the political works he is engaged in a form of nonideal theory, he is attuned to the actual range of affects that typically motivate people and to the normative differences between passions. This enables him to account for the way in which Aristotelian "mixed actions" reflect unwillingness, since they are paradigmatic cases of action from timidity, where one wills what one does not will. More generally, we see from this analysis how Spinoza, unlike Hobbes, builds into his account conceptual space for coerced volitions and degrees of willingness.[41] While the germ of the account can be found in some passages from the *Ethics*, it receives its fullest articulation in his political writings.

Still, it is important that we not treat willingness as a proxy for liberty for Spinoza. If liberty were nothing but willingness, one could liberate a slave simply by getting her to embrace the condition of servitude.[42] But of course *feeling* free (or unconstrained) and *being* free are very different things, and Spinoza's account allows for this. One can hopefully and willingly act self-destructively. Conversely, one can fearfully or constrainedly act prudently or empoweringly.[43]

But while acting in ways that one directly affirms is just one dimension of empowerment, it is nevertheless an important one. Learning to apprehend the good in one's situation, such that one can willingly embrace it, figures crucially in Spinoza's cognitive therapy. Even if the distinction between regarding something as a greater good as opposed to a lesser evil is merely notional, the more we can focus our attention on goods rather than evils, the better off we will be:

But it should be noted that in ordering our thoughts and images, we must always [by IVP63C and IIIP59] *attend to those things which are good in each thing so that in this way we are always determined to acting from an affect of joy.* For example, if someone

---

He calls this the irresistibility condition (Frankfurt 1988, pp. 38–41). The irresistibility condition may be satisfied by threats and offers alike by making one alternative eminently better than all others. But in order for a threat or offer to be coercive, one must be moved by a motive that the coercee would prefer not to have (Frankfurt 1988, p. 44). On his account, if one acts from an offer, one often acts from a motivational state that one would endorse, since one sees this as an opportunity to improve one's position. But when one acts from a threat one's "motive is not to improve his condition but to keep it from becoming worse. This seems sufficient to account for the fact that he would prefer to have a different motive for acting" (Frankfurt 1988, p. 44).

[41] This contrasts with Hobbes, for whom, as Quentin Skinner points out, "it makes no sense to speak of being coerced into acting against your will, since the will lying behind your action will always be revealed by your action itself" (Skinner 1998, pp. 7–8).

[42] Hopeful compliance conduces to servitude when it is epistemically disabling. See Lordon 2014.

[43] In a paper delivered at the University of Toronto, Hasana Sharp proposed that for Spinoza fear of solitude may give rise to salutary effects.

sees that he pursues esteem too much, he should think of its correct use, the end for which it ought to be pursued, and the means by which it can be acquired, not of its misuse and emptiness, which *only someone sick of the mind* thinks of (5p10s – my emphasis).

We find a similar expression of Spinoza's positive psychology in 4p67 and its demonstration, where he argues that rather than acting out of fear, the free man desires the good directly and "thinks of nothing less than of death," his wisdom being "a meditation on life" (4p67d). Those who act affirmatively, from some direct desire for a good, are better off, *ceteris paribus*, than those who act aversively, from fear or timidity. This is true *a fortiori* when we are talking about the difference between secure and fearful *ingenia*.

Of course, the goal of the state then is not *merely* to make citizens hopeful by simply encouraging positive thinking. As feminist Carol Hanish memorably puts it in her essay "The Personal is Political": "We need to change the objective conditions, not adjust to them."[44] For Spinoza, the point is not simply to change people's attitudes toward the state, but to change people's attitudes toward the state by changing their objective conditions; a good state will stimulate hopeful attitudes *in virtue of* good governance. *Securitas*, as Spinoza conceives of it, is epistemically well-founded, rather than propped up by an incapacitating ideology. Still, the main claim that I wish to highlight here – a claim that is absolutely central to Spinoza's analysis, but hasn't gotten its due either in Spinoza scholarship or in contemporary political philosophy – is that affective welfare is a very important dimension along which to measure civic success. It matters whether people feel enfranchised, respected, and *hopeful*.

This chapter, thus, takes us considerably deeper into Spinoza's account of affective reorientation. Since the welfare or flourishing of an individual can be measured affectively, the success of a state can be measured in terms of the affective make-up, or *ingenia*, of its citizens. By fostering *securitas* – a strong and steadfast hope – the state will have played a considerable role in liberating or empowering its citizens. We will see in Chapters 6 and 7 how this aim of promoting hopeful *ingenia* figures into in Spinoza's political prescriptions. First, though, we must turn to Spinoza's political method.

[44] See www.carolhanisch.org/CHwritings/PIP.html.

5 Statecraft and the Taming of Fortune

> Men are men and life is life, and we must deal with them as they are; and if we want to change them, we must deal with them in the form in which they exist and have their being.
>
> – Mr. Max in Richard Wright, *Native Son.*[1]

In TTP 3, in the midst of an examination of the putative "election" of the Jews, Spinoza distinguishes between three classes of things we may honorably (*honeste*) desire:

i. understanding things through their first causes;
ii. gaining control over the passions, or acquiring the habit of virtue; and finally,
iii. living securely and healthily (TTP 3.12, iii.46).[2]

Spinoza claims that Jewish election consists only "in the enduring prosperity of their state and in [other temporal] advantages" (TTP 3.19, iii.47). He repudiates the view that the Jews exceeded all others in wisdom or ethical fortitude, since "these gifts are not peculiar to any nation, but have always been common to the whole human race – unless we want to dream that formerly nature produced different kinds of men ... So in this matter, the wise man and the fool are almost equally happy or unhappy" (TTP 3.12–13, iii.46–7). After appealing once again to the homogeneity of human nature (Section 1.3), Spinoza

---

[1] Wright 1966, p. 359.
[2] These categories of desirables loosely correspond to Spinoza's three kinds of knowledge in descending order. The third kind of knowledge consists in "understanding things through their first causes," specifically grasping the essences of singular things through the essence of God (2p40s2). One who acts from reason *(ratio)*, or the second kind of knowledge, acts from virtue (4p24) and is able to gain considerable control over the passions (5p1–20). The connection between the third class of desirables – material and physical prosperity – and the first kind of knowledge is somewhat less evident. But given that (i) and (ii) can only be achieved through the power of the intellect, it would seem that the most that one can hope for insofar as one is guided by the imagination, or the first kind of knowledge, is that (iii) one could "live securely and healthily." Since the mind, insofar as it perceives things through the senses (first kind of knowledge), is said to be guided by random *(vaga)* experience, we should not be surprised that the corresponding class of desirables would be seen as depending chiefly on fortune.

proceeds to argue that Jewish exceptionalism consisted in nothing more than material prosperity.

To further undercut claims of election – whether Jewish or Calvinist[3] – Spinoza draws what appears to be a yet another line of demarcation (see Section 3.1) between ethics and politics: ethical goods, which depend "chiefly on our power alone, or on the laws of human nature alone" (TTP 3.12, iii.46), are set apart from forms of material and civil success, the attainment of which lies "chiefly ... in external things," and which are therefore "called gifts of fortune" (TTP 3.13, iii.47). This creates the impression that, unlike in ethics, little can be done to tame the effects of fortune over civil life.

In this chapter, I argue that this impression is misleading. The state can do much to mitigate the effects of fortune. But in order to do so, it must adopt institutions, laws, and procedures that are suited to the temperament or *ingenia* of the people. By examining Spinoza's accommodationist political method, I hope to establish at least three things, one of which is historical, one textual, and one philosophical. The historical point is that Spinoza's adaptive political method reveals Spinoza's affinity with the civic humanist tradition, to which I alluded in the Introduction. The textual point is that the method of politics – its remedies to fortune – is consistent with the method of ethics. So, whereas Chapter 3 made the case for the continuity of ethical and political *aims*, this chapter makes the case for the continuity of ethical and political *methods*. Indeed, I will argue that we can gain further insight into Spinoza's ethical method by looking at his account of statecraft. And we will see that Spinoza's model of nonideal theory can inform and enrich our understanding of the relationship between psychology and civic institutional design.

5.1   *Fortuna* and Its Remedies

To situate Spinoza's conception of statecraft and the remedies to fortune, it will be helpful to consider how fortune was conceived in Spinoza's time. In the medieval period, fortune was often presented as an animate force, closely associated with fate, and typically assuming a female form.[4] As Hanna Pitkin puts it, fortune functioned to "turn men's eyes away from this world where there is no justice, no correspondence between merit and reward, toward the eternal."[5]

---

[3] Leo Strauss emphasizes the extent to which Spinoza's critique of Judaism can be seen as a not-so-veiled critique of orthodox Calvinism in the seventeenth century United Provinces (Strauss 1965, especially Ch. 7).

[4] Pitkin 1984, pp. 139–40.

[5] Ibid., p. 140.

The goddess *Fortuna* was an emissary of God; hence the expression "all fortune is good fortune."[6]

In the Renaissance and early modern periods, it was more common to conceive of fortune as the source of both aid and adversity. Metaphysical chance or real (Epicurean) indeterminacy was, of course, a theological nonstarter.[7] Instead, "fortune" designated epistemic chance: that which could not have been predicted and which lies beyond our control. It was thus conceived of as something that could, at least in theory, be mitigated through the expansion of knowledge and the deployment of instruments of control. Ernst Cassirer characterizes the shifting conception of our relationship to fortune in the following way:

In the medieval doctrine of two worlds, and in all the dualisms derived from it, man simply stands apart from the forces that are fighting over him; he is, in a sense, at their mercy. Though he experiences the conflict of these forces, he takes no active part in it. He is the stage of this great drama of the world, but he has not yet become a truly independent antagonist. In the Renaissance a different image emerges ever more clearly. The old image of Fortune with a wheel, seizing men and dragging them along, sometimes raising them, sometimes throwing them down into the abyss, now gives way to the depiction of Fortune with a *sailboat*. And this bark is not controlled by Fortune alone – man himself is steering it.[8]

On Cassirer's construal, Renaissance philosophers took a less resignative, more active approach to fortune. There was broad agreement that the proper remedy to *fortuna* is the cultivation of *virtus*.[9] However, Renaissance philosophers conceived of the remedies to fortune in a wide range of ways, reflecting diverse conceptions of *virtus*. Within these diverse texts we find two prominent families of remedies, which I will refer to as the (Stoically-inspired) internal control model and the humanist civic activist model.

---

[6] Ibid. See also Pocock 1975, p. 39. This has been called the "Lord's handmaid" view of fortune (Coogan 1969, p. 167). Coogan attributes this view to Salutati and Dante, who, in Canto VII of the *Inferno*, presents *Fortuna* as "a guiding spirit, blissful and indifferent to reproof" and "turns her wheel and reveals divine dispensations" (Coogan 1969, p. 167).

[7] This led some to abandon altogether the traditional concept of fortune. See, for instance, Descartes's claim that fortune is "a chimera which arises solely from an error of our intellect" (*Passions of the Soul*, 2.145–6, in *CSM*).

[8] Cassirer 1963, pp. 76–7. See Hanna Pitkin for the prevalence of seafarer imagery in this period (Pitkin 1984, p. 141).

[9] For the classical (Roman) roots of the opposition between virtue and fortune, see Skinner 1978, p. 95. Skinner points out that St. Augustine attacks this opposition on the grounds that it places too much control for our fate in our hands. There is more than a hint of Pelagianism in the more activist Renaissance approaches to overcoming *fortuna*. See Brooke 2012 for an analysis of how Stoic conceptions of control and Augustinian criticisms thereof play out in the early modern period.

The Internal Control Model

Stoics tended to see fortune as only affecting "externals" or "indifferents" such as health and wealth. A paradigmatic statement of the Stoic approach may be found in Seneca's Epistle LXXXII to Lucilius:

> Therefore, gird yourself about with philosophy, an impregnable wall. Though it be assaulted by many engines, Fortune can find no passage into it. The soul stands on unassailable ground, if it has abandoned external things; it is independent in its own fortress; and every weapon that is hurled falls short of the mark. Fortune has not the long reach with which we credit her; she can seize none except him that clings to her. Let us then recoil from her as far as we are able. This will be possible for us only through knowledge of self and of the world of Nature.[10]

Through knowledge, one may shun fortune and thereby gain control over oneself.

Petrarch (1304–1374) revives this basic Stoic idea in the Renaissance, even claiming that bad fortune is preferable to good fortune on the grounds that good fortune breeds indolence, while poverty and physical suffering can promote something like antibodies of virtuous resistance.[11] By developing virtue in the face of adversity, one inures oneself to these potential threats to one's well-being.[12] The conception of virtue here that was to serve as a remedy is something like steadfastness or strength of mind. Poggio Bracciolini (1380–1459) adopts this account, claiming: "The strength of fortune is never so great that it will not be overcome by men who are steadfast and resolute."[13] Those who conceived of the proper remedy to fortune as strength of mind or constancy generally held rather sanguine attitudes about our ability to overcome bad fortune, since mental fortitude renders one impervious to fortune's hazards.

In the late Renaissance, one of the fullest expressions of the view that strength of mind can conquer fortune comes from the neo-Stoic Justus Lipsius (1547–1606). On Lipsius's account, as expressed through his Stoic protagonist Langius in *De constantia* (1584), fortune renders the mind inconstant, governed by mere opinion. The virtuous person, the Stoic sage, will, by contrast, live with a constant mind, which is "always matched with

---

[10] Seneca, Epistle LXXXII or "On the Natural Fear of Death," in Seneca 1962, p. 243.

[11] See Petrarch: "I think that it is more difficult to govern prosperity than adversity, and I submit that in my experience smiling Fortune is more to be feared and demonstrably more dangerous than frowning Fortune" (Petrarch 1991, prefatory epistle, pp. 5–6).

[12] See Petrarch 1991, pp. 3–4. See also Thomas More's poems on fortune (Coogan 1969, p. 169).

[13] Bracciolini, *De miseria conditionis humanae*, quoted in Poppi 1988, pp. 641–67.

Reason."[14] Only one who is mentally strong will face the vagaries of fortune with equanimity:

You will be a king indeed, free indeed, only subject to God, enfranchised from the servile yoke of fortune and affections. As some rivers are said to run through the sea and yet keep their stream fresh, so will you pass through the confused tumults of this world and not be infected with any briny saltiness of this sea of sorrow. Are you likely to be cast down? Constancy will lift you up ... Let showers, thunder, lightning, and tempests fall round about you, you will cry boldly with a loud voice, "I lie at rest amid the waves."[15]

This promise of "l[ying] at rest amid the waves" had a special lure for Lipsius's immediate audience who were living in war-ravaged Europe near the end of the sixteenth century. By casting fortune as an unpredictable and potentially destructive force, Lipsius distances his view from the more hopeful medieval portrayals of fortune as an expression of divine providence. However, his remedy shares with these older views the belief that it is folly to kick against the pricks. Instead of trying to control external matters, one should turn inward to gain control over one's emotional responses to fortune's torrent.[16]

Descartes embraces a version of this approach in the *Passions of the Soul*, where he claims: "all the troubles coming from elsewhere are powerless to harm [the soul]. Such troubles will serve rather to increase its joy; for on seeing that [the soul] cannot be harmed by them, it becomes aware of its perfection."[17] With proper training, "we easily acquire the habit of governing our desires so that their fulfillment depends only on us, making it possible for them always to give us complete satisfaction."[18] And in a 1645 letter to Princess Elisabeth, Descartes directly states that externals are incidental to happiness: "It seems to me that each person can make himself content by himself without any external assistance."[19]

There are several salient features to the response to fortune that I've canvassed thus far. First, it narrows the scope in which virtue is expressed. One flouts fortune by cordoning off one's ethical concerns to include only what is under one's full control. Second, it assumes that among the few things that *are* under one's direct control are one's judgments and affective responses. And,

[14] Lipsius 2006, I.6, p. 40.
[15] Ibid., p. 41. "Constancy" is defined as: "a right and immovable strength of the mind, neither lifted up, nor pressed down with external or casual accidents," while "strength" is defined as a "steadfastness not from Opinion, but from judgement and sound Reason" (Lipsius 2006, I.4, p. 37).
[16] See also French neo-Stoic Guillaume Du Vair (1556–1621), e.g., Du Vair 1990, esp. p. 205.
[17] *Passions of the Soul*, 2 Section 148, in CSM.
[18] *Passions of the Soul*, 2 Section 146, in CSM.
[19] 4 August 1645, CSMK, vol. 3, pp. 256–8.

finally, while this approach sees virtue as bound up with wisdom, this conception of wisdom is largely non-deliberative – one's knowledge enables one to bear fortune, but it does not require the performance of any particular actions. According to a prominent strand of Renaissance and early modern thought, then, virtue consists in strength of mind, a private, non-deliberative capacity.

The Civic Activist Model

Leon Battista Alberti (1404–1472) can be seen as a transitional figure between the internal control model of taming fortune and the civic activist approach. On the one hand, in his discussion of fate and fortune in *Dinner Pieces* (*Intercoenales*) (1439), he indicates that if one wishes to live temperately in the face of fortune, one ought to cultivate internal virtue, just as if one were tossed into the raging river of fortune, one might prudently seek out a single solid plank (representing knowledge gained through the liberal arts) rather than put oneself at the mercy of the captain of a boat (representing imperial protection): "a tranquil and free mind will rightly eschew such huge labors and the great and continuous perils of boats."[20] And in his somewhat earlier *Della Famiglia* (1433–1434), Alberti contends that "fortune is weak and powerless when it comes to taking away the least part of our character."[21]

In both of these works, though, Alberti reveals that his conception of virtue and character involves a public, civic dimension. Prudence (*prudentia*), industry (*industria*), and diligence (*diligenza*) are foremost among the virtues needed for mitigating the effects of fortune.[22] Those who are most able to conquer fortune are "ready to meet any emergency with vigilance, faith, diligence, and a sense of duty, and who will not refuse to face toils and dangers gladly for the common welfare."[23] This civic dimension is even more pronounced in *Della Famiglia*, where Alberti writes: "We shall always believe that in political affairs and in human life generally reason is more powerful than fortune ... industry, skill, persevering labors, wise counsel, honest activity, just demands and reasonable expectations do maintain and defend both republics and principalities."[24] The suggestion here is that one cannot tame fortune by retreating to an inner citadel; rather, fortune must be limited through prudent engagement in the world.[25]

---

[20] Alberti 1987, p. 25
[21] Prologue Alberti 1969, p. 29.
[22] As opposed to the conception of character that diminishes the role of deliberation, Alberti writes that "prudence and diligence are of great value in human affairs" (Alberti 1987, p. 27).
[23] Alberti 1987, p. 25.
[24] Alberti 1969, p. 30
[25] One could endorse *both* models by distinguishing between ethical and political domains. This was Lipsius's approach: at an individual level, one ought to adopt an internal control account;

Machiavelli represents the apotheosis of this activist approach to fortune. His depiction of fortune in *The Prince, Tercets of Fortune* and the *Discourses* is multifaceted. In some places, he presents it as fate or heaven's plan. Elsewhere it is portrayed as something unforeseeable and beyond one's control. In whichever guise, fortune is personified as an "unstable goddess and fickle deity."[26] There are traces of resignation in Machiavelli's response. He writes that one cannot "hope to escape her hard bit"[27] and that even if "men are able to assist Fortune" they certainly cannot "thwart her."[28] One is left with a deep sense of just how much of human well-being lies beyond one's control, despite appearances to the contrary.[29] Why not, then, spare oneself the pain of resisting fortune's irrepressible power?

Machiavelli's notoriously sexist response that one *can* gain considerable control over lady fortune, provided that one is bold with her: "because fortune is a woman ... if you want to control her, it is necessary to treat her roughly,"[30] a point that he repeats in the *Tercets*, where he claims that fortune is pleased by one "who pushes her, who shoves her, who jostles her."[31] Fortune may be the "arbiter of half of our actions,"[32] but the other half remains within our control. For this, though, one must *take* control, exhibiting *virtù*.

Machiavelli's conception of *virtù* is shorn of associations with *honestas* or honorableness.[33] It is a capacity that is not bound by strict laws and not expressed in a fixed manner; rather, *virtù* is a kind of malleable prudence that enables one to assess one's circumstances and to seize the opportunities afforded therein. As he puts it in a letter to Soderini,

[B]ecause the times and conditions often change (both generally and in particular places), and men do not change either their ideas or their methods, it happens that a man sometimes succeeds and at other times fails. Indeed, anyone who was capable of adapting to them, would always be successful (or, at least, he would be able to avoid failure), and it would then be true that a wise man could control the stars and fates.[34]

---

at the civic level, one ought to adopt an activist approach. This is also a rather natural way of reading Spinoza, though I will suggest that it is mistaken.

[26] *Tercets of Fortune*, in CWO 2, p. 746.
[27] Ibid., p. 747.
[28] *Discourses* 2.29 in *CWO* 1, p. 408.
[29] Illusions of control – over matters of success, of course, not failure – lead us to exaggerate our sense of resistance to fortune when things are going well: "hence all the evil that comes upon mankind is charged to her; but any good that befalls a man he believes he gets through his own worth" (*Tercets of Fortune, in CWO* 2, p. 746). Spinoza makes a very similar observation in the opening of the TTP (Preface.1–2, iii.5).
[30] *Prince*, Ch. XXV, p. 87.
[31] *Tercets of Fortune*, in *CWO* 2, pp. 748–9.
[32] *Prince*, Ch. XXV, p. 85.
[33] For Machiavelli's break with classical Ciceronian virtues, see Skinner 1984, pp. 214–15. See also Skinner 2000, pp. 40–3.
[34] Letter to Soderini, c. 1506; in *Prince*, p. 98.

This same theme is struck throughout *The Prince*: "[one] must be prepared to vary his conduct as the winds of fortune and changing circumstances constrain him."[35] Adaptability is perhaps the chief characteristic of *virtù*.[36]

One of the reasons that adaptability is so important is that circumstances are in perpetual flux. Political regimes are locked in the Polybian cycle of regime decay and regeneration, consigned to impermanence: "not a thing in the world is eternal."[37] Harking back to the republic of Rome, the "eternal city," Machiavelli appears to hold some hope of, at least temporarily, stopping fortune through the adoption of a (Polybian) mixed republic. But the rivers of fortune, the cycle of decay and regeneration, continually threaten whatever dikes one erects: "ability [*virtù*] brings forth quiet; quiet, laziness; laziness, disorder; disorder, ruin; and likewise from ruin comes order; from order, ability; from the last, glory and good fortune."[38] In order for a state to maintain its strength, it must resist entropy by constantly renewing or restoring itself (*Discourses* 3.1). There is no point at which the *virtù* of a state is perfect, complete; the state must constantly adapt in order to persevere.

In the *Tercets of Fortune*, Machiavelli writes that the flexible man, the true man of *virtù*, who "could leap from wheel to wheel would always be happy and fortunate,"[39] a point that he repeats in *The Prince*: "if it were possible to change one's character to suit the times and circumstances, one would always be successful."[40] And, yet, throughout his works, Machiavelli despairs of finding a man of such *virtù*: "one does not find men who are so prudent that they are capable of being sufficiently flexible ... I conclude, then, that since circumstances vary and men when acting lack flexibility, they are successful if their methods match the circumstances and unsuccessful if they do not."[41]

This pessimism is shared by Machiavelli's friend Francesco Guicciardini (1483–1540), who sees civic success as lying in the fortuitous fitness of one's character for one's times:

Even if you attribute everything to prudence and virtue and discount as much as possible the power of Fortune, you must at least admit that it is very important to be born or to live in a time that prizes highly the virtues and qualities in which you excel. Take the example of Fabius Maximus, whose great reputation resulted from his being by nature hesitant. He found himself in a war in which impetuosity was ruinous, whereas

[35] *Prince*, Ch. xviii, p. 62.
[36] See *Discourses* 3.8–3.9. See Del Lucchese 2009, p. 14.
[37] *Tercets of Fortune*, in CWO 2, p. 748.
[38] *The History of Florence*, V.1, in CWO 3, p. 1232.
[39] *Tercets of Fortune*, in CWO 2, pp. 747–8.
[40] *Prince,* Ch. xxv, p. 86. Cf. Guicciardini, *Ricordi*: "To be sure, if a man could change his nature to suit the conditions of the times, he would be much less dominated by Fortune. But this is most difficult and perhaps even impossible" (Guicciardini 1965, no. 31)
[41] *Prince*, Ch. xxv, pp. 86–7.

procrastination was useful. At another time, the opposite could have been true. His times needed his qualities, and that was his fortune.[42]

Even Francis Bacon (1561–1626) – who famously celebrated man as *faber fortunae*, architect of his own fortune[43] – recognizes the challenges and hazards involved in shaping one's fortune, since it requires precise insight into the ways that human nature is constituted:

[T]he precept which I conceive to be most summary towards the prevailing in fortune, is to obtain that window which Momus did require, who seeing in the frame of man's heart such angles and recesses, found fault there was not a window to look into them; that is, to procure good informations of particulars touching persons, their natures, their desires and ends, their customs and fashions, their helps and advantages.[44]

He proceeds to note that psychological insight in turn requires keen awareness of circumstantial particulars, the variability of which renders prudential action precarious. Like Guicciardini and Machiavelli before him, Bacon regards circumstantial adaptability as the key to shaping fortune and inflexibility its greatest impediment:

Another precept of this knowledge is, by all possible endeavour to frame the mind to be pliant and obedient to occasion; for nothing hindereth men's fortunes so much as this '*Idem manebat neque idem decebat*' [he remained the same, though it no longer suited him], men are where they were, when occasions turn: and therefore to Cato whom Livy maketh such an architect of fortune, he addeth that he had a "versatile *ingenium*" (AL, 279).

The conception of virtue – consisting in having a versatile *ingenium* – is so rare that, unless one is endowed with the preternatural capacities of Cato, one is forever vulnerable to fortune. For civic activists like Machiavelli, Guicciardini, and Bacon, adaptability might enable one to elude fortune, but such adaptability is itself elusive, as it runs contrary to the stubborn fixity of temperament and character. Consequently, fortune governs much of political life.

At this point we may highlight three features of the civic activist model that distinguish it from the internal control model. First, civic activism expands the scope of virtuous action to include the civic or public sphere – in this respect, it is more ambitious than the internal control approach. Second, in expanding the

---

[42] Guicciardini 1965, no. 31. See Guicciardini's *History of Italy* treatment of Piero de Medici. Compare with Machiavelli: "Those who because of a bad choice or natural inclination are out of harmony with the times, generally live in misfortune and their actions have a bad outcome; it is the opposite with those who are in the harmony with the times" (*Discourses* 3.8, in *CWO*, p. 450; cf. *Discourses* 3.9).

[43] See "Of Fortune" and *The Advancement of Learning* (esp. pp. 272–86) in Bacon *MW*.

[44] *The Advancement of Learning*, in *MW*, p. 273.

domain of virtue-expression, civic activism introduces greater uncertainty, as the demands of prudence are ever-shifting – they are difficult to ascertain and perhaps even harder to conform to, given the rigidity of human temperaments. So, fortune hangs over even a virtuous republic like the sword of Damocles.[45] To keep its effects at bay, a statesman must remain extremely vigilant, making "restorative" adjustments in accordance with circumstances. And, finally, because virtue requires reading one's own times, one's potential enemies, and one's countrymen accurately, the proper exercise of statecraft requires careful discernment of human affective and cognitive patterns – it requires a grasp of political psychology.[46]

5.2   Spinoza on Fortune

In order to situate Spinoza's approach to fortune within this framework, let's begin by considering how he conceives of fortune.[47] Spinoza rejects any conception of *fortuna* as divine providence, presenting fortune instead as that which is unforeseeable and beyond one's control. In the *Ethics*, he emphasizes the uncontrollability of fortune, defining matters of fortune as "things which are not in our power" (2p49s) and connecting fortune with servitude: "Man's lack of power to moderate and restrain the affects I call bondage [*servitutem*]. For the man who is subject to affects is under control, not of himself, but of fortune [*fortuna*]" (4 Preface, ii.205). But, of course, there are plenty of things that are not within one's power – like the orbits of the planets, or the process of aging – that could not reasonably be described as matters of fortune. Spinoza's characterization of fortune in the TTP looks rather more adequate, since it adds that matters of fortune are unpredictable: "by 'fortune' I understand nothing

---

[45] Del Lucchese observes that Machiavelli's account "holds no similarity to the Stoic conception, which is based on the idea of a primary inner core of man that is protected from the vicissitudes of fortune, an inner fortress to take refuge in when events take a turn for the worse ... The steadiness of will required by Machiavellian virtue diverges significantly from the Stoic conception. It is no guarantee of a protected 'place' sheltered from the changes of fortune. On the contrary, it involves the awareness that precisely because nothing is beyond the reach of fortune, no virtue can be considered absolute or transcendental" (del Lucchese 2009, p. 16). Cf. Pitkin 1984, p. 144.

[46] See Maurizio Viroli's assessment: "In Machiavelli's view, as we have seen, politics is the work of human beings, with their emotions, their temperaments, and their imaginations. Since this was so, he always did his best to understand the hearts of the princes he met, and he worked hard to explore their souls thoroughly, peering behind their masks and pretenses" (Viroli 2002, pp. 100–1).

[47] Among the few works on Spinoza that have explored his treatment of fortune in detail are Moreau 1994 (Part II, Chapter IV) and Rosenthal 1996. Rosenthal explores the Machiavellian framework behind Spinoza's analysis, while highlighting the way that Spinoza's distinct notion of virtue and the role that he accords to reason depart from Machiavelli's treatment of fortune. Some of these ideas are also expressed in Rosenthal 2001.

but God's guidance, insofar as it directs human affairs through external and unforeseen causes" (TTP 3.11, iii.46).[48]

Given that our bondage to the passions is a form of subjection to fortune, by rationally limiting the power of the passions, we thereby "conquer fortune" (4p47s). Spinoza's account of human freedom (*libertas humana*) in *Ethics* 5 thus seems to be an account of how fortune is tamed. The first half of Part 5 concerns the rational "remedies for the affects" (5p20s). The latter half focus on the "greatest satisfaction of mind" (5p27), namely, the love of God that arises from the third kind of knowledge. The account of human freedom here resembles, at first blush, the internal control model: one gains control over fortune by attending only to those things over which one has control, namely, to the power of one's intellect, which enables one to temper the passions and apprehend the deepest, most powerful truths. On this reading, the proper response to fortune is not to try to conquer worldly affairs, but rather to get one's epistemic house in order and to accept that which is not within our control. This reading is encouraged by Spinoza's earlier assertion that necessitarianism "teaches us how we must bear ourselves concerning matters of fortune, or things which are not in our power, that is, concerning things which do not follow from our nature – that we must expect and bear calmly both good fortune and bad" (2p49s2; cf. 4 app. 32).[49]

This way of conceiving of Spinoza's remedies to fortune fits with a certain virtue-ethical reading, according to which the rightness of an action is judged primarily on the basis of the motivating affect, rather than on the basis of its overt expressions or consequences.[50] For instance, he writes that "no action, considered in itself, is good or evil" (4p59 alt. dem.) and that "to every action to which we are determined from an affect which is a passion, we can be determined by reason, without that affect" (4p59). Beating one's fists up and down might be an expression of anger, but it might also be a celebration of one's physical capacities. What makes the action good or evil is not the motion itself or its consequences, but rather the adequacy or inadequacy of the idea that gave rise to the action.

Spinoza similarly emphasizes the importance of the eliciting motivational state in a letter to Willem Van Blyenbergh: "Nero's matricide, insofar as it contained something positive, was not a crime; for Orestes too performed the same outward act and had the same intention of killing his mother, and yet he is not blamed, or at least not as Nero. What, then, was Nero's crime? Nothing else than that by that deed he showed that he was ungrateful, devoid of compassion

---

[48] Compare his characterization of fortune in a letter to Bouwmeester as that which is produced by causes that are "unknown to us and foreign to our nature and power" (Ep. 37).

[49] These passages reflect Spinoza's debt to Stoicism. For more on this relationship see Miller 2015 and Debrabander 2007.

[50] See D. Garrett 1996, p. 297; Kisner 2011, p. 198.

and obedience" (Ep. 23, March 1665).⁵¹ And in the TP, he justifies divergent assessments of one and the same action on the grounds that it is "not that the act itself [that] is different, but … the one who does it is" (TP 7/27). Whether an action is virtuous or vicious depends on the character of the affect that gives rise to it. To act from virtue is to act from an active affect (see 3p59 and 3p59s) or from the joy and desire that arise insofar as one has adequate ideas. This could be taken as entailing that virtue, or strength of character [*fortitudo*], consists primarily in reforming one's own mind, or strengthening one's intellect, rather than trying to control external affairs.⁵²

I want to suggest briefly here – and more expansively in what follows – that the internal control interpretation of Spinoza fails to capture much of Spinoza's response to fortune, even in the *Ethics*. Spinoza opens *Ethics* 5 with a striking critique the Stoic account of affective self-control: "the Stoics thought that [the affects] depend entirely on our will, and that we can command them absolutely. But experience cries out against this, and has forced them, in spite of their principles, to confess that much practice and application [*usum et studium*] are required to restrain and moderate them" (5 Preface, ii.277–8). This passage is quite telling. Spinoza is admitting straightaway that his remedies will yield affective self-control only gradually and incompletely, through assiduous practice.

In fact, Spinoza was very much alive to the fact that human freedom and self-control depends critically on external causes.⁵³ If we want to live joyful and intellectually rich lives, our environment must be structured in ways that conduce to this aim. Most notably, since "there is no singular thing in Nature which is more useful to man than a man who lives according to the guidance of reason" (4p35c1), our capacity to live freely depends in no small part on the strength of our moral communities. He stresses this throughout *Ethics* 4, claiming that "[m]an, I say, can wish for nothing more helpful to the preservation of his being than that all should agree in all things that the minds and bodies of all would compose, as it were, one mind and one body" (4p18s), and that "things which are of assistance to the common society of men, or which bring it about

---

⁵¹ Spinoza is responding to the charge that if God is the cause of all events, he is responsible for all of the evil that we bear witness to. His main point here is to defend the claim that evil does not follow from the essence of any thing.
⁵² Since Spinoza identifies acting from strength of character (*fortitudo*) with acting from the "dictates of reason" (*ex dictamine rationis*) (3p59s) and "acting absolutely from virtue" with acting "by the guidance of reason" (*ex ductu rationis*) in 4p24, it might seem that acting from virtue is necessarily deliberative. However, Donald Rutherford has argued recently that the dictates "do not function as practical principles; rather, they are merely acts of understanding, or conclusions entailed by acts of understanding" (Rutherford 2010, p. 503). On this reading, knowledge gives rise to virtue without the intervention of practical deliberation. For a response to Rutherford, see J. Steinberg 2014.
⁵³ I stress this point in J. Steinberg 2009. See also Armstrong 2009b; Kisner 2011.

that men live harmoniously, are useful; those, on the other hand, are evil which bring discord to the state" (4p40).[54]

But forming bonds and bringing it about that others too love virtue and knowledge is a fraught affair. Spinoza explicitly acknowledges this point in another letter to Blyenbergh, declaring: "*of the things outside my power* [*in potestate mea non sunt*], I esteem none more than being allowed the honor of entering into a pact of friendship with people who sincerely love the truth" (Ep. 19, January 5, 1665 – my emphasis). Forging and maintaining strong interpersonal connections, which constitutes a vital part of Spinoza's conception of ethics, depends on fortune.

We get further insight into why Spinoza thought that social harmony is subject to fortune in the Appendix to *Ethics* 4:

It is especially useful to men to form associations, to bind themselves by those bonds most apt to make one people of them, and absolutely, to do those things which serve to strengthen friendships. But skill and alertness [*ars et vigilantia*] are required for this. For men vary – there being few who live according to the rule of reason – and yet generally they are envious, and more inclined to vengeance than to compassion. So it requires a singular power of mind [*singularis animi potentiae*] to bear with each according to his *ingenium* (4 Appendix, Cap. xii–xiii).

The fact that one must adapt one's actions to the circumstantial particulars renders experience critical to the proper expression of virtue. Determining what constitutes generosity in any particular instance requires *ars et vigilantia*. The singular power of mind described here sounds rather like the flexible prudence of the activist model of virtue.

We can begin to see from this brief sketch how Spinoza's approach to ethics deviates from the internal control model and resembles the civic activist account. First, Spinoza denies that virtue is absolutely under our control. This is due in part to the fact that our judgments themselves are not entirely under our control. But it is also because our power of acting depends on the health of our communities; and, while we can act in ways that strengthen our bonds with others, this requires deliberative reason so that one may adapt one's behavior to suit others' *ingenia*. Moreover, even if one is skillful and vigilant, because the *ingenia* of others will always be, to some extent, elusive and opaque, the efficacy of one's actions will depend on fortune. In terms of his relationship to the Stoics, Spinoza breaks with their view of fortune and control in at least two significant ways: (1) he denies that our judgments lie entirely within our control; and (2) he denies that things that lie outside of our judgment – i.e. external affairs – are mere (preferred) indifferents. These two points are connected: since our welfare depends on our power of judgment, and our power

---

[54] For more on the importance of sociality, see J. Steinberg 2013.

of judgment depends on external conditions, external conditions are directly connected to our welfare. So, even in the *Ethics*, the exercise of virtue depends on deliberative reason and the assistance of external things, leaving one inescapably subject to fortune. We get considerably more insight into Spinoza's activist conception of virtue by looking at the remedies for fortune spelled out in his political treatises.

5.3   The Political Remedies to Fortune

Despite Spinoza's attribution of Jewish political success to "God's external aid" (TTP 3.17, iii.48), he does not in fact think that civic welfare is primarily a function of fortune. Immediately after emphasizing the role of fortune in Jewish success, he concedes that "human governance and vigilance [*humana directio et vigilantia*]" can do much to make society "more secure, more stable, and less subject to fortune [*securior ... magis constans, minusque fortunae obnoxia*]" (TTP 3.13–14, iii.47). The Machiavellian flavor to Spinoza's account of civic remedies to fortune is most evident in Chapter 10 of the *Political Treatise*. The two prior chapters examine the foundational principles and institutions for two models of aristocracy. In Chapter 10, he turns to consider whether a properly founded aristocracy could – in the absence of external invasion – persist in perpetuity or whether it is necessarily susceptible to disintegration. He approvingly quotes Machiavelli as claiming that with the state, as with the body, "something is added daily which eventually requires treatment" (TP 10/1; Machiavelli, *Discourses* 3.1). Like Machiavelli, Spinoza maintains that these accretions, left untreated, imperil the state, and, "If there's been no provision for dealing with this problem, the state won't be able to last by its own excellence [*virtute*], but only by good luck [*sola fortuna*]" (TP 10/1). Relying on the traditional opposition of virtue and fortune, Spinoza claims that the former is exercised through the restoration of the state to its foundations either through the wisdom and prudence of the laws (*consilio et prudentia legum*), or by a man of singular virtue (*aut viri eximiae virtutis*). Spinoza's concern here is to sketch an account of civic virtue in the form of laws and institutions that, when properly administered, render the state impervious to internal destruction (TP 10/1).

The subsequent discussion of these remedies is quite revealing. While the Romans appointed a temporary dictator to regulate the conduct of senators and ministers, Spinoza maintains, in keeping with the rule that one "ought to adopt remedies which agree with the nature of the state [*cum imperii natura conveniant*]" (TP 10/1), that such an approach would be ill-suited for a peaceful Aristocracy, where it would only proliferate fear and jeopardize security. Instead, he proposes the appointment of a council of syndics to perform this function. Despite his faith in the syndic council, he concedes that their remedies cannot be spelled out in an *a priori*, one-size-fits-all manner. Rather, if the state is to be preserved, it must be maintained by reason and "by men's common affects" (TP 10/9), which can only be achieved by adopting measures that suit the customs and *ingenia* of a given people (TP 10/7), "tak[ing] special care [*in eo apprime vigilari*]" that "subjects do their duty voluntarily rather than because the law compels them to. For a state which provides only fear as the motive for men's actions will lack vices rather than possess virtue" (TP 10/7–10/8) (Sections 4.3–4.4).

The power and *securitas* of a state, then, depends on the judgments of a collection of individuals regarding matters that are by their very nature changeable and uncertain. What I want to highlight here is that while political judgment may be informed by rational precepts and historical examples, it must also be attuned to circumstantial particulars; remedies must be dynamic enough to respond to the turns of fortune's wheel. Underpinning this response to fortune is a methodological realism.

The Principle of Accommodation

Spinoza's commitment to political realism is announced in the very opening paragraph of the TP, where he echoes Machiavelli by railing against those who "conceive men not as they are, but as they would like them to be," maintaining that they have "never conceived a Politics which could be put to any practical application" (TP 1/1).[55] Good governing practices are formed in light of the passions, which are "inconvenient" but "necessary" features of human nature *as it really is* (TP 1/4): "I've contemplated human affects – like love, hate, anger, envy, love of esteem, compassion, and the other emotions – not as vices of human nature, but as properties which pertain to it in the same way heat, cold, storms, thunder, etc., pertain to the nature of the air" (TP 1/4; cf. 3 Preface). And just as it would be foolish to ignore meteorological conditions when deciding what to wear outside, it is foolish to ignore affective conditions of participants when determining how to structure a state or how to interact with others. Spinoza's methodological principle of accommodation[56] may be expressed in the following way: commands and teachings should be accommodated to the *ingenia* of affected parties, such that these commands and teachings elicit optimal (epistemic and affective) responses.[57]

Accommodation may be formal or substantive – that is, one might accommodate one's language or mode of presentation to suit one's audience, or one might accommodate the content of the message itself. We find an early

---

[55] Compare *Prince*, XV.

[56] Spinoza uses the verb *accommodare* in this manner throughout his writing. To cite just a few examples: Ep 32; 4p4c; 4 app. 6–7; 5p7d; TTP Preface.18, iii.9; TTP 2.31, iii.37; TTP, 4.17, iii.61; TTP 5.7, iii.70; TTP 14.3, 173

[57] See J. Steinberg 2014.

endorsement of formal accommodation in the *Treatise on the Emendation of the Intellect*, a work composed in the early 1660s, though it remained unfinished at the time of Spinoza's death in 1677. Here, Spinoza advances his version of Descartes's "provisional moral code" (DM III; AT VI/22 ff.), offering a set of "rules of living" (*regulae vivendi*), the first of which is "to speak according to the power of understanding of ordinary people, and do whatever does not interfere with our attaining our purpose. For we can gain a considerable advantage from this, if we yield as much to their understanding as we can. Moreover, in this way, they will give a favorable hearing to the truth" (*TdIE*, Section 17). And just a few lines later, in the third rule, Spinoza recommends "conforming to those customs of the community that do not conflict with our aim" (*TdIE*, Section 17).[58]

The composition of the TTP is sometimes itself regarded as a grand exercise in linguistic accommodation. In it, Spinoza moderates his naturalistic metaphysics to suit an audience of liberal Christian theologians.[59] Indeed, he not only enacts his realist principle in this work, he also endorses it as part of the method of instruction:

[M]en would rather be taught by experience than deduce all their perceptions from a few axioms and connect them together. It follows that if someone wants to teach a doctrine to a whole nation – not to mention the whole human race – and wants everyone to understand him in every respect, he is bound to prove his doctrine solely by experience, and for the most part to accommodate [*accommodare*] his arguments and the definitions of his teaching to the power of understanding of ordinary people, who form the greatest part of the human race. He should not connect his arguments, or give definitions, according as they serve to connect his arguments better. Otherwise he will write only for the learned, i.e., he will be intelligible only to very few men, compared with the rest (TTP 5.36 – 37, iii.77).

Moreover, the very existence of the state can be seen as a kind of accommodation or workaround for our deep-seated irrationality:

If human nature were so constituted that men desired most what is most useful, there'd be no need of skill to produce harmony and loyalty. But it's evident that human nature isn't at all like that. As a result, it's been necessary to set up a state,

---

[58] Cf. Descartes's first maxim of his provisional code of ethics: one should "obey the laws and customs of [one's] country" (DM III; AT VI/23). See also his correspondence with Princess Elisabeth: "[I]t is also necessary to examine in particular all the mores of the places where one lives in order to know just how far they must be followed" (Descartes, Letter to Elisabeth, AT 4: 295 in CSMK). It should be acknowledged that the Stoics, too, adopted some version of the principle of accommodation. But while they viewed conforming to customs as a preferred course of action, they did not conceive of it as essential to one's virtue. Spinoza, however, thinks that that flexible, prudential action can directly contribute to one's welfare.

[59] Strauss 1988; Yovel 1989, Ch. 5.

so that everyone – both those who rule and those who are ruled – does what's for the common well-being, whether they want to or not. That is, it's been necessary to set it up so that everyone is compelled to live according to the prescription of reason, whether of his own accord, or by force, or by necessity (TP 6/3; cf. TTP 5.20–1, iii.73).

Civil mechanisms are only necessary to keep us upright because we are not perfectly rational.

In subsequent chapters, I will consider some of the ways in which Spinoza's accommodationism operates in his theory of statecraft, contributing to his defenses of toleration (Chapter 6) and democratic governance (Chapter 7). Sometimes this takes the form of accommodating universal, or at least pervasive, features of human psychology, like the natural vindictiveness, envy, and hyperbolic discounting of the future that make the state necessary in the first place. Other times, it takes the form of accommodating existing paths and predilections, respecting the customs, regime-form, and prevailing ethos, or shared *ingenia*, of a particular civic body. This form of accommodation reveals that Spinoza is a theorist of path dependence (TTP 18, iii.226–8; TP 9/14).

Given that Spinoza thinks that what is politically best must be determined in light of what is possible (see Introduction), it should not be all that surprising that Spinoza elevates the political writings of statesmen – trained in the art of practical politics – above the writings of philosophers: "Political Practitioners [*politici*] have written much more successfully about Political affairs than Philosophers have. Since they've had experience as their teacher, they've taught nothing remote from practice" (TP 1/2). Experience keeps one attuned to what is psychologically possible. It is thus essential to successful accommodation: "the more we have observed and the better we know the customs and character [*mores et conditiones*] of men – which can best be known from their actions – the more cautiously [*cautius*] we will be able to live among them and the better we will be able to accommodate [*accommodare*] our actions and lives to their *ingenia*, as much as reason allows" (TTP 4.19, iii.62). For Spinoza, as for Machiavelli and Bacon, good governance requires flexible prudence, and flexible prudence requires attunement to the circumstances of one's times. Spinoza calls this awareness of one's circumstances "vigilance" (*vigilantia*).

Vigilantia and Civic Virtue Institutionalized

In the *Ethics*, Spinoza claims that vigilance is required to "bear with each according to his *ingenium*" (4 Appendix, Cap. xiii) and to guard against excessive forms of joy and desire (4 Appendix, Cap. xxx). Vigilance also figures prominently in his discussion of political remedies to fortune. In TTP

Chapter 3, he claims that "human governance and vigilance [*humana directio et vigilantia*]" can do much to tame fortune and establish security (*securitas*):

[T]o form and preserve a social order requires no small talent and vigilance. So a social order which for the most part is founded and directed by prudent [*prudentibus*] and vigilant [*vigilantibus*] men will be more secure, more stable, and less subject to fortune [*magis constans, minusque fortunae obnoxia*]. Conversely, if a social order is established by men of untrained intelligence, it will depend for the most part on fortune and will be less stable (TTP 3.14, iii.47).

And in the subsequent chapter he cites vigilance once more as a check on the power of fortune. He embraces the Solomonic view that "when knowledge shall enter into your heart, and wisdom shall be pleasant to you, then your providence [*mezima*] will watch over you and prudence will guard you" (TTP 4.45, iii.67–8), noting that "strictly speaking, *mezima* means thought, deliberation, and *vigilance*" (TTP 4.45, iii.68n31).[60] He proceeds to reinforce the importance of vigilance, claiming that "the happiness and peace of one who cultivates the natural understanding does not depend on the rule of fortune (i.e., on God's external aid), but chiefly on his internal excellence (i.e., on God's internal aid), because he preserves himself chiefly by being watchful [*vigilando*], by acting, and by planning well" (TTP 4.46, iii.68). The emphasis on vigilance, prudence, and deliberative action suggests once more that his allegiances are closer to the civic activist account than to the internal control model.

Vigilance, then, is one of central virtues by which fortune is tamed. However, Spinoza does not think that the peace and security of the state should be made to depend on the vigilance of an individual:

[Civic harmony comes about] if the affairs of the state are so arranged that nothing which concerns the common well-being is committed absolutely to the good faith of any one person. For no one is so alert [*vigilans*] that he doesn't sometimes lose focus; and no one has such a powerful and unimpaired mind that he is not sometimes broken down and apt to be overcome, especially when the greatest strength of character is needed (TP 6/3).

The solution is to institutionalize vigilance, to make it a function of the mechanisms of the state, such that it does not depend on the antecedent virtue of any one individual. Institutions must be structured so that vigilance is exhibited in the whole of the state. He writes:

It's the duty of the sovereign, as everyone will admit, to know the situation and condition [*statum et conditionem*] of the State, to look out [*vigilare*] for the common well-being

---

[60] For an illuminating discussion of how Maimonides's account of providence resembles, and might have informed, Spinoza's naturalistic surrogate, see Nadler 2014.

of all, and to bring about whatever is useful for the majority of his subjects. But since one person alone can't review everything, and can't have his mind always alert, and concentrated on deliberation ... the Monarch must have Counselors (TP 7/3).

The watchful council is described elsewhere as "the mind's external senses, as it were the body of the Commonwealth, through which the mind conceives the condition of the State, and does what it decides is best for itself" (TP 6/19). A vigilant mind-body politic thus requires a great many officials, whose alertness is encouraged by good institutions: "affairs must be arranged so that the Public servants consult their own interests most when they look out [*invigilant*] most diligently for the common good" (TP 8/24). The details of how this is to be achieved will be the concern of Chapters 6 and 7 of this study.

5.4   Accommodation in the *Ethics*

We saw above (Section 5.2) that, even for Spinoza, ethical affairs are inescapably subject to fortune. One's welfare depends considerably on the strength of one's social bonds, which remains, to some degree, out of one's control. Moreover, as a general metaphysical fact, one always remains subject to the power of external causes (see 4p4) and, consequently, to the passions. One needs a method to overcome these vulnerabilities. In ethics, as in politics, accommodation is a critical part of the method, as those who have not accommodated their theories to suit actual conditions have "written Satire instead of Ethics" (TP 1/1).

Useful, non-Utopian ethics involves encouraging forms of action and affects that are nonideal.[61] Spinoza makes this point in *Ethics* 4p54s, where, after demonstrating that humility and repentance are not good *per se*, he writes:

Because men rarely live from the dictate of reason, these two affects, humility and repentance, and in addition hope and fear, bring more advantage than disadvantage. So since men must sin, they ought rather to sin in that direction. If weak-minded men were all equally proud, ashamed of nothing, and afraid of nothing, how could they be united or restrained by any bonds? The mob is terrifying, if unafraid. So it is no wonder that the prophets, who considered the common advantage, not that of the few, commended humility, repentance, and reverence so greatly. Really, those who are subject to these affects can be guided far more easily than others, so that in the end they may live from the guidance of reason, that is, may be free and enjoy the life of the blessed.[62]

What is good in a particular context may not be what is good *per se*. This gives rise to the problem of second-bests (see Introduction): we cannot neatly derive what is good under nonideal circumstances from what is best under

---

[61] See J. Steinberg 2014.
[62] Compare with the claim of 4p50s that even if pity is not a virtue, those who are guided by neither reason nor pity are inhuman. See J. Steinberg 2013.

ideal conditions. In order to determine what is good in a particular context, one must have a reasonably good grasp of others' *ingenia*. This requires *experientia* or knowledge of temporally-fixed particulars.

Perhaps surprisingly, even the free man must accommodate the *ingenia* of others, as circumstances require. Near the end of *Ethics* 4 Spinoza writes: "a free man who lives among the ignorant strives, as far as he can, to avoid their favors" (4p70). The demonstration runs as follows: if a free man were to receive a favor from an ignorant person, he would seek "not to repay men with benefits which are equivalent in [other men's] eyes, but to lead himself and the others by the free judgment of reason, and to do only those things which he himself knows to be most excellent" (4p70d). Unfortunately, though, the free man's "superior" payment – one might imagine, say, philosophical instruction – would assuredly be resented. Thus, the free man will avoid favors, so as not to be the object of hatred. Based on the demonstration, then, it would seem that the free man would avoid the problems associated with accommodation by refusing the favors of the ignorant.

However, Spinoza acknowledges in the scholium that the free man cannot consistently refuse favors, since even the ignorant can, in times of need, "bring human aid," and if one persistently avoids favors, one will appear supercilious, thereby provoking scorn such that "in the very act of avoiding their hate, [he] would incur it" (4p70s). Consequently, if the free man is to avoid contempt, he will occasionally have "to return thanks to them according to their own *ingenia*" (4p70s). Even the free man must bend to the *ingenia* of the ignorant.[63] This helps to explain Spinoza's approval of Paul, whom he regards as the most philosophical of the Apostles, as Paul was a Greek among Greeks, and a Jew among Jews (TTP 3.46, iii.54; TTP 5.24, iii.88–1 Corinthians 9:20–2).

Finally, we should note that accommodationism is not confined to interpersonal affairs. Acquiring a habit of virtue also requires *intra*personal accommodation, adopting strategies to compensate for one's own cognitive foibles. In the rich scholium to 5p10, Spinoza describes a method for exploiting the

---

[63] In a letter to Descartes, Princess Elisabeth of Bohemia supplies a vivid example of the frustrating bind of a philosopher living amongst the ignorant, compounded by gendered expectations of a patriarchal society: "In order to profit from the particular truths of which you speak, it is necessary to know exactly all the passions we feel and the prejudices we have, most of which are imperceptible. In observing the customs of the countries where we are, we sometimes find some very unreasonable ones that it is necessary to follow in order to avoid even greater inconveniences. Since I have been here [in Riswyck] I have experienced a very trying illustration of this truth. For I was hoping to profit from this stay in the country by having more time to employ in study, and I have found here without comparison, less leisure than I ever had at The Hague, because of the distractions of those who don't know what to do with themselves. And even though it is very unjust of them to deprive me of real goods so that I might give them imaginary ones, I am constrained to abide by the impertinent established laws of civility so that I do not acquire any enemies. Since I began writing this letter I have been interrupted more than seven times by these annoying visits" (September 30, 1665, AT 4: 301 in Shapiro 2007).

resources of the imagination, on which our thinking so deeply depends, to serve rational ends. He writes:

The best thing, then, that we can do, so long as we do not have perfect knowledge of our affects, is to conceive a correct principle of living [*ratio vivendi*], or [*seu*] sure maxims of life [*dogmata vitae*], to commit them to memory, and to apply them constantly to the particular cases frequently encountered in life. In this way our imagination will be extensively affected by them, and we shall always have them ready (5p10s).[64]

In order to overcome *fortuna* – or to gain control over the affects – it is not enough to *have* adequate ideas, one must also adopt a method for potentiating these ideas (Section 8.4), which involves accommodating general features of human psychology, such as our reliance on the imagination, while also targeting one's more idiosyncratic cognitive–affects failings (5p10s). This accounts for Spinoza's insistence that ethical and intellectual perfection requires persistent meditation and habituation (see 5p10s; *TdIE*, Section 7; Ep. 37). It also helps to explain Spinoza's proposal that everyone "accommodate" the dogmas of the faith to suit "his own power of understanding ... interpret[ing] them for himself, as it seems to him easier for him to accept them without any hesitation, with complete agreement of the heart, so that he may obey God wholeheartedly" (TTP 14.32, iii.178). And what encourages one person's faith may be quite different from what encourages another's.

All of this requires the ability to track one's own cognitive quirks and deficiencies, vigilantly attending to one's own *ingenium*. Accommodation is thus no less necessary for ethical development – both for strengthening social bonds and for adopting personalized metacognitive strategies for acquiring virtue – than it is for civic strength. And, as accommodation depends on experience, the specter of fortune thus haunts the cultivation and exercise of virtue in ethics in the very same way, even if perhaps not to the same degree, that it limits the efficacy of rational political action.

5.5   Rhetoric and Reconstitution

In Chapter 3, I began to make the case that on Spinoza's account the aim of politics is continuous with that of ethics. Here I am claiming that the method of politics is continuous with the method of ethics. Politics and ethics seek to diminish fortune by adapting rational principles to suit to the *ingenia* of

---

[64] See J. Steinberg 2014. In a similar vein, Herman De Dijn notes that the "real life also for the rational man, is a life of *struggle*, of confrontation, with victories and defeats, a struggle in which both personal strength *and* fortune (EVp10s) play the central roles. Trying to act and live under the guidance of reason is an attempt 'to conquer *fortune* as much as possible' (EIVp47S)" (De Dijn 2004, p. 45). See also Yovel 2004 and Gatens and Lloyd 1999.

affected parties. This accommodationist method is rhetorical in the Baconian sense of "apply[ing] Reason to Imagination for the better moving of the will"[65] Persuasion requires accommodation.

Virginia Cox, in her essay "Rhetoric and Ethics in Machiavelli," calls attention to Machiavelli's application of the rhetorical method to politics:

> In Machiavelli's Florence, as in the classical world, rhetoric offered a sophisticated model for a complex, power-oriented civic practice: power-oriented in the sense that the orator's mission was to mold his listeners' responses and work on their wills. Machiavelli's genius lies in the transformative political use he proposes for this practice.[66]

Cox proceeds to trace the roots of the very notion of adaptive prudence that typifies *virtù* back to classical rhetoric, particularly the work of Quintilian, who wrote: "In practice [in oratory], almost everything depends on causes, times, opportunity, and necessity. Hence a particularly important capacity in an orator is a shrewd adaptability since he is called upon to meet the most varied emergencies."[67] Cox shows that the accommodationist features of Machiavelli's account are reminiscent of the "dialectical relationship of agency and context embodied in the sophistic-rhetorical notion of *kairos*, or harmonization with the moment: as with Quintilian, the orator's art is seen to rest crucially in his capacities of adaptation and response."[68] In seeking *effectual truths* rather than idle abstractions, and in highlighting the need to adapt to one's times and to adopt instruments of persuasion that are suited to one's audience, Machiavelli's political writings exhibit a distinctly rhetorical character.

Spinoza's approach to politics is rhetorical in precisely the same way. Effective governance and useful theorizing about governance must be nonideal: it must engage people according to their *ingenia*, acknowledging "the truth of the concrete," as Antonio Negri puts it.[69] I am not the first to highlight the rhetorical dimensions of Spinoza's political thought. Fokke Akkerman has drawn attention to the rhetorical structure of the preface to the TTP.[70] And, more recently, Michael Rosenthal has argued that in addition to being a work of rhetoric, designed to persuade the reader by way of carefully chosen images suited to affective constitution of the expected reader, the TTP also serves as a "handbook of rhetoric."[71] Rosenthal's analysis of the two fold rhetorical

---

[65] The Advancement of Learning, in MW p. 238; Machiavelli, Discourses 3.39.
[66] Cox 2010, p. 173. See also Garver 1987.
[67] *Institutio Oratoria*, 2.13, Cited in Cox 2010, p. 175n4.
[68] Cox 2010, p. 182.
[69] Negri 1997, p. 222.
[70] Akkerman 1985.
[71] Rosenthal 2003b, p. 251. Rosenthal focuses specifically on what Spinoza's discussion of prophecy – with its emphasis on persuasion and the use of narratives and parables – reveals about the political method.

character of the TTP – as a work of rhetoric and as a work *about* the rhetorical method – is very compelling. What I have suggested above is that this view of politics as rhetorical extends to *both* of his political works and to the *Ethics*. The style of the TP is, of course, markedly different from that of the TTP. But this is precisely what we should expect from a rhetorician seeking to persuade two very different audiences: liberal theologians in the TTP and philosophers in the TP. And if the TP is less obviously a work of rhetoric, the endorsement of the rhetorical method is at least as pronounced in this work, which is concerned precisely with articulating institutions and procedures suited to the affective–cognitive make-up of situated subjects.

5.6   Spinoza's Methodological Synthesis: A Coda

While the "rhetorical" construal of Spinoza's political method harmonizes with the realist opening to the TP, it seems to jar with the geometrico-deductive approach to political theory articulated later in the same chapter (TP 1/4; cf. TP 1/7).[72] If politics is a craft – rhetorical, accommodationist – and political affairs are subject to (epistemic) fortune, how can we also have deductive scientific knowledge of the state? As I read him, Spinoza intends to join a deductive scientific approach to politics with rhetorical accommodationism, advancing a hybrid model of political theory that seeks to incorporate the most plausible features of Machiavellian and Hobbesian methods, while avoiding their deepest flaws.

To appreciate the distinctiveness of Spinoza's account, let's briefly consider some of the ways in which Spinoza's method differs from Machiavelli's. Machiavelli's method should be understood in light of the humanist privileging of rhetoric over philosophy. Following Petrarch, many humanists distinguished philosophy, which occupied itself primarily with conceptual clarification, from rhetoric, which aimed at action.[73] They elevated the latter over the former in part on the grounds that, unlike philosophy, rhetoric sought the improvement of mankind as a whole. When Machiavelli, in announcing his professedly radical methodological aims in *The Prince*, Ch. XV, distances himself from those who theorize about "how [people] ought to live" while neglecting how people *actually* act, he is criticizing philosophers precisely because their aims are merely theoretical rather than useful. Machiavelli is not – or, at least, is not primarily – a political *philosopher*.[74] His project is rhetorical, action-oriented, not scientific or merely theoretical.

---

[72] The "deductive" character of the work has been cited as evidence that Spinoza remains outside of the Machiavellian paradigm (Pocock 1987, p. 438) and as evidence that the method of the TP is radically unlike that of the TTP (Balibar 1998, p. 50).

[73] See Seigel 1966, p. 35.

[74] See Crick 2003, p. 48.

Machiavelli has been characterized as a political scientist, who turns to the annals of history to extract lessons from the many "experiments" recorded therein. Indeed, one scholar has gone so far as to declare that "it was he, not Francis Bacon, who invented the inductive method."[75] But while Machiavelli claims to have arrived at certain general axioms through his study of historical particulars, it is in my view quite misleading to treat him as an inductive scientist, as if he were seeking causal explanations through the tabulation of historical events. His analysis of history does not purport to be systematic; his portrayal of historical events and figures is highly stylized, even mythologizing. He selectively culls and curates his materials, fashioning exemplars of greatness and folly.[76]

Machiavelli's use of history is too desultory and tendentious to supply anything like scientific insight into human nature or the nature of political action. Moreover, he seems to lack any interest in constructing a larger theoretical framework. He does, of course, appeal to universal rules and maxims, rooted in the uniformity of human nature. But this uniformity seems to be invoked only in order to justify his use of history.[77] He never embeds these rules or maxims within anything like an overarching theory; nor does he evince any hope of supplying a general science of human motivation and social history. Instead, he remains fundamentally a particularist, "reasoning by examples," as one scholar puts it,[78] in order to cast light on some concrete problem in Florentine politics.

Contrast this with Hobbes, who casts his methodological stance in similarly revolutionary terms.[79] While Machiavelli thinks that the reason that political thinkers have failed to offer useful advice is because they have been too focused on abstract theoretical matters, Hobbes thinks that the failure to make progress in civil science has to do precisely with the theoretical inadequacies of existing accounts, inadequacies shared by Machiavelli and his scourges alike. He claims, in *De Cive*, to provide the first *scientia* of the *civitas*. For Hobbes – inspired by Euclid and the possibility of geometrical clarity, which is responsible for almost all that "distinguishes the modern world from the barbarity of the past"[80] – *scientia* consists in causal or genetic knowledge. So

---

[75] Walker 1950, p. 92.
[76] Machiavelli deliberately molds his heroes (Cesare Borgia, Scipio, Moses, Cyrus, etc.). See Hanasz 2010, p. 12.
[77] Crick claims that "these remarks are almost meaningless. What does he mean by 'human nature'? – This is never clear" (Crick 2003, p. 51). For a contrasting view, see Butterfield 1962.
[78] François Regnault, in "La pensée du prince," cited in Gregory Elliott's preface to Althusser's *Machiavelli and Us*, xvi; see *Prince*, Ch. IX, p. 36.
[79] Hobbes boldly claims to provide the first scientific account of the *civitas*, claiming the Civil Philosophy is "no older (I say it provoked, and that my detractors may know how little they have wrought upon me) than my own book *De Cive*" (*De Corpore*, Epistle Dedicatory, in *EW* I, ix).
[80] *De Cive*, Epistle Dedicatory, p. 4.

rather than following the "conventional structure of rhetorical discourse," he views the commonwealth "as taken apart" so as to conceive of how it might have been generated and what grounds a standard of justice (*De Cive*, Preface to the Readers, p. 10). This affords us a kind of maker's knowledge of the state, allowing for a stable knowledge of the causes of, and remedies for, civil dissolution:

[I]f the patterns of human action were known with the same certainty as the relations of magnitude in figures, ambition and greed, whose power rests on the false opinions of the common people about right and wrong [*jus et iniuria*], would be disarmed, and the human race would enjoy such secure peace that (apart from conflicts over space as the population grew) it seems unlikely that it would ever have to fight again.[81]

Spinoza shares Hobbes's enthusiasm for Euclidean clarity, and he thinks that we can have scientific or causal knowledge of the foundation of the state (TP 1/4; TP 1/7), the nature and scope of "right" (*ius*), "law" (*lex*), and "authority" (*potestas*) (TP, Chs. 2–4) of the civil and moral good (TP, Ch. 5). And, as we will see in more detail in Chapters 6 and 7, Spinoza invokes the laws of psychology of the *Ethics* (especially *Ethics* 3) in order to derive lessons about political laws and institutions. Spinoza even adopts Hobbesio-Euclidean methodological tools to support Machiavellian claims, such as the claim that all humans share one and the same nature.[82] One can, then, have deductively sound, scientific knowledge of certain features of civil life and human nature, especially conditional (if–then) knowledge.[83]

However, Spinoza is far less sanguine than Hobbes about the potential for the *practical application* of scientific knowledge. Political affairs are far too dynamic and require far too much experiential knowledge (of circumstantial particulars) to arrive at fool-proof manuals for the remediation of civil dissolution, which is why he repeatedly cautions against taking his particular remedies for fortune as infallible guides, noting instead that measures must be adopted that accord with the customs and *ingenia* of the people. As he acknowledges in the TTP, even while we know that the success of a state depends upon the virtue (*virtus*) and trust (*fide*) of the subjects, because of the plasticity of human nature, "it's not so easy to see how they must be led so that they constantly maintain their loyalty and virtue" (TTP 17.13, iii.204).

To be sure, Spinoza thinks that demonstrative knowledge can be useful. Knowing that right and authority are reducible to power relations

[81] *De Cive*, Epistle Dedicatory, p. 5.
[82] See Machiavelli, *Discourses* Preface, in *CWO* 1, p. 124; *Discourses* 1.11, p. 163; *Discourses* 1.39, p. 278; *Discourses* 3.43, p. 521.
[83] See A. Garrett 2012.

is vitally important if such authority is to be maintained. And rational insight into human psychology – for example, the fact that people resent being governed by perceived equals – can undoubtedly guide the practice of governance. However, as I have suggested above, and argued in more depth elsewhere,[84] even if one can derive practical principles from these demonstrative truths, these principles do not supply *specific* prescriptive guidance. To determine what is best in a particular set of circumstances, one must know a lot about the particular constitutions and tendencies of those affected. So, while a great deal can be done to gain control over civil affairs, and while theoretical knowledge contributes mightily to successful social regulation, politics is nevertheless bound to be imprecise, subject to fortune. And, in stressing the dynamic, adaptive, and, in practice, imprecision of governance, Spinoza has more in common with Machiavelli than he does with Hobbes.

Conclusion

We are now in a position to appreciate the three main points that I set out to establish in this chapter. The first (historical) point is that Spinoza's political method reflects his connection to the Renaissance humanist tradition.[85] Like the civic activists, Spinoza's approach to taming fortune is deliberative and adaptive or rhetorical. The second (textual) point is that Spinoza's political method is continuous with, and sheds light on, the ethical method, both of which require vigilance and flexible prudence.

A full analysis of the third (philosophical) point concerning how Spinoza's nonideal method might be instructive to a contemporary philosophical audience would require entering more deeply into the contemporary terrain than befits this work. Still, I think we can gesture at a few attractive features of Spinoza's account here, taking into account the claims of my previous three chapters. The state's sole aim is to increase the causal power of its citizens (Chapter 3), unimpeded by juridical constraints (Chapter 2). This involves shaping the affective make-up of citizens, promoting *securitas* over fear (Chapter 4). We see from this that affects are both part of the relevant input for political reasoning and output for political action. Consequently,

---

[84] J. Steinberg 2014.

[85] We might also point out the connection between Spinoza's method and the pedagogical method embraced by Juan Luis Vives. As I noted in Chapter 1, Spinoza's prominent reliance on the concept of *ingenium* might well be owed to Vives, who, in his seminal work on education, *De Tradendis Disciplinis*, adopts as one of its core pedagogical tenets the need to formulate instructions relative to the *ingenia* of the pupils (see Book II, Ch. 3). Pedagogy and rhetoric – both of which aimed at moral development – were closely connected in the late Renaissance.

I call Spinoza's method "dynamic realism": it is realist because civic decisions must be accommodated to existing *ingenia*; but it is dynamic since the accommodation here is in the service of reconstituting or reshaping these very *ingenia*.

There are several compelling features of Spinoza's dynamic realism. Here, I will mention just three. First, it provides us with a textured account that enables us to drive a wedge between realism and conservatism, which are all too often assimilated. Methodological realism requires only that normative decisions be made in light of a realistic understanding of circumstantial particulars, including, most importantly, psychological features of affected parties. Conservatism, on the other hand, entails either that it is not possible (descriptive conservatism) or not desirable (normative conservatism) to significantly alter present conditions. While realism adopts a present-state-respecting starting point, conservatism pursues a present-state-preserving end point. Ultimately, what determines whether one's method is conservative or progressive is not whether or not one's starting points are sensitive to concrete realities, but rather whether – and to what extent – one thinks that reshaping these concrete realities is *possible* and *desirable*. While there are, as we shall see, some conservative features of Spinoza's thought, his realism functions not to inhibit reform, but to make genuine reform possible.

Second, Spinoza's dynamic realism reveals the *normative* significance of the affects. Affects are not mere impediments or mental detritus that must be worked around since they cannot be swept away by the force of reason; rather, they are indicators of power and welfare. In order to measure the success of a polity, we must, then, look to the affective make-up of its citizens. This suggests the possibility of a constructive link between political philosophy and psychological research on affects and welfare.

And, finally, Spinoza's method unifies politics, psychology, and metaphysics in a way that, while out of fashion, raises a worthy challenge to the anti-systemic, divide-and-conquer approach to philosophical analysis.

Let's briefly take stock of the vision of politics that has been advanced at this point. Chapters 2 and 3 provide a conception of the normative bedrock of Spinoza's politics: he eliminates judicial or deontological restrictions on action, removing all limitations on the advancement of the one true aim of the state: freedom or empowerment. Chapter 4 provides a nuanced account of the affective side of freedom or empowerment. Chapter 5 reveals that accommodationism is the overarching methodological principle for the advancement of freedom. In order to liberate or empower its citizens, the state must adapt to circumstances, including the actual *ingenia* of its subjects. Taking the normative and methodological features together yields a dynamic form of realism, according to which civic structures and decisions must be suited to existing *ingenia,* but with the aim of reconstituting or reshaping these very *ingenia.* The reconstitution of essences is possible because, as we saw in Chapter 1, human *ingenia* are plastic. We will now turn to consider how Spinoza thinks that statecraft can reform or transform the psychological make-up of citizen-subjects.

6 From Superstition and Persecution to True Religion and Toleration

[I]f the spirit of religion join itself to the love of wonder, there is an end of common sense; and human testimony, in these circumstances, loses all pretensions to authority. A religionist may be an enthusiast, and imagine he sees what has no reality: He may know his narrative to be false, and yet persevere in it, with the best intentions in the world, for the sake of promoting so holy a cause: Or even where this delusion has not place, vanity, excited by so strong a temptation, operates on him more powerfully than on the rest of mankind in any other circumstances; and self-interest with equal force. His auditors may not have, and commonly have not, sufficient judgment to canvass his evidence: What judgment they have, they renounce by principle, in these sublime and mysterious subjects: Or if they were ever so willing to employ it, passion and a heated imagination disturb the regularity of its operations. Their credulity encreases his impudence: And his impudence overpowers their credulity.

– Hume, "Of Miracles"[1]

In 1665 Spinoza wrote a letter to the Secretary of the Royal Society, Henry Oldenburg, to explain what compelled him to compose the work that would become the *Tractatus Theologico-Politicus*. He offered three reasons. One of these is personal: he wished to defend himself from the charge of atheism. The vitriolic response to the work reveal how spectacularly unsuccessful he was on this score. The other two reasons have a broader compass. He meant to oppose "the prejudices of theologians," which he claims "are the greatest obstacle to men's being able to apply their minds to philosophy" and to defend the "freedom of philosophizing and saying what we think," for "the preachers suppress it as much as they can with their excessive authority and aggressiveness" (Ep. 30). The former is a worry about superstition; the latter about persecution. These two maladies are mutually supportive and share a common basis: an empowered religious caste.

Consequently, Spinoza aims to safeguard the state from the destructive impact of the clergy. On my reading, this is the guiding directive of the TTP. In this chapter, I will advance an interpretation of this work as

---

[1] Hume 1975, pp. 117–18.

a sustained, multilayered, systematic attack on clerical power that seeks to liberate citizens from destructive passions – like fear, ambition, pride, envy, and hatred – that arise out of, and in turn sustain, corrupt institutions. I hope to show that Spinoza evinces a keen appreciation of the interplay of civic institutions and affects, remaining thoroughly realist in his method: we must understand the psycho-social roots of ideological corruption – understood here in terms of widespread superstition and persecution – in order to protect against it.

Of course, the aim is *ingenia* reorientation – his realism is, after all, dynamic – and genuine peace and *securitas* require more than just the rooting out of bad civic institutions. This chapter, on the TTP, emphasizes the prevention of corrupt and corrupting institutions, while Chapter 7, which focuses primarily on the TP, explores how the adoption of salutary institutions promotes harmony and rationality. Together, these two chapters reveal the coherence and complementarity of Spinoza's political treatises, supplying at least a partial answer to the question of why Spinoza wrote a second political treatise: the TP completes the project of *ingenia* reform. Nevertheless, the TTP has a methodological pride of place, since no good institutions can be erected as long as superstition and persecution persist. As Leo Strauss aptly puts it, "the critique of the prejudices of the theologians is the necessary prolegomenon to philosophy as such."[2] So we will begin, as Spinoza does, with a critique of clericalism.

The chapter will be organized as follows. After sketching the theologico-political context in which the work was written (Section 6.1), I turn to Spinoza's analysis of the psychosocial origins of superstition and persecution (Section 6.2), which arise when an overly powerful clergy primes and exploits certain deep psychological proclivities. The remedy, then, is to dismantle clerical power, first by restricting the domain over which religious leaders *could* preside (Section 6.3), and then by depriving them of authority altogether (Section 6.4). Finally, I turn to the additional arguments for the freedom to philosophize that Spinoza advances in the concluding chapter of the TTP, showing how they arise from his psychological realism (Section 6.5) and that they admit of a certain amount of *ingenia*-relativity (Section 6.6).

6.1   The Theologico-Political Context in Brief

Spinoza portrays the Dutch Republic of his day in strikingly incongruous ways. On the one hand, paraphrasing Tacitus, he writes: "Since, then, we happen to have that rare good fortune – that we live in a Republic in which everyone is granted complete freedom of judgment, and is permitted to

---

[2] Strauss 1965, p. 112.

worship God according to his *ingenium,* and in which nothing is thought to be dearer or sweeter than freedom" (TTP Preface.12, iii.7; cf. TTP 20 title and TTP 20.40, iii.246).[3] On the other hand, as the letter to Oldenburg cited above indicates, he saw clerical intolerance as an imminent threat to liberty. And immediately after singing the praises of Dutch liberty, he sounds a warning cry that at least partially belies the image of the United Provinces as a beacon of liberty: "Many, with the most shameless license, are eager to take away the greater part of that right, and under the pretext of religion to turn the heart of the multitude (who are still at the mercy of pagan superstition) away from the supreme powers, so that everything may collapse again into slavery" (TTP Preface.13, iii.7).

While some have resolved this tension by reading Spinoza's encomium of Dutch liberty as ironic, a bitter swipe at the intolerant magistracy, or as in some way disingenuous,[4] I think that we should understand this passage as operating proleptically,[5] fostering a certain civic self-conception in order to bring reality closer to that very ideal, much as the Batavian myth of independence functioned during the Dutch Revolt.[6] In Austinian language, the assertion of Dutch liberty is performative and not merely constative.[7]

Spinoza is intervening here in the protracted struggle over Dutch identity that shaped much of the political debate in the United Provinces after it established independence from Spain.[8] On the one hand, there were those who thought that, having fought for their own freedom from the oppressive and intolerant Spanish Hapsburgs, the Dutch republic was a commonwealth founded on the principle of confessional freedom. Their vision was, in some respects, the law of the land. The Dutch Republic took a relatively permissive approach to religious practice, allowing Lutherans, Mennonites, Anabaptists, Collegiants, Quakers, and even Jews and Catholics to practice their faiths, even if it initially denied full citizenship rights to the latter two groups. And the freedom of religious practice was protected in at least some of the provinces by Article XIII of the *Union of Utrecht* (1579), one

---

[3] As Curley notes in his translation, this is an allusion to Tacitus's *Histories* 1.1.4. This same passage is invoked in Toland's *Pantheisticon* (1720) and Hume's *Treatise* (1738). For more on the significance of this passage in early modern thought, see Russell 2010, Chapter 7.
[4] Jonathan Israel considers a range of interpretations of Spinoza's praising of Dutch liberty in Israel 2002. He attributes the reading of this remark as an "ironic protest" to M. Francès, K.O. Meinsma, and E. Balibar, among others (Israel 2002, p. 149n7).
[5] As when one tells a child that she is too smart to engage in foolish behavior in order to encourage the fulfillment of this description. For more on proleptic mechanisms, see Williams 1995; Fricker 2014.
[6] See van Gelderen 1992.
[7] See Austin 1975.
[8] Mout 1997, p. 40.

of the foundational documents of the republic.[9] By praising Dutch freedom, Spinoza is lending his weight to the tolerationist model of national
identity.[10]

However, there were also those who viewed the nascent republic as an
unreconstructed Calvinist state, regarding the Dutch revolt as an essentially
Calvinist uprising against a Catholic oppressor. Those who saw the Dutch
Republic as a fundamentally Calvinist state sought for the Reformed Church
to have a greater influence over civic life. As Gerrit Groenhuis puts it, "for the
orthodox Calvinists the justification for the Dutch Republic was as the 'abode
of the Bride'; in other words, the State existed for the sake of the Church... The
temporal as well as the ecclesiastical authorities should abide by God's plan."[11]
The theocratic pretensions of the Calvinists are expressed by Article XXXVI
of the *Belgic Confession*, which codified the main doctrines of the faith:
"[t]he government's task is not limited to caring for and watching over the
public domain but extends also to upholding the sacred ministry, with a view
to removing and destroying all idolatry and false worship of the Antichrist."[12]
Civic authorities are positioned to do God's work on earth, including punishing heretics. Consequently, on this vision, anti-Socinian laws and laws against
blasphemy and heresy more generally were an essential, not an aberrant, part
of a Calvinist Republic.

The struggle between tolerationists and Calvinist hardliners over national
identity, confessional freedom, and the relationship between church and state
persisted throughout the seventeenth century, taking a number of different
forms. The conflict between the Remonstrants and the Counter-Remonstrants
in the early decades of the century set the terms for much of the subsequent dispute. The Remonstrants were followers of Jacobus Arminius (hence their other
designation: "Arminians") who articulated the ways in which they deviated
from orthodox Calvinism in a formal "Remonstrance" in 1610. One of their
core tenets was that faith is expressed in the conscience of the individual and is
therefore not subject to the coercive power of the state. The Remonstrants were
opposed by the conservative Gomarists (followers of Franciscus Gomarus),
or Counter-Remonstrants. This theological dispute quickly took on public
significance, pitting the Remonstrant Arminians, who counted among their
early supporters the Advocate of the States of Holland Johan Oldenbarnevelt

---

[9] "[E]ach person shall remain free in his religion and...not one shall be investigated or persecuted
because of religion, as is provided in the Pacification of Ghent" (see www.constitution.org/cons/
dutch/Union_Utrecht_1579.html).

[10] If the magistrates did not share something like this conception, the work would have had no
chance of avoiding censure. Unsurprisingly, as it turns out, the TTP was expeditiously banned.
For more on the banning of the work, see Israel 1995b.

[11] Groenhuis 1981, p. 125; See also Mout 1997, p. 44.

[12] See www.legacy.fordham.edu/halsall/mod/1562belgicconfession.asp.

and a young Hugo Grotius, against the Counter-Remonstrant Gomarists, who received the support of the Stadtholder, Prince Maurits. For a little over a decade (roughly 1607–18), the dispute raged on, radiating outward from Amsterdam and Utrecht. Finally, in 1618, a national synod, the Synod of Dort, convened to define more precisely the parameters of public faith. The fallout from the Synod of Dort was disastrous for the Arminians. The Synod rejected the grounds of remonstrance, affirming the doctrines enshrined in the *Belgic Confession*. Oldenbarnevelt was put to death, and Arminians throughout the country were purged from town councils and universities.[13]

This episode cast a long shadow over Dutch political life. The middle of the century witnessed an aftershock that centered on university life. Once again, two theologians were at the heart of the debate: Johannes Cocceius, a liberal theology professor at Leiden, and Gisbertus Voetius, Dean of the University of Utrecht. Disputes between Cocceians and Voetians began over abstruse theological matters, but expanded into more general disagreements about the relationships between religion, natural philosophy, and politics. The Voetians led the assault on the Cartesian philosophy being taught in the universities. They thought that the new science advocated by Descartes, with its mechanistic view of the material world, posed a threat to Christianity.[14]

Spinoza's philosophy was criticized by *both* the Voetians and the moderate Cocceian-Cartesians. But it was the Voetians who posed the greatest threat to Spinoza and his circle, since Voetius had argued in his *Politica Ecclesiastica* for the persecution of Anti-Trinitarians.[15] And his followers were bent on punishing freethinkers and reining in philosophers, invoking his theology to justify the expansion of blasphemy laws.

Spinoza witnessed the effects of these blinkered campaigns. His intellectual circle included Collegiants whose meetings were described by the Amsterdam Reformed consistory as "Socinian gatherings, in which Quakers and Boreelists mingle."[16] He also saw his friend Ludwig Meijer's *Philosophia S. Scripturae Interpres* viciously condemned upon its publication in 1666, and their mutual friend Adriaan Koerbagh tried and sentenced for blasphemy for publishing his libertine ideas in two treatises in 1668. In the more scandalous of the two – *Een Bloemhof van allerley lieflijkheyd* (A Flower Garden of all Kinds of Loveliness) – Koerbagh ridiculed a number of traditional religious doctrines and practices, while advancing his own shocking views, among which were: Jesus is not divine; God is identical with nature; everything is necessitated by the laws of nature (the laws of God); and miracles are impossible. These are

---

[13] See Israel 1995a, pp. 452ff.
[14] Nadler 1999, pp. 151–2 and 308–10.
[15] Israel 1995a, pp. 912–3.
[16] Ibid., p. 913.

all positions that Spinoza consistently endorsed. However, while Spinoza was famously cautious, Koerbagh was not, publishing the works in Dutch – and thereby making them accessible to the general literate public – under his own name. During his subsequent imprisonment under squalid conditions Koerbagh became ill, and he died soon thereafter (in 1669). It is generally supposed that it was Koerbagh's imprisonment and death above all else that precipitated the publication of the TTP.[17]

Finally, any analysis of cultures of intolerance in Spinoza's time would be incomplete without mentioning his own treatment by the Amsterdam Rabbinate. He was, of course, cast out of the Jewish community in Amsterdam in 1656 when the council of elders issued a particularly caustic *cherem*, uncharacteristically leaving no room for repentance and readmission. Such a decisive expulsion would have carried enormous social costs for anyone. And even while Spinoza proved to be remarkably resilient, thriving philosophically and socially in exile, he was surely sensitive to the impact of persecution, having seen its traumatic effect on others, like Uriel da Costa who committed suicide after being expelled from the very same Amsterdam Jewish community when Spinoza was just eight years old.[18]

Between the schisms and witch-hunts that marked Dutch theologico-political life in the seventeenth century and his own experience with the Amsterdam Rabbinate, Spinoza was acutely aware of the threat posed by religious intolerance. In later sections, we will see how he draws on this well of experience – sometimes encrypted as biblical history – to corroborate his case against ecclesiastical authority.

6.2   The Psychosocial Basis of Civic Corruption

The Psychosocial Roots of Superstition

Spinoza's realism leads him to diagnose disorders so that he can propose suitable remedies. To treat civic corruption in the form of mass superstition and intolerance, one must first understand its source. It is no wonder then that Spinoza directly takes up this diagnostic challenge in the preface to the TTP, starting with superstition.

While Spinoza does not offer a tidy definition of superstition, one can extract a general account from his desultory observations. Superstition is a perversion of religion that is particularly bound up with idolatry and divination.[19] It consists in trying to understand God's will or his plan by relying on signs or images, such as the entrails of animals. It is doubly confused in that it involves

---

[17] Nadler 1999, p. 170.
[18] For more on da Costa and the Amsterdam Jewish Community, see Yovel 1989.
[19] For context, see Cameron 2010; James 2009.

a confused, anthropomorphic, providential conception of God,[20] and it seeks to understand God's operations via haphazardly associated images (Section 1.2). Superstition thus involves projecting confused features of one's own mind onto God, implicating the divine in our own lunacy (E 1, Appendix, ii.79), interpreting nature as if "[it] were as crazy as [we] are" (TTP Preface.3, iii.5).[21] In short, superstition is presented as a disorder of the mind, an addiction to the prognosticative power of images.[22]

This malady of mind leads to misology, or the hatred of reason. The superstitious are so dependent on the imagination that they "call [reason] blind, and human wisdom vain" (TTP Preface.4, iii.5). Superstition thus "teaches men to scorn reason and nature, and to admire and venerate only what is contrary to both of these" (TTP 7.4, iii.97–8) and to "hate no one more than those who cultivate true knowledge and true life" (TTP 2.2, iii.30). Superstition sustains itself by generating a misologistic, anti-philosophical mindset.

Like so many thinkers before and after him, Spinoza identifies fear as the reason "why superstition arises, lasts, and increases" (Preface.5, iii.6).[23] Spinoza is not merely parroting a humanist bromide here; this diagnosis springs directly from his psychology. People generally desire uncertain things (see TdIE, Section 6). When they are able to obtain these goods, they are proud and resistant to counsel. But when fortunes turn, they are filled with fear and anxiety. Still, our minds are buoyant. Because we strive to imagine those things that increase our power of acting (3p12–3p13), the more intensely we are pressed upon by fear, the more anxiously we will seek sources of hope (3p25). This leads us in times of fear to scour our environment for portents of some good, irrespective of the epistemic merits of these signs (TTP Preface.2, iii.5).

Fear thus renders people credulous, leading them to recklessly seek sources of hope. Spinoza claims in the *Ethics* that it is precisely the readiness to believe – a readiness that is primed by fear – that gives rise to superstition (3p50s). Since "anything whatever can be the accidental cause of hope or fear," our environment abounds with such "omens" to which the anxious may turn

---

[20] In Balling's translation of *Metaphysical Thoughts* (Appendix to PCP), we find Spinoza claiming that the attribution of a free will to God is "the sole cause of superstition, and perhaps of much knavery" (*CM*, Ch. VII, ii.261).

[21] Cf. "[A]s if the whole of nature were as senseless as they are" (TTP Preface, Section 2).

[22] Cf. Locke's and the Cambridge Platonists' descriptions of "enthusiasm."

[23] Susan James shows that this view has its basis antiquity and was revived in the Renaissance (James 2012, p. 15). We may add that it had quite a long and illustrious afterlife consequent to the TTP. See for instance La Bruyère, *Les Caractères* (1688): "La superstition semble n'être autre chose qu'une crainte mal réglée de la Divinité"; and Hume, "Of Superstition and Enthusiasm." A late flourishing of this idea may be found in Russell's claim that "fear is the main source of superstition, and one of the main sources of cruelty" (see the epigraph to Chapter 4). And Alexander Lesser notes that "the Murray Dictionary defines superstition in general as 'religious belief or practice founded upon fear or ignorance'; and specifically, 'an irrational religious belief or practice,' or 'an irrational religious system'" (Lesser 1931).

(3p50). This leads people to place their trust in uncredentialed authorities.[24] This is the first stage of Spinoza's account of superstition:

FEAR → CREDULITY

By maintaining that superstition arises from a heedless credulity born from fear, Spinoza indicates that superstition is not merely a feature of our benighted past; it is something to which everyone is prone by nature (TTP Preface.7, iii.6; cf. 3p50s).

Still, unreliable sources of hope are bound to let people down without further buttressing: "As easy, then, as it is to take men in with any superstition whatever, it's still just as difficult to make them persist in one and the same superstition" (TTP Preface.8, iii.6). Stable forms of superstition are possible only when affects are manipulated and mobilized to serve political ends. It is maintained "only by hope, hate, anger, and deception" (TTP Preface.7, iii.6). He illustrates this by appealing to his favorite scourge, the Turks:

To avoid this evil [of inconstancy], immense zeal is brought to bear to embellish religion – whether the religion is true or illusory – with ceremony and pomp, so that it will be thought to have greater weight than any other influence, and so that everyone will always worship it with the utmost deference. The Turks have succeeded so well at this that they consider it a sacrilege even to debate religion; they fill everyone's judgment with so many prejudices that they leave no room in the mind for sound reason, nor even for doubting (TTP Preface.9, iii.6–7).[25]

In order to preserve their position, the powerful "keep men deceived" and "cloak in the specious name of Religion the fear by which they must be checked, so that they will fight for slavery as they would for their survival" (TTP Preface.10, iii.7). Superstition is stabilized and political power is preserved when the general anxiety that gives rise to credulity is redirected and repackaged under the respectable banner of "religion."

While Spinoza's account here is short on details, it is easy to imagine what he has in mind. By keeping people perpetually afraid – particularly by promoting fear of damnation[26] – choking off alternative sources of hope and positioning themselves as saviors, the politically powerful keep the masses fixed to *their* images, *their* ideology, thereby motivating the multitude to do their

---

[24] Spinoza writes to Burgh that he has pledged credulity to other men, placing his trust in others rather than in himself (Ep. 76).

[25] Compare this with his remarks about the Catholic Church: "I grant that the organization of the Roman Church, which you praise so highly, is well-designed politically, and profitable for many. I do not believe there is any order more suitable for deceiving ordinary people and controlling men's minds, unless it would be the order of the Mahommedan Church, which surpasses it by far. For from the time this superstition began, no schism has arisen in their Church" (Ep. 76).

[26] See once again Spinoza's letter to Burgh, where he identifies "fear of Hell" as "the single cause of superstition" (Ep. 76). See Nadler 2005.

bidding. The powerful evade responsibility for disappointment by stoking and redirecting the anger and hatred of the masses, establishing a common enemy to serve as the scapegoat, namely, "heretics," especially those who prize reason and challenge the hegemonic ideology. In something like this way, affective resources are called upon to keep people mired in superstition.

This account adds another layer to the account of the origin of stable superstition.

MASS FEAR → MASS CREDULITY

MASS CREDULITY + POLITICIZATION OF RELIGION → STABLE SUPERSTITION

While general fear and anxiety breed widespread credulity, it is the mobilization of religion for political ends that shores up otherwise unstable systems of belief. The powerful use their elevated status to manufacture, intensify, and redirect the very passions that breed a superstitious cast of mind in the first place. The result is a vicious cycle of fear and superstition. Politically ginned-up anxiety bolsters superstition, and superstition stupefies the mind, intensifying anxieties about one's future state, rendering one more susceptible to the abuse of religion – and around and around we go.

The Psychosocial Roots of Persecution

In the paragraph that follows his eulogy of Dutch liberty, Spinoza turns to diagnose how it is that in the name of Christianity – a religion of "love, gladness, peace, restraint, and good faith toward all" – people engage in the "bitterest hatred toward one another" (TTP Preface.14, iii.8). He seeks to understand the origin of the pervasive intolerance that he witnessed (Section 6.1). His account is as follows:

What's the cause of this evil? Doubtless that religion has commonly consisted in regarding the ministries of the Church as positions conferring status, its offices as sources of income, and its clergy as deserving the highest honor. For as soon as this abuse began in the Church, the worst men immediately acquired a great desire to administer the sacred offices; the love of propagating divine religion degenerated into sordid greed and ambition; and the temple itself became a Theater, where one hears, not learned ecclesiastics, but orators, each possessed by a longing, not to teach the people, but to carry them away with admiration for himself, to censure publicly those who disagree, and to teach only those new and unfamiliar doctrines which the common people most wonder at. This had to lead to great dissension, envy, and hatred, whose violence no passage of time could lessen" (Preface.15, iii.8).

Spinoza cites two main reasons why the elevated position of the church gives rise to intolerance: (1) when religious offices are endowed with prestige and power, they attract "the worst men," and (2) those who hold such offices are further encouraged to grandstand and induce wonder in the common people.[27] To understand the roots of intolerance, I think we must home in on the invocation of ambition (*ambitio*) here.[28] It is to intolerance what fear is to superstition. To see this, we must turn to Spinoza's analysis of the psychology of disagreement.

Here it is worth recalling a couple of general features of Spinoza's psychology. First, because evaluative judgments are nothing but affects (Section 1.1), evaluative disagreements are just expressions of different affective relationships toward the same object. Second, the doctrine of the imitation of affects entails that, other things being equal, when one imagines that another (like her) disagrees with her judgment, she will, *to some extent*, feel what the other feels and, consequently, judge as the other judges (E3 DA xxxiii) (Section 1.2). Spinoza calls this emulation (*aemulatio*). So, when we encounter someone who has a different affective relationship to some object from ours, we undergo a "vacillation of mind" (*fluctuatio animi*) (3p17, 3p31), leaving us torn between contrary affects/judgments. External conflict is internalized as a form of cognitive dissonance.

While Spinoza obviously does not have a formal theory of cognitive dissonance, he does acknowledge something like this phenomenon. We see this, for instance, in 4p17s, where Spinoza is elaborating on his claim that true knowledge may be overpowered by the passions. Here he quotes two classical sources. Scholars almost invariably focus on the first, a quote from Ovid ("I see and approve the better, but I follow the worse"), while ignoring the second, from the Ecclesiastes: "He who increases knowledge increases sorrow." The latter passage echoes Spinoza's claim a few lines earlier that "the true knowledge of good and evil stirs up conflict in the mind." Acquiring knowledge induces conflict by generating affective dissonance, leaving one internally conflicted. If, for instance, one's striving has been directed toward the boundless acquisition of wealth, but one comes to see this as a specious *summum bonum*, this recognition may provoke feelings of frustration, regret, and shame as one's idea of how one should live jars with one's awareness of how one has lived. While this revelation may lead one to pursue nobler ends, the recognition in itself does not guarantee that one's desires will be revised in its light, and the initial effect of such knowledge is to "increase sorrow" and "stir up conflict."

This internal conflict may be seen as an expression of a more general feature of Spinoza's psychology, namely, ideological preservationism. The general

---

[27] Cf. "... he who knows how to censure more eloquently and cunningly the weakness of the human mind is held to be godly" (E3 Preface).

[28] Others have also emphasized the role of ambition in generating intolerance. See Matheron 1969; Rosenthal 2001; 2003a.

principle that all things strive to persevere in their being applies to individual ideas as well as systems of ideas (i.e., minds) that function collectively.[29] All ideas and ideational systems strive to resist oppositional forces. We seek to affirm what we affirm and love what we love with the utmost constancy.[30] This explains why disagreement and vacillation are unwelcome disturbances (3p31; 4p17s). Cognitive dissonance arises when an idea constrains or opposes some antecedent idea. Representing one's acquisitiveness as folly entails experiencing a disruption of one's erstwhile desires.

Spinoza maintains that such cognitive dissonance is unstable: when we are torn by contrary affects, "a change will have to occur, either in both of them, or in one only, until they cease to be contrary" (5a1; cf. Ep. 32). There are four main ways in which the dissonance that arises through disagreement might be diminished: (1) *Toleration*; (2) *Epistemic Convergence*; (3) *Affective Convergence*; and (4) *Hatred*. Let's briefly consider the first three ways in with conflicts may be resolved.

> *Toleration*: One suspends one's judgment when one "perceives the inadequacy of one's view" (2p49s).
>
> *Epistemic Convergence*: One or both parties modify their beliefs based on exposure to new evidence and arguments.
>
> *Affective Convergence:* One or both parties modify their beliefs out of a love of esteem (*gloria*) and a sense of shame (*verecundia*), accommodating their beliefs to the others' beliefs in order to win their approval.

While these ways of reducing dissonance certainly play a role in overcoming quotidian disputes, their efficacy is limited by a prominent feature of human psychology: ambition.

Ambition is a protean concept for Spinoza.[31] His first gloss of term is as the "striving to do something (and also to omit doing something) solely to please men" (3p29s). Just two propositions later, however, Spinoza construes ambition as a more specific "striving to bring it about that everyone should approve his love and hate" (3p31s). This is the primary sense in which Spinoza uses ambition in the *Ethics*: the desire that others "live according to [one's own] *ingenium*" (ibid.).[32]

Spinoza takes the desire to have others conform to one's own values and judgments to be a pervasive feature of human psychology (5p4s). In light of

---

[29] Diane Steinberg makes this point in D. Steinberg 2005.

[30] See James: "[I]ndividuals and communities develop attachments to their imaginatively-grounded beliefs and habits which in turn make them resistant to change" (James 2011, p. 185).

[31] See Section 1.2. See also Matheron 1969, pp. 159ff.

[32] This is the *ambition de gloire* in Matheron's treatment (Matheron 1969, p. 168). Bacon, "Of Vain-Glory," in *MW*, p. 444.

ideological preservationism, it is easy to see why. We are by nature averse to modifying our judgments. So when we disagree with others, the resulting dissonance prompts us to strive to get them to conform to our *ingenia*. So, while one might revise or restrict the scope of one's beliefs in response to new evidence or social pressure, natural ambition renders us resistant to such change. We strive to have others defer to us and to judge in accordance with *our* judgments, which gratifies our pride and self-esteem.[33] Toleration and deference to others implies a lack of power to compel them, which induces a sense of humility (3p55s) or impotence against which human nature "strains" (3 DA xxix; 3p55s). Moreover, modifying an antecedent judgment typically requires amending a whole constellation of interlocking judgments, which collectively function as a barrier to belief revision. And the more deeply entrenched one's evaluative judgments are, the more resistant one will be to adapting. Matheron describes this condition well: "in reality the feelings we experience through affective contagion do not inscribe themselves on a blank slate. Even before we know what others love or hate we already have our own system of values, which, sinking its roots into our character and our history, does not allow itself to be modified without resistance."[34]

Ambition contributes to the persistence of disagreement, with disputants digging in their heels, redoubling their efforts at altering others' judgments. When disagreements persist, dissonance is reduced only through hatred. Hatred overrides the imitation of affects, which is the source of dissonance in the first place (3p27d; 3p23), enabling one to retain one's viewpoint without internal conflict. Spinoza thus concludes that "when all alike want [others to live according to his *ingenium*], they are alike an obstacle to one another, and when all wish to be praised, or loved, by all, they hate one another" (3p31s).[35] Hence, the fourth mode of reducing cognitive dissonance:

> *Hatred:* One comes to hate the person with whom one disagrees, in which case the imitation of affects is overridden and dissonance is overcome.

From this analysis, we see that, as with superstition, the roots of mutual intolerance are in human nature – in fear and ambition, respectively.[36]

But to admit that there are deep psychological roots of superstition and persecution is not to concede the inevitability of widespread ideological

---

[33] We are all inclined toward love of esteem and self-love (*Acquiescentia in se ipso*) as "the mind strives to imagine only those things which posit its power of acting" (3p54) and to avoid restrictions on this power (3p55).

[34] Matheron 1969, p. 166 – my translation of "[e]n réalité, les sentiments que nous éprouvons par contagion affective ne s'inscrivent pas sur une table rase. Avant même de savoir ce que les autres hommes aiment ou haïssent, nous avons déjà notre propre système de valeurs, qui, plongeant ses racines dans notre caractère et notre histoire, ne saurait se laisser modifier sans résistance".

[35] Matheron 1969, p. 172.

[36] Rosenthal 2001, p. 544.

corruption. Civic institutions determine whether or not the seeds of super-stition and intolerance yield gnarly, noxious fruit. One institutional defect in particular accounts for general superstition and persecution: an overly powerful clergy.

Ambition and Mass Persecution

In several places in the TTP, including the brief analysis of the emergence of civic discord in the name of religion cited above, Spinoza underscores the role of ambition.[37] Here he is conceiving of ambition as a distinctive character trait, a kind of "excessive desire for esteem" (3 DA xliv) – an obsession that so dominates the mind that it may be regarded as a "species of madness" (E4p44s; cf. 3p56s; 5p10s).[38] This cast of mind is expressed as a zealous and unyielding pursuit of converting others to one's own *ingenium*.

Ambition is bound up with two other affects: pride and envy. Pride and ambition are both expressions of excessive desire for esteem. The main differ-ence between pride and ambition consists merely in whether or not this desire for esteem has been gratified: the ambitious excessively seek esteem, while the proud (*superbum*) excessively revel in it (3 DA xxix; 3p30s; 5p10s).[39] This explains why Spinoza treats ambition and pride more or less interchangeably in the TTP. Since esteem is a relational good, the ambitious or proud rejoice both when their own standing is increased and when the standing of others is diminished (3p55s). Excessive lovers of esteem are thus envious, envy (*invidia*) being defined as "hate [*odium*] insofar as it so affects a man that he is saddened by another's happiness and, conversely, glad at his ill fortune" (3 DA xxxiii; cf. 3 DA xxxix; 3p24s).

The combination of ambition, pride, and envy makes excessive lovers of esteem hateful and intolerant. They not only seek relentlessly to impose their judgments on others, they also strive to diminish the standing of others. As Spinoza warns in *Ethics* 4, just one proposition after declaring that "it would take too long to enumerate all of the evils of pride here" (4p57s):

[H]e who exults at being esteemed by the multitude is made anxious daily, strives, acts, and schemes, in order to preserve his reputation. For the multitude is fickle and inconstant; unless one's reputation is guarded, it is quickly destroyed. Indeed, because everyone desires to secure the applause of the multitude, each one willingly

---

[37] *TTP Preface*.15, iii.8; TTP 7.4, iii.97; TTP 20.30, iii.242.

[38] This excessive love of esteem is to be contrasted with ordinary self-love, or *acquiescentia in se ipso*, which is assuredly a good thing (see 3p55s).

[39] Spinoza characterizes pride as "thinking more highly of oneself than is just" (3 DA, xxvii; 3p26s). Since pride is also supposed to include excessive love of esteem, it is quite possible that Spinoza intends "thinking more highly of oneself than is just" to comprise both overestimation *and* valuing esteem more than is appropriate.

puts down the reputation of the other. And since the struggle is over a good thought to be the highest, this gives rise to a monstrous lust of each to crush the other in any way possible (4p58s).

The account strongly resembles the analysis of the emergence of intolerance in the TTP Section 9, where Spinoza writes of religion degenerating into "sordid greed and ambition" (TTP Preface.15, iii.8) in which pastors sought "not to teach the people, but to carry them away with admiration for himself, to censure publicly those who disagree" resulting in "great dissension, envy [*invidia*], and hatred, whose violence no passage of time could lessen" (TTP Preface.15, iii.8). A similar sentiment is expressed in his characterizing of the fickle and easily corrupted masses: "everyone thinks that he alone knows everything, and wanted everything to be done according to his *ingenium*... from love of esteem [*gloria*], he disdains equals, and will not put up with being ruled by them. From envy for the greater praise or better fortune someone else receives – these things are never equal – he wishes the other person ill, and is delighted when bad things happen to him" (TTP 17.7, iii.203). No wonder, then, that Spinoza characterizes the proud as "burdensome to all" (3p30s).[40]

To make matters worse, excessive lovers of esteem are also among the most susceptible to superstition. As they "immoderately desire uncertain things" – namely, the esteem of the fickle masses – they are "most thoroughly enslaved to every kind of superstition" (TTP Preface.4, iii.5). As they are also particularly ideologically protective and egocentric, they are unwilling to learn from disagreement, and instead "accommodat[e] Scripture to their worst customs" (TTP 18.9, iii.223). Spinoza reinforces this connection between ambition and superstitious distortion throughout the TTP (see especially TTP 7.1–4, iii.97; TTP 20.21, 242).

The link between ambition and superstition helps to explain why the ambitious direct their intolerance at philosophers, since, as we saw above, superstition breeds misology. Philosophers are the natural ideological enemies of superstitious, ambitious individuals. This tension between hidebound lovers of esteem and philosophers is exacerbated by the fact that the ambitious seek to surround themselves with "parasites, or flatterers" who inflate their sense of self-importance (4p57). Consequently, the excessive lover of esteem "hates the presence of the noble," who are not taken in by mere appearances (4p57 and 4p57d) and who securely abide by their judgment: "[T]he proud man must be envious (see IIIP55S) and hate those most who are most praised for their virtues...he takes pleasure only in the presence of those who humor his

---

[40] Cf. TTP 20.42, iii.246. Cf. 4p35s. Julie Cooper is undoubtedly right that "Spinoza is a critic, rather than a champion, of pride" (Cooper 2013, p. 72).

weakness of mind and make a madman of a fool" (4p57s). The proud perceive the rational as troublesome insubordinates.[41]

When given a rostrum, ambitious people spread their antipathy toward reason, encouraging others to disparage and revile philosophers and philosophy (Preface.15, iii.8). They manufacture fear, perpetuating widespread superstition and insecurity by targeting free-thinkers as a threat to common morality and civic life. By ramping up their attacks on philosophers, these powerful, hateful, and fractious individuals achieve greater fame for themselves, while diverting civil discontent onto the rational.

A powerful clergy is able to propagate its message precisely when ordinary people are rendered insecure and credulous. As Michael Rosenthal aptly puts it "if at least some people in adversity are ready to believe anything, then there will be some who will be ready to give them something to believe. Indeed, this is a fertile ground for those who are…desirous to convert others to their own beliefs and practices."[42] And the more successful clerics are in setting themselves apart from the common people – presenting religion as fundamentally mysterious and in need of decryption by the luminous few – the more capable they are of inspiring wonder or devotion rather than envy. While in general people, out of ambition, resist governance by equals (TTP 17.13, iii.203), envy gives way to devotion when one ceases to regard the other as an equal (3p55c) and instead one "wonders" at the other's singular powers. If politically empowered, a superstitious and intolerant few can spread their irrational and hateful ideology to the insecure and credulous masses, who are primed for their message.[43]

We see from this that Spinoza was deeply attuned to the psychological impact of civil institutions. If a people are to live in security and peace, the power of the clergy must be curtailed. This is the directive around which so much of the TTP is structured, since if the state is to protect the masses from ideological corruption – the primarily concern of the critical or protective side of *ingenia* reform – it must attack the conditions in which mass superstition and persecution thrive by limiting the authority of the clergy.

6.3   Spinoza's Anticlericalism I: Faith and the Separation Thesis

Spinoza seeks to restrict the power of the clergy in several ways. The first nineteen of twenty chapters of the TTP can be seen as constituting a

---

[41] Nadler observes that the free person is steeled against emotional manipulation by the clerics (Nadler 2005, p. 216).

[42] Rosenthal 2003a, p. 325.

[43] We will see that many of these considerations apply to imbalances of political power in general, thus paving the way for his defense of relative egalitarianism (Section 7.2). But the propagation of superstition and misology make the power of religious authorities distinctly dangerous.

two-stage argument for limiting clerical power. The first fifteen chapters diminish the scope of theological interest, and the subsequent four chapters make the case against coercive religious authority. We will consider these arguments in turn over the course of the next two sections (Sections 6.3 and 6.4). In what follows I offer only a schematic overview of the arguments of these chapters. Fortunately, comprehensive and insightful analyses of TTP have already been written.[44] I will confine my efforts to delineating the basic argumentative strategy of these chapters, casting this analysis in a somewhat new light.

The first stage of Spinoza's anticlerical argument is to separate faith from philosophy. This thesis – which, for convenience, I will refer to as the Separation Thesis[45] – is described as the "main purpose of this whole work" (TTP 14.5, iii.174). For the failure to distinguish philosophy and faith leads to "absurdities, disadvantages, and harms" (TTP 15.43, iii.188).

The Separation Thesis is, at its core, a repudiation of the view that Scripture gives us knowledge of God (his nature and his will) and of the operations of nature. The religious disputes that shook the Dutch Republic in the Seventeenth Century (Section 6.1) turned on metaphysical interpretations of Scripture. Spinoza challenges a methodological assumption on which these interpretations depend, namely, that the bible is a special kind of text, one whose claims must be true on account the text's divine origin. To assume *ex ante* that this text is the unvarnished word of God is to commit a form of idolatry, which Spinoza rails against, both in the Preface, where he criticizes superstitious common people who "worship the books of Scripture rather than the Word of God itself" (TTP Preface.25, iii.10), and in Chapter 12, where he accuses those who "worship likenesses and images, i.e. paper and ink, in place of the Word of God" (TTP 12.5, iii.190) of converting religion into superstition.

Scriptural idolaters divide into two camps. One camp, which Spinoza dubs the "dogmatists" (*dogmaticis*) (TTP 15), assumes that Scripture is an unerring source of *rational* metaphysical knowledge. According to this group – which includes Moses Maimonides and Spinoza's friend Ludwig Meyer[46] – the claims of Scripture must be adapted to accord with reason. While the dogmatists are right to regard reason as the ultimate arbiter of metaphysical knowledge, they are wrong to treat the bible as if it were written for philosophers rather than common people (TTP 7.75–87, iii.113–16). To assume *ex ante* that this

---

[44] James 2012; Nadler 2011.
[45] Spinoza's Separation Thesis should be distinguished from the Separation Thesis of Dutch Cartesians, like De Raey and Wittich, who regard philosophy as an autonomous field of study, but deny that this exhausts the scope of metaphysical knowledge, allowing that Scripture can contribute to our understanding of Nature. For more on De Raey and Wittich, see Douglas 2015.
[46] Spinoza calls Maimonides "the first person among the Pharisees" (TTP 15, iii.180); but his critique clearly also implicates Meyer's *Philosophy as the Interpreter of Holy Scripture*.

particular text is unfailingly rational is to abdicate reason, which demands that the credibility of a text be established through its content, not brutely assumed.

The second form of Scriptural idolatry assumes *ex ante* that Scripture is an unerring source of metaphysical knowledge while denying that reason is the only standard for metaphysical knowledge. Spinoza refers to those who commit this form of idolatry as the "skeptics" (*scepticis*), and they are represented in the TTP by Rabbi Jehuda Al-Fakhar.[47] This view subordinates reason to faith, claiming that when philosophy and Scripture conflict, it is Scripture to which we must defer. Spinoza agrees with the skeptics that there can be genuine incongruence between what Scripture and reason maintain, but denounces the way that they "want to make reason, [God's] greatest gift, a divine light, subordinate to dead letters – which men's wicked conduct could have corrupted" (15.10, iii.182).[48] This is the height of epistemic absurdity.

In order to oppose both forms of Scriptural idolatry, Spinoza advances a distinct interpretative method. Curiously, though, Spinoza does not articulate his interpretative method until Chapter 7 of the TTP, after having already made a number of bold interpretative claims. How are we to account for the placement of the chapter on method?[49]

My proposal is that Spinoza, cleverly and subtly, bootstraps his way to a radically naturalistic interpretation of Scripture. He starts with a minimal methodological stance that distils down to the rejection of Scriptural idolatry. Once liberated from this prejudice, we find that Scripture advances a great many untenable claims if we take it to be primarily a work of metaphysics. Having challenged the revelatory potential of Scripture, Spinoza can then put forth a more robustly naturalistic method in TTP 7. And when we approach Scripture with the naturalistic method in hand, we discover that it is an utterly fallible, human text. This leads to an interpretation of Scripture as fundamentally concerned with justice and piety rather than metaphysical truth.

We may break this structure down into five steps:

1. Adopt a minimal, naturalistic interpretative method (Preface).
2. Cast doubt on Scripture as the source of revealed knowledge (Chapters 1–6).

---

[47] J. Samuel Preus suggests that Al-Fakhar is a stand-in for Descartes and Bacon (Preus 2001, p. 194).
[48] Using reason to include the intellect in general. He adds "I am amazed that it should not be thought a crime to speak disparagingly of the mind" (TTP 15.3, 183).
[49] The odd placement of Spinoza's chapter on method has received very little discussion in the secondary literature. An exception is Strauss, who claims that Spinoza inverts the expected order of analysis by using his critique of revelation to support his critique of Scripture. Strauss gets things partially right here but he ignores the two-way dependency between the naturalistic method and the rejection of Scripture as metaphysics (1965). Rosenthal also addresses the issue in passing in Rosenthal 2003b, where he claims that the chapter on interpretation strategically follows the affective disruption that precedes it (p. 161). This view seems congenial to mine; but I hesitate to infer much from a few brief remarks.

3. Advance a more robust interpretative method (Chapter 7).
4. Demonstrate that Scripture is a thoroughly fallible, human document; decisively reject the view of Scripture as a work of metaphysics (Chapters 8–12).
5. Propose an alternative conception of faith and the function of Scripture (Chapters 13–15).

Let's briefly consider each of these steps in the progression of the argument.

Step 1: The Minimal Method (Preface)

In the Preface to the TTP, Spinoza clearly delineates the methodological assumption that he opposes:

[Most] presuppose, as a foundation for understanding Scripture and unearthing its true meaning, that it is everywhere true and divine. So what we ought to establish by understanding Scripture, and subjecting it to a strict examination, and what we would be far better taught by Scripture itself, which needs no human inventions, they maintain at the outset as a rule for the interpretation of Scripture (TTP Preface.19, iii.9).

Against such Scriptural idolatry, Spinoza resolves to "examine Scripture afresh, with an unprejudiced and free spirit, to affirm nothing about it, and to admit nothing as its teaching, which it did not very clearly teach me" (TTP Preface.20, iii.9). This is his version of the Calvinist *sola scriptura* principle. But, of course, it would be a rhetorical non-starter for Spinoza to open with even the regulative assumption that Scripture is just a text like any other. Consequently, he cannot yet avail himself of the full naturalist method. Instead, he proposes the more modest approach of reading Scripture with an "unprejudiced and free spirit," adopting a proscriptive minimal method that demands only that we not assume *ex ante* that: (1) all of the claims of Scripture are true, and (2) the text purports to give us metaphysical knowledge.

Step 2: Critique of Revelation (Chapters 1–6)

With this minimal method in place, Spinoza turns to consider what we learn from Scripture about revelation, starting with an analysis of prophets and prophecy. We learn from Scripture that prophets grasp the divine only via the imagination, which is, of course, the lowest form of cognition for Spinoza (2p40s2). Spinoza does not conceal his epistemological commitments here. He castigates those who do not value "natural knowledge" because it is common to all (TTP 1.2, iii.15), and stresses that "Prophecy is inferior to natural knowledge" as the former depends on the latter to certify its claims (TTP 2.5, iii.30).

Echoing his claim from the *Ethics* that ideas of the imagination tell us more about the condition of the imaginer than they do about the objects imagined (2p16c2), Spinoza asserts here that prophecies reveal more about the temperament and "cast of imagination [*dispositione imaginationis*]" of the prophet than they do about Nature or God's will (TTP 2.12, iii.32). And when we look to prophets for metaphysical knowledge, we wind up in a muddle, as they contradict one another. Fortunately, we need not take the claims of prophets as revealing truths about God and God's works. What the text consistently shows is not that prophets were insightful, but that they were morally upright, having minds "inclined only to the right and the good" (TP 2.10, iii.31). This is an abrasive opening. Just two chapters in and Spinoza is gesturing toward the conclusion that Scripture is not suited to reveal deep truths about God or Nature, but, rather, aims only at moral instruction.

Spinoza extends his critique of revelation in Chapters 3–6, where he confronts the status of Jewish election, Mosaic laws, divine providence, divine law, and the existence of miracles. Here he proceeds somewhat differently than he does in the first two chapters, offering compact statements of central features of his metaphysics that seem to conflict with how Scripture is ordinarily understood: God is not anthropomorphic; God acts from a fixed and immutable nature (TTP 4.37, iii.65; TTP 6.25, iii.86); and God does not love one part of creation more than the rest (TTP 3.12, iii.46–7). To the extent that Scripture contradicts these tenets it is the source of metaphysical confusion.

Still, much of what looks like confused metaphysics can be attributed to the cramped perspectives of the characters. Adam conceives of God as a kind of supreme legislator who issues violable edicts "because of a defect in his knowledge" (TTP 4.27, iii.63). The same holds for the Israelites, who view God confusedly as one who issued edicts for their special benefit (ibid.). Joshua wonders at the appearance of the sun standing still only because he is ignorant about planetary motion and parhelia (TTP 6.55, iii.92). And when Scripture actually relays the views of those who are held to be wise, like Solomon and Christ, we find that their ideas agree with reason. From Solomon, for instance, we learn that everything follows from the laws of nature (TTP 6.67, iii.95) and that true happiness lies in knowledge and virtue (TTP 4.41–50, iii.66–8). Christ is presented as having grasped God's laws adequately as eternal truths rather than as commands (TTP 4.31–4, iii.64–5).

Moreover, naturalistic explanations are available to account for apparent violations of metaphysical principles. Jewish election can and should be understood as the civic flourishing of a stubborn, slavish people that is explicable in terms of the laws of social coordination (TTP 5.17, iii.73). What are reported as miraculous from one perspective is often recounted elsewhere with reference to the natural causes, as when we learn that the locusts reach Egypt on account of a massive gale (TTP 6.46, iii.90). And finally, according to Spinoza, some of what look like claims of divine interventions in the operations of nature appear that way only because we lack knowledge of Hebrew figures of speech (TTP 6.59–63, iii.93–4). Based on such considerations, Spinoza concludes that "If you attend thoroughly to these things, and to the fact that Scripture relates many things very briefly, without any circumstances, and in a way almost muti- lated, you will find almost nothing in Scripture which can be demonstrated to be contrary to the light of nature" (TTP 6.64, iii.94; cf. TTP 6.69, iii.96–7; TTP Preface.24, iii.10).[50]

We should not infer from this that Spinoza sides with the dogmatists. He does not operate with an *antecedent* assumption that Scripture cannot gain- say reason, as he expressly concedes that his naturalistic reconstructions might not agree with "the writer's intention" (4.39, iii.66). And even if a care- ful interpretation of Scripture could reveal that its claims agree with reason, this would not make the bible is a philosophical text. At its core, Scripture is a collection of narratives written for common people: "Since the whole of Scripture was revealed first for the use of a whole nation, and eventually for the use of the whole human race, the things it contains must necessarily have been accommodated chiefly to ordinary people's power of understanding and proved by experience alone" (TTP 5.38, iii.77). The thrust of Scripture is non- philosophical – it presents, at least on the surface, a confused view of God, suited to the apprehension of its readers. This conclusion, gleaned from the first six chapters, challenges the auratic status of Scripture.

Step 3: The Full Interpretative Method (Chapter 7)

Having exposed the problems with Scriptural idolatry, puncturing the ideal of Scripture as an unerring guide to metaphysical truths, Spinoza is positioned to explicate his full interpretative method in TTP 7. The central proposal of this rich chapter is that we approach Scripture in a way that is consistent with the interpretation of nature (TTP 7.6, iii.98). As I see it, there are two main features of this proposal, which help to set up the subsequent interpretation. First, in order to understand the meaning of Scripture, we must "prepare a straightfor- ward history of Scripture" (TTP 7.7, iii.98).[51]

This requires that we learn about the conditions behind its composition (the "life, character, and concerns of the author" [7.24, iii.102]) and that we gain familiarity with the language in which the text was written (TTP 7.44, iii.106). Second, in order to grasp the meaning of the texts, we must examine Scripture

[50] In a commentary on this chapter, Steven Nadler raised questions about the sincerity of these remarks, in part because they seem to undercut Spinoza's attempt to distance himself from the dogmatists. For his own attempt at explaining away this tension, see Nadler 2013.
[51] This is not true of philosophical texts that proceed through a series of simple and intelligible steps, like Euclid's *Elements* (7.17, 111).

as we do nature, beginning with that which is "universal and common to the whole" and then proceeding to less universal things (TTP 7.27–9, iii.102–3).[52] These two parts of Spinoza's naturalistic method enable him to complete the case against Scripture as metaphysics, while enabling us to identify Scripture's true meaning.

Step 4: The Full Rejection of Scripture as Metaphysics (Chapters 8–12)

In the subsequent cluster of chapters, Spinoza deploys the naturalistic method to challenge a host of traditional claims about Scripture and its authorship. The overarching claim of these chapters is that our knowledge of the history of Scripture is "not only incomplete, but also quite faulty" (TTP 8.2, 118). Scripture is an artifact through and through, a potpourri of fables assembled to suit the interests of its editors. Spinoza denies that Moses was the sole author of the Pentateuch (TTP 8),[53] questions the authorship of Joshua, Judges, Ruth, Samuel, and claims that the canonical books of the Old Testament were fixed by a fallible council of Pharisees (TTP 10.46–7, iii.150).[54]

Having argued that Scripture is a patchwork and utterly human document, Spinoza pivots to preempt the accusation that this renders Scripture profane. He maintains, first, that the most general teachings of Scripture – simple truths about God (that he exists, is omnipotent, etc.) and the core teachings of morality (TTP 12.37, iii.165–6) – are consistent with reason and "inscribed by divine agency in men's hearts, i.e., in the human mind" (TTP 12.2, iii.158). Moreover, he argues, "nothing is sacred or profane or impure in itself, outside the mind, but only in relation to the mind" (TTP 12.12, iii.160). The sacredness or profanity of a text is determined by its effects on the reader. Just as "words have a definite meaning only from their usage" (TTP 12.11, iii.160), texts as a whole acquire their significance functionally. A text is sacred only insofar as it moves people to devotion and adherence to God's word. The implication is clear: those who would turn Scripture into a superstitious doctrine and promote hatred and conflict are the real heretics – they make the text profane. Spinoza aims restore Scripture's sacred status by distilling Scripture to its core salutary teachings.

---

[52] It is frequently observed that Spinoza follows a Baconian method here, as we compile data in order to apprehend definable essences (TTP 7.6, iii.98) (Preus 2001, p. 181).

[53] Spinoza recapitulates the evidence set forth by Ibn Ezra (1089–1167), and repeated by La Peyrère and Hobbes, which includes the decisive fact that it describes Moses's death and burial (TTP 8, iii.121) and continues to relate events that occurred thereafter.

[54] Spinoza claims that "we must necessarily admit that in thus making this selection they took the word of God as their criterion" (TTP 12.9). Elsewhere, though, he questions their good faith (TTP 10.3).

Step 5: Faith and the Separation Thesis (Chapters 13–15)

Chapters 13–15 complete the case for the Separation Thesis. When, in accordance with the naturalist method, we look to Scripture to find the prevalent teachings that operate as its "universal principles," we discover that the central teachings exhort obedience to God and love of one's neighbor – the latter being the whole of the law (e.g., TTP 14.9, iii.174).[55] This leads Spinoza to embrace a functional conception of the faith [*fides*] as just that set of beliefs that conduce to justice and charity. While there is some thin content to faith in the sense that there are doctrines of the universal faith that one must acknowledge in order to exhibit obedience to God (TTP 14.29, iii.178), these dogmas are left deliberately indeterminate, so that they may be accommodated according to the *ingenia* of the individual (TTP 14.32, iii.178). Faith does not require that one's beliefs have any *specific* content; it simply requires commitment to certain very general principles without which Spinoza thinks – rightly or wrongly – justice (*justitia*) and loving-kindness (*caritas*) are not possible. The crucial point here is that Scripture does not demand that one form a true understanding of God; it merely requires commitment to whatever set of ideas begets justice and charity (TTP 13.24, iii.171).

We can now appreciate the full force of Spinoza's Separation Thesis. Unlike Dutch Cartesians who maintained that faith and philosophy constitute autonomous, complementary domains of knowledge, Spinoza demotes the epistemic status of faith. Despite Spinoza's language of separation, faith does really not have its own jurisdiction, since philosophy confirms and grounds the very moral principles that are central to faith. If faith has a unique social role, it is as a source of moral instruction for those who are incapable of reason. Faith and reason are only partially separate and certainly not equal. The Separation Thesis diminishes the scope over which a clergy could preside.

Because Scripture does not require particular beliefs, and because the moral message of the bible is apparent on its face, there is no need for an interpretative vanguard to decipher the "true" message of Scripture. Instead of acting as interpreters of divine mysteries, the role of the clergy is restricted to promoting the bible's message of justice and charity.

Toleration, Humility, and the Positive Civic Function of Religion

After completing the case for the Separation Thesis, Spinoza observes: "how salutary this Doctrine is, how necessary in the republic, if people are to live

---

[55] Spinoza notes this when he first articulates the method in Chapter 7: "a unique and omnipotent God exists, who alone is to be worshipped, who cares for all, and who loves above all those who worship him and who love their neighbor as themselves, etc. Scripture, I say, teaches these and similar things everywhere, so clearly and so explicitly that there has never been anyone who disputed the meaning of Scripture concerning these things" (TTP 7.27–8, iii.102).

peacefully and harmoniously, how many, and how great, are the causes of disturbance and wickedness it prevents" (TTP 14.34, iii.179). This is not merely because a true conception of faith diminishes the pretensions of the clergy, but also because the promotion of such faith diminishes the pride and envy that fuel intolerance and hatred.

The natural pride and ambition that make us "alike an obstacle to one another" (3p31s) is not easily restrained. Once we are strongly affectively disposed toward something, we will generally seek to impose this judgment on others. As noted in passing above, however, this ambition may be checked by perceiving the inadequacy of one's own judgments (2p49s). This happens when one has a higher-order idea that offsets the lower-order judgment. For instance, since affects constitute evaluative judgments (Section 1.1), to the extent that I crave an afternoon whiskey, I judge it to be good. However, knowing something about the distortive and misguiding character of the passions in general (Sections 1.2 and 3.2), and thinking about the total effects of whiskey-drinking in a more rational, time-neutral way (the sleepiness and incapacitation), I might be able to perceive the inadequacy of my initial judgment and resist the craving. Perceiving the inadequacy of one's first-order judgment can lead one to suspend this judgment and check the impulse to convert.

However, this can only be part of the story, since not all forms of toleration include the erosion of one's own commitment. One can refrain from imposing one's judgment on others even while retaining the full force of one's judgment *for oneself.* In such cases, one may still perceive the inadequacy of the *scope* of one's judgments. After all, good and evil are not absolute features of the world: "one and the same thing can, at the same time, be good, and bad, and also indifferent. For example, music is good for one who is melancholy, bad for one who is mourning, and neither good nor bad to one who is deaf" (E4 Preface). While the main contours of a good, empowering life are going to be similar for all humans, whether or not a particular thing is good depends on the *ingenium* of an individual at a particular time. This higher-order recognition of the *ingenium*-relativity of concrete goods can help to check misguided efforts at conversion.

Unfortunately, just as it is a "rare virtue" to "suspend judgment" (TP 7/27), so too it is a rare virtue to limit the scope of one's judgments. Such epistemic humility needs social support. This is where Spinozistic faith comes in, as it encourages us to recognize the *ingenia*-relativity of the good:

[B]ecause men vary greatly in their *ingenia*, because one is content with these opinions, another with those, and because what moves one person to religion moves another to laughter, from these considerations, together with what has been said above, I conclude that each person must be allowed freedom of judgment and the power to interpret the foundations of faith according to his own *ingenium*. We must judge the piety of each person's faith from his works alone (TTP preface.28, iii.11).

He proceeds to stress the plasticity of *ingenia* and its significance for his conception of faith once again in TTP 14: "No one doubts that the common *ingenia* of men is extremely variable, and that not everyone is equally satisfied by all things. Opinions govern men in different ways: those which move one person to devotion, move another to laughter and contempt" (TTP 14.22, iii.176–7). Because of the diverse ways in which the human mind can be constituted (Sections 1.2–1.3), what encourages obedience to God in one person may be quite distinct from what encourages it in another.[56] A proper understanding of faith allows that Scripture "was accommodated to the grasp of the common people, so everyone is permitted to accommodate it to his own opinions, if he sees that in that way he can obey God more wholeheartedly in matters of justice and loving-kindness" (TTP 14.3, iii.173). One can, as Susan James puts it, adopt particular narratives suited to motivate one to act in accordance with moral principles.[57] A proper conception of faith thus not only supports the freedom to philosophize at the civic level, it promotes personal toleration, encouraging individuals to check the brash supposition that what is good for them is good for another.

When Spinoza declares that "the worship of God and obedience to him consist only in Justice and Loving-kindness, *or* in love towards one's neighbor" (TTP 14.27, iii.177) is one of the seven universal dogmas of faith, he is effectively making the adoption of this conception of faith a necessary precept of citizenship. And in so doing, he is promoting that a policy of toleration, such that one's doesn't take one's own specific religious beliefs as prescriptive for all of humanity. Public faith, properly understood, helps to erode pride.[58]

The other chief salutary function of public religion lies in its capacity to boost national solidarity. We see this in Spinoza's analysis of universal religion (TTP 14; TP 8/46ff), which is a kind of antidote to exclusivist religions. Spinoza attacks exceptionalism throughout the TTP, claiming that:

[W]hoever views himself as more blessed because things are well with him, but not with others, or because he is more blessed and more fortunate than others, does not know true happiness and blessedness. The joy he derives from that comparison comes from envy and a bad heart... So someone who rejoices for that reason rejoices because of an evil occurring to someone else. He is envious and evil, failing to know either true wisdom or the peace of true life. (TTP 3.1–2, iii.44)

[56] See Rosenthal 2001, p. 551.
[57] James 2010, especially p. 252.
[58] This coheres with Spinoza's approval of the prophets who commended humility along with other Christian virtues because "those who are subject to these affects can be guided far more easily than others, so that in the end they may live from the guidance of reason, that is, may be free and enjoy the life of the blessed" (4p54s). See James 2011, p. 189. For more on Spinoza on humility and the critique of pride, see Cooper 2013 and Soyarslan (forthcoming).

He ascribes this mentality explicitly to "the Hebrews," who "used to boast that they were superior to all others, indeed, who were accustomed to disdain all others, and hence distain knowledge common to all" (TTP 1.41, iii.27); but he quite evidently has a more proximate opponent in mind: Calvinist exceptionalists. The universal religion aims at once to break the harmful effects of exceptionalism, while encouraging a degree of social cohesion. However thin the seven "doctrines of the universal faith" may be, they provide some sort of common ground to which all citizens may appeal, rather than fixating on difference. This is even more clear in the case of the "national religion" of the Aristocracy described in TP 8/46–8.

There is a precarious balance here. Civil religion must be thin enough to accommodate a wide range of beliefs, while being thick enough to promote a sense of cohesion. While one might reasonably doubt whether the norms of tolerance and solidarity can be jointly satisfied, this seems to be Spinoza's aim. A proper conception of faith – with its public and private dimensions – can mitigate the place of pride and envy in civil life, replacing superstition, parochialism, and hatred with tolerance and, to a degree, solidarity.

6.4 Spinoza's Anticlericalism II: The Single Authority Thesis

While the first fifteen chapters limit the intellectual authority of the clerics, relegating them to moral guides, the subsequent four chapters (Chapters 16–19) complete the case against clerical power, depriving them of political authority altogether. Sovereign authority consists just in the capacity to maintain dependency (Section 2.5), inducing subjects to unreservedly commit to living according to its judgments and way of living (*ratio vivendi*). Like Hobbes, Spinoza thinks that sovereign authority is incompatible with clerical authority.[59] Spinoza advances several arguments for the indivisibility of civil authority. For instance, near the end of TTP 16, he claims that if matters of religion were not under sovereign right, there could be no common law:

[I]t's certain that if no one were bound by law to obey the supreme power in the things he thought pertained to religion, then the right of the state would depend on the varying judgment and affect of each person. For no one would be bound by a statute which he judged was contrary to his faith and superstition. So under this pretext everyone could assume a license to do anything. In this way, the right of the state would be completely violated. From this it follows that the supreme power, which, both by divine and by natural law, has the sole responsibility of preserving and protecting the rights of the state, has the supreme right to maintain whatever it judges concerning religion (TTP 16.61–3, iii.199).

---

[59] Hobbes, *Lev.*, Ch. 29, p. 228.

Spinoza is essentially claiming here that in order for a state to remain a state, the sovereign must retain full authority over matters of faith.[60] He offers another variant of this argument in Chapter 19, where he aims to establish that "right concerning sacred matters belongs completely to the supreme powers" (TTP 19 title, iii.228). After declaring that the arguments for separating secular and religious authorities are "so frivolous they don't deserve to be refuted" (TTP 19.34, iii.234), he nevertheless attempts to expose the absurdity of divided authority:

Everyone knows how highly the people value the right and authority regarding sacred matters, and how much weight everyone attaches to the utterances of the one who has it. So we can say that the person who has this authority has the most powerful control over their hearts. *Anyone who claims to take this authority away from the supreme powers is trying to divide the sovereignty.* This will necessarily give rise to quarrels and disagreements which can never be restrained, as happened before between the Kings and Priests of the Hebrews. *Indeed, anyone who wants to take this authority away from the supreme powers is trying (as we've already said) to make himself sovereign.* For what can the supreme powers decide, if this right is denied to them? Certainly nothing concerning war and peace, nor any other business, if they are bound to wait for the opinion of someone else, who is to tell them whether what they judge to be advantageous is pious or not. On the contrary, everything will happen according to the decree of that person who has the right of judging and deciding what is pious or impious, sacrilegious or not (TTP 19.40–2, iii.235 – my emphasis).

If the clergy possessed independent authority, the sovereign would be unable to exercise its essential function of making the law (see TP 4/1). Ecclesiastical authority is in this way an existential threat to the state (Section 7.1).[61]

With this argument for sovereign indivisibility in place, Spinoza can argue that clerics lack theological as well as civic authority. The general content of divine law, as expressed by Scripture – the simple command to love one's neighbor and to worship God – is intelligible to all, without the need for priestly mediation. And the sovereign alone determines the specific ways in which piety, or the love of one's neighbor, is to be expressed (TTP 19.24, iii.232), for there is no standard of piety apart from what the sovereign codifies into law. Consequently, "no one can practice piety rightly nor obey God, unless he obeys all the decrees of the supreme power" (TTP 19.27, iii.233). The content of divine law thus collapses into the content of justice, leaving clerics without even an independent realm of expertise. At best, priests are boosters of the state, and their sermons should serve civic ends.

In addition to the philosophical arguments for a single authority, Spinoza draws on the history of the Hebrew state to illustrate the danger of clerics

[60] Cf. TP 3/3.
[61] See J. Steinberg 2018b.

who seek to usurp authority from the civil sovereign. After describing how the Hebrew state survived and even flourished through Moses's leadership (TTP 17; cf. TTP 5), Spinoza examines the decline of the Hebrew state in Chapter 18, which confirms his psychosocial analysis of origin of intolerance (Section 6.2): "there were no sects in their Religion until after the high Priests in the second state had the authority to make [religious] decrees and to handle the affairs of the state. To make this authority permanent, they took for themselves the right to rule, and in the end wanted to be called Kings" (TTP 18.6, iii.222).[62] After acquiring power, these clerics "began to seek the glory of his own name both in religion and in other matters, determining everything by priestly authority and daily issuing new decrees, concerning ceremonies, the faith, and everything else, decrees they wanted to be no less sacred and to have no less authority than the laws of Moses" (TTP 18.8, iii.222). And when the high priests disagreed with one another, they forced the magistrates to take sides, breeding toxic factional conflict and "deadly superstition" (TTP 18.9, iii.222).

Spinoza's entire account of the decline of the Hebrew commonwealth can be read as a very thinly veiled warning about the dangers of Calvinist fanaticism in the United Provinces. The decision to use the Hebrew state as an object lesson for ideological corruption carried significant rhetorical force, as the history of the Israelites was woven into the self-conception of Dutch Calvinists as a chosen people.[63] It is as if Spinoza is saying here, "if you are going to model your identity on the Israelites, don't forget what brought about the destruction of their state."

Spinoza makes the lessons for the Dutch Republic explicit in the concluding chapter:

[W]hen the religious controversy between the Remonstrants and the Counter-Remonstrants was being stirred up by the Politicians and the Estates of the provinces, in the end it degenerated into a schism, and many examples made it manifest that laws passed to settle Religious controversies aggravate people more than they correct them, that some people take unlimited license from them, and moreover, that schisms don't come from a great zeal for truth (a source of gentleness and consideration for others), but from an overwhelming desire for control (TTP 20.41, iii.246).

This is how Spinoza understood the aftermath of the Synod of Dort: it did not so much extinguish the conflict as intensify disputation and empower the consistory to punish their opponents. Calvinist clerics are represented as modern Pharisees, ambitious and superstitious men who "have everywhere persecuted men distinguished for their integrity, famous for their virtue, and on that

---

[62] He also claims that the Pope "gradually began to bring all of the kings under his control" (TTP 19.17, 235).

[63] See Rosenthal 1997; Schama 1987, pp. 231–4; Nadler 1999, pp. 283–4.

account, envied by the mob – publicly denouncing their opinions and inflaming the savage multitude in their anger against them" (TTP 18.24, iii.225).

Spinoza's analysis of the decline of the Hebrew state and its resonances in the Dutch Republic completes the case against clerical authority. The Separation Thesis reduces the scope of theological interest, while the claim for a single authority denies clerics the right to make law or even specify the content of divine law. The historical analysis highlights the dangers of granting clerics power to which they are not entitled, corroborating the psychosocial analysis of superstition and intolerance.

The prescription matches the diagnosis. Given how "ruinous it is, both for religion and for the Republic, to grant the ministers of sacred affairs the right to make [religious] decrees or to handle the business of the state" (TTP 18.22, iii.225), it is essential "to grant the supreme powers the right to distinguish between what is permissible and what is not" (TTP 18.27, iii.226). The power of the clergy must be curtailed if pride and intolerance, fear and superstition, are to be held in check.

6.5   Prudential Arguments for Toleration

While the attack on clerical authority constitutes the core of Spinoza's defense of toleration,[64] it does not give us a reason to oppose moral legislation as such. It doesn't explain what is wrong with Isaiah Berlin's characterization of Spinoza as one who thinks that "all irrationality, heteronomy, passion, which resist or darken reason, must be removed, or at the very least controlled, by rational self-understanding, education and also legislation – that is, if necessary, the sanction of force, of coercive action."[65] In fact, Spinoza does *not* think that the state should seek to expurgate irrationality and vice by coercive means. But given that a strong state is required to protect against ideological corruption, what justifies limiting the exercise of sovereign power in the way that Spinoza does?

The answer comes in the concluding chapter, where Spinoza finally makes good on what he purports to do in the subtitle of the work, namely, to demonstrate "that the republic can grant freedom of philosophizing without harming its peace or piety, and cannot deny it without destroying its peace and piety." Rather than putting forth a principled basis for civic toleration by invoking rights as limits on the legitimate exercise of sovereign power or by maintaining that goods are intersubjectively incommensurable, Spinoza advances a battery of psychologically grounded, prudential arguments for allowing people

[64] For another interpretation along these lines, see Laursen 1996.
[65] Berlin 1993, p. 298. See J. Steinberg 2010b.

to think and express themselves as they see fit.[66] Two main lines of argument emerge: (1) there are natural limits to the sovereign's power to regulate belief and action; and (2) attempts to regulate belief and action typically backfire. Let's consider these in turn.

Natural Limits of Sovereign Authority

Spinoza opens his case for the freedom to philosophize in TTP 20 by pointing to the limits of sovereign authority, claiming that no one can be compelled to transfer their judgment to another, which is "why rule over minds is considered violent, and why the supreme majesty seems to wrong its subjects and to usurp their rights whenever it tries to prescribe to everyone what they must embrace as true and reject as false" (TTP 20.3, iii.239). When, earlier in the work, Spinoza claims that "simplicity and honesty of heart are not instilled in men by the command of laws or by public authority, and absolutely no one can be compelled by force or by laws to become blessed [*beatus*]" (TTP 7.90, iii.116), he is effectively denying that rational beliefs can be coerced. This is because, more generally, the sovereign lacks the power or right to compel judgment.

Spinoza's claim about the inefficacy of state control over minds depends on his account of belief-formation. What we believe is a function of the relative power or intensity of ideas,[67] which is determined by a range of factors over which we lack direct, voluntary control. And, as noted (Section 6.2), we are ideological preservationists, clinging to our beliefs unless confronted by a force strong enough to dislodge them. Consequently, belief-revision, for Spinoza, is quite demanding. Even when we have true ideas, such ideas, on their own, are often too weak to restrain the confused ideas that oppose them (4p14–17). The limitations of belief-revision also lie behind Spinoza's claim that we never have absolutely control over the passions – that we are always, to some extent, subject to fortune. Our *ingenia* are largely the product of our experiential histories, subject to influences beyond our control, and are not easily modified (Section 1.2).

---

[66] Spinoza's was not the first low country theorist to offer a prudentialist defense of toleration. Near the end of the sixteenth-century Justus Lipsius and Dirk Coornhert were embroiled in a polemic about toleration and the need for confessional unity. Lipsius had argued for a policy of *mixed prudence*, allowing that in certain instances the right and expedient thing for a sovereign to do is to impose confessional uniformity on a people. Coornhert claimed against Lipsius that permitting religious freedoms, and freedom of expression more generally, actually strengthened political stability (Mout 1997, p. 42). While Lipsius and Coornhert sought theological cover for their positions, a significant strand of their dispute concerned whether or not confessional pluralism is politically stable. Spinoza in some measure accepts the terms of this debate, positioning himself firmly on Coornhert's side.

[67] See J. Steinberg 2018a; Cf. Section 8.4.

These considerations help to explain why sovereign right or power is limited vis-à-vis judgment. One typically cannot change judgment by fiat, irrespective of the source, since, as Michael Rosenthal puts it in his interpretation of Spinoza, "to successfully change a belief requires that we take into account the complex chain of events and circumstances that led to the formation of that belief in the first place,"[68] and commands alone do not sufficiently alter the underlying conditions of belief-formation. Because of the obstinacy of human *ingenia*, there is ineradicable variegation to human beliefs – "men's minds differ as much as their palates do" (TTP 20.4. iii.239) – and attempts to compel uniformity belief by law are generally ineffective.

Moreover, because, as Spinoza puts it in the *Ethics*, "men have nothing less in their power than their tongue" (E3p2s), speech also lies beyond the scope of coercible activity:

[N]o one can surrender his freedom of judging and thinking what he wishes, but everyone, by the greatest natural right, is master of his own thoughts, it follows that if the supreme powers in a republic try to make men say nothing but what they prescribe, no matter how different and contrary their opinions, they will get only the most unfortunate result. Not even the wisest know how to keep quiet, not to mention ordinary people. It's a common vice of men to confide their judgments to others, even if secrecy is needed (TTP 20.8, iii.240).

As surprising as it is for a descendant of Marrano Jews to claim that people cannot easily conceal their beliefs, this is his view, at least at the outset of TTP 20.

Since Spinoza does not extend this argument from legislative impotence to the realm of behavior, it tempting to assume that Spinoza is relying on a strict distinction between physical, outward actions and mental, inward beliefs.[69] Reading Spinoza in this way makes his treatment of speech – as more like conscience and less like action – even less plausible. Moreover, such a distinction would seem to violate Spinoza's mind-body parallelism by entailing disparate treatment of (coercible) physical actions and (non-coercible) mental states.[70]

Fortunately, though, Spinoza's argument does not depend on the dichotomy between physical/outer states and mental/inner states. The "obedience" that the state *can* compel is characterized as an "internal action of the soul" (Section 3.3); conversely, Spinoza explicitly admits the possibility of

---

[68] Rosenthal 2003a, p. 330.
[69] This view was something of a mainstay among early-modern tolerationists. See Grotius: "for every individual is judge over his own religious conviction, the Church itself decides on the faith of the Church inasmuch as it is public, except for him in whose hand and power all public bodies lie" (Grotius *OHWP*, p. 189). Scholars have sometimes read Spinoza in this way. According to Henry Allison, Spinoza's defense of toleration depends on a "rigid separation of thought and action" (Allison 1975, p. 178). Rosenthal claims that Spinoza operates with a sharp distinction between "outer religion" or physical welfare and "inner religion" or epistemic welfare which lies beyond the scope of the state (Rosenthal 2003a, p. 326). See also Smith 1997, p. 144.
[70] Della Rocca 2008a, pp. 223–4.

"seditious opinions" (see TTP 20.20, iii.242). The distinction that Spinoza is after can be cashed out entirely in terms of different kinds of belief. While most beliefs are relatively impervious to alteration by force, there is a species of belief that is more responsive to coercive pressure, namely, beliefs about the utility of performing some action. The state may not be able to bring it about by law that I hate philosophy, but it can bring it about that I represent the activity of reading philosophy aversively, by annexing penalties to such behavior.[71] In this way, Spinoza can defend the claim that the state possesses a greater control over actions than it does over ordinary belief without adopting the metaphysically dubious dichotomy of the private mind and the public body.

The line between what is and is not susceptible to coercion is, thus, blurry. Due to doxastic intransigence, individual judgments cannot be *entirely* subjected to sovereign control. Nevertheless, Spinoza himself concedes that "someone can get prior control of another person's judgment in many ways, some of them almost incredible" (TTP 20.4, iii.239) and that "hearts are to some extent under the control of the supreme power, which can bring it about in many ways that men believe, love, and hate whatever it wants them to" (TTP 17.9, iii.202; cf. TTP 20.2, iii.239). And if the state can inspire averse representations of violent, hateful actions, why not at least try to inspire averse representations of hateful and destructive thoughts?[72]

Backfire and Resistance

The case against legislative overreach is concentrated in the middle sections of TTP 20 (TTP 20.24–36, iii.243–5). In these passages, Spinoza claims that "anyone who wants to limit everything by laws will provoke more vices than he'll correct" (TTP 20.24, iii.243). Sumptuary laws, for instance, which aim to limit "extravagant living, envy, greed, drunkenness, and the like" (ibid.), only foster these vices. This observation is reprised in the TP: "all laws which can be violated without wronging anyone else are objects of derision. Far from reining in men's desires and lusts, they make them stronger. We always strive to have what is prohibited, and desire what we're denied" (TP 10/5).

To understand why moral legislation typically backfires we must return once again to ambition and ideological preservationism. We generally strive to have

---

[71] Della Rocca arrives at a similar conclusion, claiming that "the state, by restricting actions, is in the business of restricting thought after all," from which he concludes that "on his own terms, Spinoza seems to have no good reason to draw the sharp line he does between thought and speech, on the one hand, and action in general, on the other" (Della Rocca 2008a, p. 224). *Pace* Della Rocca, I'm not convinced that he was after a sharp distinction in the first place.

[72] We should not underestimate Spinoza's *illiberalism*. He admits that too much liberty destroys the state (TP 3/3), and he seems to deny that civil liberties are good in themselves, claiming in the TP that an Aristocracy should permit only those freedoms that "must necessarily be granted it from the constitution of the state itself" (TP 8/5).

others live according to our *ingenia* and we bristle when they seek to impose their judgments on us.[73] Consequently, people typically become defiant when their judgments are treated as criminal:

> For the most part men are so constituted that they endure nothing with greater impatience than that opinions they believe to be true should be considered criminal and that what moves them to piety toward God and men should be counted as wickedness in them. The result is that they dare to denounce the laws and do what they can against the magistrate; they don't think it shameful, but quite honorable, to initiate rebellions and attempt any crime for the sake of this cause (TTP 20.29, iii.244).

By seeking to coerce conformity of *ingenia*, the state inspires greater resistance and hatred, which, as noted above (Section 6.2), is often the path of least resistance to reducing cognitive dissonance. Outlawing forms of thought and expression only further alienates offenders and deepens existing schisms.

Finally, in what might be an attempt to grapple with the problem of *conversos* or Marranos noted above, Spinoza notes that even if the state could successfully regulate expression, it could not do so without undermining the conditions under which trust and *securitas* are possible. If people were prohibited from expressing their sincere opinions, they "would think one thing and say something else. The result? The good faith especially necessary in a Republic would be corrupted. Abominable flattery and treachery would be encouraged, as would deceptions and the corruption of the liberal studies" (TTP 20.27, iii.243; cf. TTP 14.20, iii.176).

The enactment of moral legislation would undercut its own aims, destroying trust, promoting vice and resistance, and generally destabilizing the state. The flipside to this analysis is that by granting citizens the freedom to think and speak as they wish – the freedom to philosophize – they will more willingly and hopefully uphold the institutions of the state. Granting the freedom to philosophize contributes to the goal of governing in such a way "they seem to themselves not to be led, but to live according to their own *ingenium* and from their own free decision" (TP 10/8). Liberal governance promotes precisely the kind of affective buy-in, commitment to the state, and *feeling* of freedom that Spinoza regards as personally and politically salubrious (Section 4.4). Moreover, such freedoms are "especially necessary" to the flourishing of the arts and sciences (TTP 20.26, iii.243), and, as we will see in Chapter 7, they enhance the epistemic capacities of individuals and social bodies (Section 7.3).

---

[73] This is especially the case with men of private station: "the Prophets, as private men, aggravated people more than they corrected them by the freedom with which they warned, reproached, and censured them. On the other hand, when these same people were warned or criticized by their Kings, they were easily set right" (TTP 18.13, iii.232; cf. TTP 19.45, iii.236).

6.6   Dynamic Realism, *Securitas*, and Relativity

Spinoza's treatment of the relationship between religion and the state and his defense of political freedoms exemplify his dynamic realism. If the state is to promote peace and security, it must weaken the forces that stoke fear and pride into superstition and persecution, it must also encourage a brand of faith that conduces to personal humility and toleration, and it must protect freedoms of thought and expression, so that people feel free and secure, rather than oppressed and resentful. The entire analysis here hinges on Spinoza's account of human psychology.

Spinoza's case for toleration admits of a degree of relativity. Rather than offering a principled argument for civil liberties, Spinoza defends them just insofar as they conduce to the aims of peace, security, and empowerment. The extent to which civil liberties promote these aims will vary according to the *ingenia* of the people (see e.g., TP 7/2). Spinoza illustrates this in his analysis of Mosaic statesmanship. Moses established a state religion that included a great number of laws – ceremonial, dietary, etc. – that would have been perceived as oppressive if adopted in the United Provinces. However, for the Hebrew people, who were accustomed to slavery and not yet capable of self-rule, such interventionist legislation "must have seemed no longer bondage, but freedom" (TTP 17.89, iii.216) – these laws fostered social cohesion and material prosperity.

The utility of a piece of legislation thus hinges in part on how it will be received by subjects, which in turn depends on custom and expectation.[74] As Spinoza astutely notes, "nothing is more difficult than to take freedom away from men again, once it has been granted" (TTP 5.22, iii.74). The more one comes to expect a certain good, the more disappointed one will be when this good is removed. So, while the freedom-loving Dutch would regard moral legislation as oppressive, the Hebrews, accustomed as they were to obedience, did not.

Some see the absence of a clear principle for delimiting the scope of toleration as a limitation of Spinoza's account. Lewis Feuer complains that "there are no reserved rights upon which the individual can insist…this is the final weakness in Spinoza's political theory; his doctrine pleads for wisdom but merges into quiescence rather than deed."[75] Edwin Curley shares Feuer's frustration: "If we cannot make sense of the idea that people have a natural right to such things, then we seem to be handicapped in the criticism we want to make of the Roman conduct (or of a tyrant's treatment of his own people). That the notion

---

[74] The source of the command may also go a long way in determining how effective it is. Moral commands are more grating and destabilizing when they come from religious figures than when they come from the civil authority (see TTP 18.13, iii.223; TTP 19.45, iii.236).

[75] Feuer 1958, p. 114

of natural right (not coextensive with power) disappears in Spinoza seems to me still to be a defect in his political philosophy, sympathetic though I may be to the arguments which lead to that result."[76]

However, as I see it, the circumstance relativity of Spinoza's account might actually be one of its virtues. Consider Spinoza's approach in relation to a prominent challenge for liberals today, namely, how far one should tolerate hate speech, or speech that vilifies or degrades someone on the basis of their identity. Like religious bigotry, hate speech may be seen as undermining peace by feeding the zeal of the ignorant and allowing for the stigmatization of members of groups that are often already vulnerable and marginalized. On the other hand, there is some hope that, at least in a relatively enlightened society, hate speech may strengthen the resolve of the citizenry in opposing racism and bigotry. And, moreover, restricting speech may well have the consequence of making people who are accustomed to broad liberties more resentful toward government. So how far should a sovereign that wants to promote peace tolerate hate speech?

Spinoza would argue that to take a principled, once-and-for-all stance would be naïve and imprudent. Instead, one should consider the receptivity of the citizenry to such regulation, weighing the harms wrought by its admission on the target group against the likelihood of resistance or backfire in the case of regulation. In countries where there is a dominant ethos of liberty – i.e., where people are accustomed to a very tolerant state with minimal intervention – the regulation of hate speech might be more destabilizing or disharmonizing than it would be countries where there is a dominant ethos of fraternity. Accommodating a people's *ingenia* certainly makes legislating rather complicated. But, given the complexity of the phenomena, perhaps a little messiness is to be expected. Governance is, once again, a craft and not a deductive science.

[76] Curley 1996, p. 335.

7   The Affective and Epistemic
Cases for Democracy

[H]ow do you break down resistance on the part of powers that be toward citizens becoming participants in decision making? I don't have any cut pattern, except that I believe that people, when informed about the things they are concerned with, will find a way to react. Now, whether their reactions are the most desirable at a given stage depends, to a large extent, upon whether the people who are in the controlling seat are open enough to permit people to react according to the way they see the situation. In organizing a community, you start with people where they are.

— Ella Baker, "Developing Community Leadership"[1]

Spinoza's commitment to democracy is often portrayed as tenuous and uneasy. Lewis Feuer, for instance, claims that Spinoza's democratic theory was "divided against itself," due to his "feelings of withdrawal" and "mistrust of the multitude."[2] Leo Strauss paints Spinoza as a reluctant democrat with a very dim view of the masses, who are separated from the wise by an "unbridgeable gulf."[3] And Douglas Den Uyl and Steven Smith characterize him as an "unsentimental" and somewhat grudging democrat.[4] Such interpretations are supported by Spinoza's dismissive remarks about the common people, especially in the TTP (see e.g., Preface.33–4, iii.12). Nevertheless, Spinoza's commitment to democracy in the TTP is beyond dispute.

However, two other questions remain unsettled:

1. Was Spinoza *consistently* committed to democracy? Did he remain convinced of the superiority of democracies when he composed the *Political Treatise*?
2. To the extent that he is a consistent democrat, how does he justify this preference?

The first question is often thought to be difficult to answer in part because the *Political Treatise* remained unfinished at the time of Spinoza's death in 1677,

---

[1] Quoted in Mueller 2004, p. 84.
[2] Feuer 1958, p. 103.
[3] Strauss 1965, p. 245ff.
[4] Den Uyl 1983, pp. 162–3; Smith 2003, p. 132.

leaving off just a few paragraphs into what would likely have been two chapters devoted to democracy. Feuer raises the possibility that it is no mere accident that the chapters on democracy remain unfinished: "Did he come to a dead halt, unable to affirm that democratic faith which had animated the *Tractatus Theologico-Politicus*? Did he stop before an insoluble, insuperable problem, baffled by the mob, by the shadows of the slaves dancing around the mangled body of John de Witt?"[5] Feuer is referring to the brutal murders of Johan de Witt, the republican Grand Pensionary (chief statesman and legal advisor), and his brother Cornelius at the hands of a zealous mob in 1672 – an incident that, according to Feuer, left Spinoza with an even deeper distrust of the masses.[6] Feuer takes this event to have spurred Spinoza to write a less democratic work, the TP.

Commentators have expressed similar doubts about the consistency and force of Spinoza's defense of democracy. Yitzhak Melamed, for instance, claims: "it is not at all clear [in the TP] what his preference is between democracy and aristocracy."[7] He proceeds to portray Spinoza's defense of democracy as naïve, undergirded by reasoning that is "not particularly impressive."[8] Like Feuer and Strauss, Melamed claims that "for the most part, [Spinoza] despises and fears the masses,"[9] rendering him ambivalent toward democracy. And Raia Prokhovnik agrees with Feuer that Spinoza positively abandoned his advocacy of democracy by the time he wrote the TP, maintaining that there is a "marked shift in the course of Spinoza's political writings, away from democracy."[10] She places most of the weight of her claim on Spinoza's apparent approval in TP of certain form of decentralized aristocracy.[11]

In this chapter, I defend the view that Spinoza was a consistent and perceptive democrat. To see this, we must look beyond the tiny fragment of TP Ch 11 that constitutes his formal commentary on democracy, considering his analysis of other ideal regime forms, which are themselves marked by broad participation and the diffusion of political power. As Étienne Balibar puts it, the TP

---

[5] Feuer 1958, p. 151. Matheron and Balibar also speculate that the incompleteness of the chapters on democracy in the TP may tell us something about Spinoza's conflicted attitude toward democracy. Matheron suggests that Spinoza might have struggled to reconcile the repressive force of *imperium* with a democracy (Matheron 2011a, pp. 228–9), while Balibar writes that "we watch him die before this blank page," as he confronted the problem of citizenship (Balibar 1989, p. 128).

[6] Feuer 1958, Ch. 5. The murders of the de Witts apparently elicited uncommon outrage in Spinoza. According to one famous account, Spinoza had to be restrained by his landlord from taking a sign that read "*ultimi barbarorum*"(ultimate of barbarians) to the site of the massacre (Freudenthal 1899, p. 201).

[7] Melamed 2013b, p. 271.

[8] Ibid., p. 272.

[9] Ibid., p. 271.

[10] Prokhovnik 1997, p. 109; cf. Prokhovnik 2004, p. 210.

[11] For an opposing view, with which I agree, see McShea 1968, p. 123.

gives us more than just a theory of democracy, it gives us a "theory of democratization, which is valid for *every* regime."[12] Rather than forsaking democracy in the TP, Spinoza seems to *expand* his theory of democracy to apply to other regimes. And he adopts a more, not less, favorable view of the masses in this work. As Curley observes in the notes to his translation, Spinoza for the most part drops the disparaging references to the *vulgus*, with its connotations of crudity and ignorance, opting instead for the more neutral *multitudo, plebs,* or *populi*.[13] And he sets up for critical reappraisal the very Tacitean reproach that "there's moderation in the common people...they're terrifying, unless they themselves are cowed by fear" (TP 7/27) that he endorses in the *Ethics* (4p54s) and which Melamed takes to reflect Spinoza's view – arguing in the TP that *if* this is true, it is only because the common people are subjugated and denied access to knowledge by the institutions of the state.

Moreover, when Spinoza directly compares the relative virtues of democracy and aristocracy in the *Political Treatise* he maintains that democracy is most absolute form of government (TP 8/3; TP 11/1). One of the reasons that this is not taken as decisive evidence of Spinoza's commitment to democracy – as I think it should be – is that it is not entirely clear what "absolutism" consists in for Spinoza. In Section 7.1, I unpack Spinoza's conception of political absolutism, showing that, on his revisionist account, civic harmony covaries with sovereign absolutism. Consequently, the claim that democracies are most absolute should be understood as a direct endorsement.

After answering the first question noted at the beginning of this chapter, I turn to the second – *why* Spinoza thinks that democracies are maximally absolute, or best – in Sections 7.2 and 7.3. Here I present a view of Spinoza's democratism that contrasts with interpretations of Spinoza as a principled egalitarian or republican. Rather than arguing that equality and/or liberty are *intrinsically* and *exclusively* secured through democratic governance, Spinoza maintains that democracies promote affective buy-in (Section 7.2) and enhanced individual and collective rationality (Section 7.3). In place of a tidy, principled defense of democratic egalitarianism, Spinoza advances a complex, psychologically-rich analysis of the relationship between civic participation and empowerment. This analysis of democratic institutions constitutes the heart of the *constructive* side of the project of *ingenia* reform, as it shows how civic institutions can contribute to the *securitas* of the people. Here, as elsewhere, Spinoza insists that institutions must be accommodated to the character or *ingenia* of the people (Section 5.3), which requires vigilance or psychological attunement. But while Spinoza shows how realism can sponsor democratism, his political psychology

[12] Balibar 1998, p. 121.
[13] Curley, "Editorial Preface" to TP, pp. 499–500. Hasana Sharp also pointed this out in her comments on my manuscript.

fails him critically when he defends the exclusion of women from democratic participation. In these passages, he abandons his thesis that the systemic differences between humans betray the effects of socio-political power (Section 1.3), relying instead upon on a rigid and untenable essentialism (Section 7.4).

7.1   Political Absolutism[14]

To see why Spinoza's claim that democracies are most absolute amounts to an endorsement, we must explore in some detail his conception of sovereign absolutism and its vexed relationship to tradition.

The Absolutist Tradition

The concept of absolute power emerged in the early modern period as a way of the reconceiving of civil authority in an age of religious conflict. While there is no one single early modern theory of sovereign absolutism, there is broad consensus about some of its core features.[15] These properties are perhaps best exemplified in the works of two of the most celebrated early modern absolutists: Jean Bodin and Thomas Hobbes.[16]

Bodin and Hobbes adopt what might be dubbed a logic of ultimacy, arguing that relations of legal dependency must terminate in some legal body that is itself independent, *legibus solutus*. To be a sovereign is precisely to be a lawgiver and *not* a subject – to be an unbound binder, as it were – for, if a "sovereign" were bound by (human) laws, such laws would have to proceed from some higher (human) legal body, in which case the "sovereign" would not be sovereign. Bodin expresses the logic of ultimacy in the following way:

No matter how much power they have, if they are bound to the laws, jurisdiction, and command of someone else, they are not sovereign...We may thus conclude that the first prerogative (marque) of a sovereign prince is to give law to all in general and each in

---

[14] Parts of this section are based on J. Steinberg 2018b.

[15] J. P. Sommerville traces some of the common features of absolutist texts, while conceding that "there was no *single* absolutist theory" (Sommerville 1991, p. 348). Kossmann 1987 and Franklin 1991 also highlight the difficulties with trying to identify a tidily bound conception of absolute sovereignty. When I refer to "conventional absolutism" below, I do not wish to deny the real variation between these texts or to insist on a standard of purity. Rather, I am treating absolutism as a cluster concept that includes among its central characteristics the legal independence and indivisibility of sovereign authority, however these features are interpreted.

[16] Bodin's *Les Six Livres de la République (République)*, written in 1576, is the *locus classicus* of early modern political absolutism. In the subsequent century, Thomas Hobbes advanced his own defense of absolute sovereignty in three major political works: *Elements of Law* (1640), *De Cive* (1642), and *Leviathan* (1651). Despite important differences between Bodin's and Hobbes's analyses of the basis for, and scope of, sovereign authority, there are striking similarities in how they conceive of sovereignty itself. And in the *Elements of Law*, Hobbes directly endorses Bodin's case against the divisibility of sovereign power (*EL*, Ch. 27, pp. 166–7).

particular. But this is not sufficient. We have to add "without the consent of any other, whether greater, equal, or below him." For if the prince is obligated to make no law without the consent of a superior, he is clearly a subject; if of an equal, he has an associate; if of subjects, such as the senate or the people, he is not sovereign.[17]

Hobbes agrees that law must spring from an unconditioned source, a power that is subject to no other mortal power (Hobbes, *De Cive*, 6.18, p. 88).[18] Legislation must terminate in some unlimited or independent lawgiving body: the absolute sovereign.

The logic of ultimacy entails indivisibility, since if sovereignty could be divided, there would be no ultimate unbound binder. While there can be multiple pretenders to sovereignty, there can be only one unsubordinated and unlimited lawgiver.[19] Because the powers of sovereign are inseparable and incommunicable, the sovereign can no more split or devolve its legislative authority than it could separate quadrilaterality from a square. The very concept of sovereignty entails indivisibility and immiscibility.[20]

Finally, on this account, sovereign authority is irresistible. Where sovereignty is absolute, subjection must also be absolute, since those who are bound to the law lack all countervailing authority or right by which resistance could be justified. This point was crucial to Bodin's and Hobbes's political interventions. Bodin's *Les Six Livres de la République* aimed to counter Huguenot resistance theory during the French Wars of Religion. And Hobbes's earlier political writings (*The Elements of Law* and *De Cive*) were written to lend support to the royalist cause in the crisis preceding the English Civil War, while *Leviathan* aimed at peace and absolute obedience in the tumultuous aftermath.[21] Irresistibility, then, along with Independence and Indivisibility constitute what we might call the three "I"s of absolutism.

Spinoza and the three "I"s of Absolutism

Spinoza embraces variants of all three of these features. In passages that leave many contemporary readers puzzled and discomfited, Spinoza claims, in both of his political treatises, that the sovereign possesses total authority to prescribe law and that subjects are absolutely bound to obey. For instance, in the *Political Treatise*, he writes: "We see, then, that no citizen is his own master. Each is subject to the control of the Commonwealth, and bound to carry out all

[17] Bodin, *République*, 1.10, p. 49.
[18] Cf. *De Cive*, 6.13; *Lev.*, Ch. 20, p. 144.
[19] *République*, 2.1, pp. 103-4; Hobbes, *De Cive*, 11.6.
[20] Bodin, *République*, 2.1, pp. 103–4. Hobbes, *Lev.*, Ch. 29, p. 228. Cf. *EL*, Ch. 27, pp. 166–7.
[21] Hobbes's local political interests in the interregnum period in which *Leviathan* was published are somewhat murky. Jeffrey Collins has argued that *Leviathan* was written in support of Cromwell's Erastian ecclesiology (Collins 2005).

its commands. He has no right to decide what's fair or unfair, pious or impious" (TP 3/5).[22] Subjects have absolutely submitted themselves to the will of the sovereign and are thus bound to obey the laws issued by the sovereign. The fact that he repeats such claims at various points in both of his political treatises reveals his enduring commitment to independence and irresistibility.

Spinoza also consistently defends the *indivisibility* of sovereign authority. He argues in the TTP that subjects could not maintain rights for themselves "without dividing, and thereby destroying, the sovereignty"(TTP 16.27, iii.193). A similar claim is made in the TP, where he writes that if a sovereign were to cede its right to determine what is law, the very integrity of the commonwealth would be threatened (TP 3/3). Elsewhere in the same work, he unequivocally asserts that "sovereignty ought to be indivisible" (TP 7/25; cf. TP 6/37).

His case against divided authority seems to be underwritten by the absolutist logic of ultimacy. As we saw in Section 6.4, Spinoza, like Hobbes before him, disqualifies clerical claims to authority. He maintains that if the civil authority needed the blessing of religious authorities in order to make law, it would not be sovereign at all, as "everything will happen according to the decree of that person who has the right of judging and deciding what is pious or impious, sacrilegious or not" (TTP 19.40–2, iii.235). On Spinoza's account it is up to the sovereign alone to determine what is pious and what is not (TTP 19.Preface, iii.228).[23]

Spinoza's commitment to the three "I"s of absolutism makes him look like a rather conventional absolutist. However, this picture fits uneasily with Spinoza's adoption of constitutional limits – *"fundamenta"*[24] or foundational laws – on the exercise of power, his advocacy of forms of mixed governance or power-sharing,[25] and, to a certain degree, his democratism. It is tempting, then, to interpret Spinoza as walking back his commitment to absolutism.[26] But this fails to make sense of why, in both of his political works, he would give the impression of embracing a position that he ultimately does not accept.

---

[22] See also TTP Preface.30, iii.11; TTP 16.25, iii.193; TP 2/16; TP 6/39.

[23] See also TTP 16, iii.198–200).

[24] Also referred to as *fundamenta imperii* and *lex imperii*.

[25] Spinoza concludes his analysis of monarchy with a discussion of the history of the Aragonese monarchy, which, as he notes, thrived when the monarchical power was "counterbalanced" by a "supreme council, like the Ephors of the Spartans" (TP 7/30). Spinoza's sympathy with the diffusion of power is even more apparent in his analysis of aristocracies, where he recommends the institution of three sovereign councils (supreme council, senate, and syndic) with distinct functions. In Spinoza's preferred model of aristocracy, sovereignty is shared by a number of cities, each with their own governing council or councils (TP 9/15; TP 10/10). Compare with the discussion of tribal power-sharing in the Hebrew state, which, Spinoza claims, resembles the situation in the United Provinces (TTP 17.54, iii.210). See Cooper 2017.

[26] See Susan James's claim that Spinoza "offers a sequence of ameliorative arguments" (2012, p. 252).

I propose that Spinoza sincerely and consistently endorses the core features of conventional absolutism; however, when these features are joined to a proper conception of authority, we get a very different account of what absolutism entails and how it is realized. In a sense, he does for "absolute sovereignty" in the political works what he does for concepts like "substance" or "God" in the *Ethics*, opening with a recognizable, even anodyne, gloss on a concept and then proceeding to draw out revisionist implications – transfiguring the concept from within a common framework. We get a clearer sense of the revisionist implications of Spinoza's conception of sovereign absolutism and their significance for his defense of democracy by examining in more depth Spinoza's conception of the function of the sovereign.

Absolute Sovereignty and Civic Harmony

Outside of the state, the power of individuals is merely nominal, not actual (TP 2/15). So, people bind themselves to a common authority, a common *ius*, without which, Spinoza argues, men cannot live (TP 1/3).[27] As we saw in Section 2.5, authority is formed when one puts oneself under the power (*sub potestate*) of another, creating a patterned dependency between the subject and that authorized body. This authority sets the laws, the common way of life or *ratio vivendi*[28] in virtue of which a collection of individuals can live together in a commonwealth, as a single people rather than as a mere aggregate (TP 3/3). Spinoza's insistence that the authority that unifies a people, binding them by a common law, must itself be absolute and indivisible is an expression of his view that – to put it epigrammatically – it takes one to make one: it takes a unified, absolute authority to make a unified people.

This view of sovereignty may be seen as a rejection of spontaneous coordination. Spinoza maintains that rational spontaneous coordination, while something of an ideal (E4p18s), is simply not an option on a large scale.[29] In emphasizing the significance of a central authority, he also denies the possibility of passionate spontaneous coordination. To be sure, there is sense in which the civil order *does* arise out of the passions. We are led, by the passions, to unite in order to overcome our natural individual weakness, a process that is facilitated in part by the imitation of affects.[30] Spinoza thus breaks with Hobbes

---

[27] See also: TP 3/3; TP 1/3; TP 2/13; TP 2/15.

[28] It is telling that in the TTP, Spinoza presents (civil) law as a "*ratio vivendi* man prescribes to himself or to others for some end [*finem*]" (TTP 4.5, iii.58). The claim that laws "bind" the people into a single body politic can be found in later chapters. See, for instance, his claim that "it's necessary that all the Patricians be so bound by the laws that they compose, as it were, one body, governed by one mind" (TP 8/19).

[29] TP 6/3; TP 1/5; TP 2/6; TP 2/8; TTP 5.20–1, iii.73; *Ethics* 4 p37 s2.

[30] See Matheron 2011.

by asserting that the commonwealth is, *in this sense*, natural, and allowing that man may be called a "social animal" (TP 2/15). But while he regards the commonwealth as a natural outgrowth of the passions, Spinoza does not think that civic unity arises without any further intervention. People must be made civil (TP 5/2), and it is the sovereign's job to make them civil by uniting them in a civic body.

To see what is distinctive about this position, we may contrast it with Antonio Negri's interpretation of Spinozistic sovereignty. Negri takes Spinoza to be advancing a radical conception of sovereignty in the *Political Treatise*, constituted by the direct dynamic activity of the people as a whole, whether this collective action is marked by consensus or conflict.[31] Sovereignty is, as he puts it, "reduced and flattened onto the *multitudo*."[32]

Negri's interpretation is insightful, if somewhat elusive. But it is also misleading. The suggestion that sovereign authority can be reduced to unmediated mass action ignores the crucial distinction between the body that defines (*definire*) authority and the body that holds (*tenere* or *habere*) it, which is enunciated in what is the foundational text for Negri's interpretation of TP 2/17:

> This right, which is defined by the power of a multitude [*multitudinis potentia definitur*], is usually called Sovereignty [*imperium*]. Whoever, by common agreement, has responsibility for public Affairs – that is, the rights of making, interpreting, and repealing laws, fortifying cities, and making decisions about war and peace, etc. – has this right absolutely [*absolute tenet*].

The *potentia multitudinis*, which "defines" sovereign right, is the material basis of the state: it is the power from which civil authority derives. But the material is shaped into a single, unified body politic by the sovereign – be it monarchical, aristocratic, or democratic in structure[33] – which alone has the right to *issue* the *rationes* by which the people act, setting laws and making decisions about war and peace (see e.g., TP 4/1–4/2; TTP 20.15, iii.241).

This role distinction between the sovereign and the multitude is reflected in Spinoza's metaphor of the sovereign as the "mind" or "will" of the commonwealth. The masses must be guided (*ducitur*) by a governing body to which they have consented (TP 6/1; cf. TP 5/2). The sovereign is "the mind of the state, by which everyone ought to be guided [*imperii veluti mens sit, qua omnes duci debent*]" (TP 4/1; cf. TP 3/5). So, when Spinoza writes of the commonwealth

---

[31] Negri 1991, p. 202.
[32] Ibid., p. 198; Negri 1997, p. 227.
[33] It must take one of these forms, since "experience has shown all the kinds of State which might conceivably enable men to live in harmony" (TP 1/3). Spinoza takes the distinctions between these forms seriously, allowing that they have different structures, different fundamental institutions. So, *pace* Negri, Spinoza does not claim that the people hold sovereignty in all regimes; this would render irrelevant differences between regimes that he insists upon (see TP 7/25).

being guided as if by a single mind (e.g., TP 2/16; TP 3/2; TP 3/7), I take it that he is upholding the very functional distinction between the sovereign and the people, the governors and the governed, that Negri collapses.[34]

What distinguishes Spinoza's conception of sovereign absolutism from conventional versions is just that Spinoza regards authority as a thoroughly natural phenomenon – it consists, once again, in patterned dependency (Section 2.5). To the extent that the common *ratio* is disrupted, the sovereign lacks authority (TP 3/3). On this view, sovereignty extends as far, and only as far, as it is able to promote obedience or compliance. It is at this point that the *potentia multitudinis*, as the material basis of the state, plays a role in *defining* sovereign power. The state is a "natural thing" (*res naturalis*) (TP 4/4), bound by the laws of nature (TP 4/4). The multitude "defines" sovereign right in the sense that it limits or constrains the ways in which sovereignty may be exercised. We saw this in Section 4.2, where we examined Spinoza's claim that:

[T]hings most people resent are less within a Commonwealth's Right. For certainly men are guided by nature to unite in one aim, either because of a common [hope or] a common fear, or because they long to avenge some common loss. Because the Commonwealth's Right is defined [*definitur*] by the common power of a multitude, it's certain that its power and Right are diminished to the extent that it provides many people with reasons to conspire against it (TP 3/9).

The more a sovereign inspires fear and indignation, the more it diminishes its own power or authority as sovereign.

So, while the sovereign plays an irreducible role in unifying the people, the exercise of sovereignty is in fact profoundly constrained by the defining power of the people. Consequently, while there is a functional distinction between the sovereign and its subjects, there is a sense in which law-making is a two-way street: it requires a body that declares the law *and* a body that complies. The process of exercising and preserving sovereign authority is thus highly dynamic, requiring that the sovereign govern in ways that minimize fear, indignation, and resistance (see TP 2/15; TP 8/5). This conception of sovereign power carries substantial revisionist implications for Spinoza's absolutism.[35]

To fully appreciate the normative significance of Spinoza's account of sovereign absolutism, we must return once more to TP 5/2–5/3:

If wickedness is more prevalent in one Commonwealth than in another, and more sins are committed there, this surely comes from the fact that the [more wicked] Commonwealth hasn't provided adequately for harmony, hasn't set up its laws wisely

---

[34] In this respect, I side with Balibar, who rejects Negri's interpretation of sovereignty as unmediated mass action, declaring instead that Spinoza is a theorist of the "modern State apparatus" (Balibar 1989, p. 125).

[35] For this, see J. Steinberg 2018b.

enough, and so, *hasn't obtained the absolute Right of a Commonwealth [neque ius civitatis absolutum obtinuerit]*...just as the subjects' vices, and their excessive license and stubbornness, are to be imputed to the Commonwealth, so, on the other hand, their virtue and constant observance of the laws are to be attributed most *to the virtue of the Commonwealth and its absolute right"* (TP 5/2–5/3).

To the extent, and only to the extent, that the sovereign has obtained absolute right[36] – "absolutism," strangely enough, being something that comes in degrees (TP 6/8; TP 7/23) – it will beget civic harmony, or establish a common *ratio*.[37] Moreover, the extent to which a state is harmonious is primarily a function of the extent to which state or sovereign power is absolute. The onus for maintaining order and indeed its own authority is placed squarely on the sovereign (TTP 16.30, iii.194; see Section 2.6).

Since civic unity – understood in terms of harmony (*Concordia*), peace (*pax*), and *securitas* (see TP 8/7) – is an unmistakable political ideal, so too is sovereign absolutism, in virtue of which this unity is possible. The upshot, then, is that when Spinoza claims that democracies are the most absolute forms of governance, he is assuredly revealing a preference. The fact that democracies are the most absolute form of government is evidence that they are the best form of government. What remains to be seen is *why* Spinoza thinks that democracies are most absolute.

7.2   Spinoza's Psychological Defense of Democracy: The Affective Dimension

Those who question Spinoza's commitment to democracy often situate their readings against portrayals of him as an exuberant and principled democrat for whom egalitarian and participatory institutions are good simply in virtue of being egalitarian and participatory, quite apart from the consequences. Jonathan Israel advances a principled egalitarian interpretation of Spinoza. On his reading, Spinoza respects the "equal weight" of human interests[38] and regards non-democratic regimes as degenerate deviations from natural equality.[39] This interpretation helps to ground Israel's thesis that Spinoza is the great progenitor of the radical enlightenment.

---

[36] Since Spinoza is referring here to the legislative body, it is evident that the by the "absolute right of the commonwealth" he means the "absolute right of the sovereign."

[37] The first part of the passage establishes that disunity entails the lack of sovereign authority: absolute sovereign authority is *sufficient* for unity. The second part of the passage establishes that unity entails absolutism: absolute sovereign authority is *necessary* for unity.

[38] See Israel 2010b, p. 92.

[39] See Israel 2001, pp. 272 and 203n9. For a more thorough canvassing of liberal and "Marxian" interpretations of Spinoza's egalitarianism, see Lord 2014.

Negri also puts forth a principled egalitarian reading, claiming that that this is reflected in Spinoza's conception of sovereignty as the dynamic (constituent) power of the multitude in the TP: "what is claimed here is a republican right and what is proposed is the very condition of democratic politics. An equal right for all."[40] The equality that Negri envisions is something like equal participatory power, an ideal that is aligned with the republican tradition, which took political participation to be a component of liberty.[41] According to a standard republican line, one is free if and only if one does not stand under the arbitrary will of a *dominus*, which is possible in and only in a well-structured republic.[42] The interpretation of Spinoza as a principled egalitarian thus often feeds into an interpretation of him as a principled republican.[43]

I will argue that while Spinoza was a republican and, to some degree, an egalitarian, his commitment to democratic institutions is thoroughly consequentialist, reflecting his dynamic realism: because of certain features of human psychology, democratic institutions tend to foster powerful, joyful *ingenia*. As a political psychologist, Spinoza offers grounds for defending democracy that have been, to some extent, neglected by the more principled, ideal-theoretical approaches common today.

There are two dimensions to Spinoza's defense of democracy as the most absolute regime-form. The first may be loosely dubbed "affective." According to this line of argumentation, egalitarian and participatory institutions diminish envy and resentment, replacing these negative affects with *securitas*, or hopeful, willing compliance (Section 4.3). The other dimension is epistemic: democratic institutions foster greater rationality at both the collective and individual levels. I will start here with the affective dimension, taking the interpretation of Spinoza as a principled democrat as a foil.

Let's consider the evidence for the reading of Spinoza as a principled democrat. Like other early modern republicans, Spinoza appeals to the twin principles of natural liberty and equality to ground his opposition to arbitrary, hierarchical governance. Three specific passages from the TTP support the reading of Spinoza as a principled democrat. The first comes from TTP Ch. 5,

---

[40] Negri 1997, p. 234.

[41] The norms of equality and liberty were very closely related in early-modern anti-despotic thought. In his case against despotism, for instance, the seventeenth-century English republican Algernon Sidney appeals to "natural freedom" and "natural equality" more or less interchangeably (DCG, p. 313).

[42] Skinner 1998, p. 23; Wirszubski 1950.

[43] See, for instance, James' observation that most scholars "underestimate the republican antecedents of [Spinoza's] analysis of freedom" (James 1996, p. 209n4). Quentin Skinner also claims that standard interpretations "underestimate the extent to which Spinoza is restating classical republican ideas, especially as developed by Machiavelli in the *Discourses*" (Skinner 1984, p. 217n35), the liberty of self-governance being one of the primary ideas. See also Prokhovnik 2004 and Smith 1997 (especially p. 164). My own reading of Spinoza and the republican tradition is most fully elaborated in J. Steinberg 2008.

where, after observing that in a democracy alone "no one is bound to be subject to his equal" (TTP 5.23, iii.74), Spinoza writes:

1. [S]ince obedience consists in someone's carrying out a command solely on the authority of the person who commands it, it follows that obedience has no place in a social order where sovereignty is in the hands of everyone and laws are enacted by common consent, and that whether the laws in such a social order are increased or diminished, the people nevertheless remains equally free, because it does not act from the authority of someone else, but by its own consent [*non ex authoritate alterius sed ex proprio suo consensus agit*] (TTP 5.25, iii.74).

In a democracy, one participates in one's own governance, retaining one's natural liberty or authority rather than standing under the right of another. This sounds like a clear endorsement of the republican ideal of liberty.

The second passage is from TTP, Ch. 16. Here, as in TTP, Ch. 5, Spinoza maintains that what makes democracies best is precisely that by participating in our own governance, we best preserve our natural equality and natural freedom:

2. With this I think I have shown sufficiently clearly what the foundations of the democratic state are. I preferred to treat it before all others, because it seemed the most natural state, and the one which approached most nearly the freedom nature concedes to everyone. In it no one so transfers his natural right to another that in the future there is no consultation with him. Instead he transfers it to the greater part of the whole Society, of which he makes one part. In this way everyone remains equal, as they were before, in the state of nature (TTP 16.36, iii.195).

Spinoza also invokes human nature and the "natural condition" of equality to defend the superiority of liberal, democratic governance in the third and final text invoked in support of the principled interpretation, from the concluding chapter (Ch. 20) of the TTP:

3. There can be no doubt that this way of governing is best, and has the least disadvantages, since it's the one most compatible with men's nature. For we've shown that in a democratic state (which comes closest to the natural condition) everyone contracts to act according to the common decision, but not to judge and reason according to the common decision. Because not all men can equally think the same things, they agreed that the measure which had the most votes would have the force of a decree, but that meanwhile they'd retain the authority to repeal these decrees when they saw better ones. The less we grant men this freedom of judgment, the more we depart from the most natural condition, and the more violent the government (TTP 20.37–8, iii.245)

In this passage, Spinoza connects democratism with liberalism, arguing that the participatory or consultative aspects of democracy are most in keeping with our natural authority over our actions.

In addition to these texts, there are contextual reasons to expect Spinoza to offer a principled defense of democracy. The argument that republics alone preserve one's natural liberty, equality, or authority was a mainstay of defenses of popular governance through early-modern Europe.[44] And this argument figured prominently in the work of two of the figures who most influenced Spinoza: Niccolò Machiavelli and Pieter De la Court.[45] Given that Spinoza praises the former as a "wise man" and an advocate of freedom (TP 5/7), it is tempting to suppose that he embraces the conception of freedom advocated by the *"acutissimus Florentinus"* (TP 10/1; cf. TP 5/7).

I want to suggest, however, that Spinoza's commitment to republican liberty and equality as ideals is half-hearted at best. The most striking "principled" defenses of democracies in the TTP are undercut by claims that he makes elsewhere in the same work and are altogether absent from the TP.[46] Moreover, a deeper inquiry into Spinoza's reasons for valuing equality and participation in governance reveals that he prizes them primarily for their psychological effects.

Take, for instance, Spinoza's claim in TTP, Ch. 5 that in a democracy (and only in a democracy) one retains one's natural authority (*authoritas*). This assertion, which he does not explicitly repeat anywhere else,[47] is incompatible with claims he makes in the very same work about authority.[48] For instance, he asserts in TTP, Ch. 17 that irrespective of what kind of state one lives in, when one is compelled – through whatever motive – to comply with the commands of sovereign, one acts from the right or authority (*ex authoritate*) of another (TTP 17.5–7; see Section 2.5). He repeats this point in the TP, drawing no distinction in this respect between republics and other forms of governance (TP 3/5; cf. TP 2/9–2/10).

---

[44] One even finds traces of this view in the pamphlet literature in support of the Dutch Revolt from the Spanish Hapsburgs at the end of the sixteenth century, and in the Dutch republican literature that emerged in the middle of the seventeenth century (van Gelderen 1992). While these works do not contain the sort of careful, sustained republican theorizing that one finds in, say, Machiavelli or Harrington, they do present a nostalgic vision of ancient Batavian freedom, which was secured when their ancestors (the tribal *Batavi*) parried the advances of the Romans.

[45] See, for instance, Machiavelli, *Discourses*, II.ii, p. 280. And De la Court referred to monarchs as "base and slavish opposers of Liberty" (*TI*, p. 12). He maintained that the Dutch people "became not free but by the death of the last stadtholder and captain general" (*TI*, p. 11) for only then were they "subject to none of what quality soever, but only to reason, and to the laws of their own country" (*TI*, p. 381).

[46] The closest passage to an endorsement of republican freedom of which I am aware is his claim that "once equality has been set aside, the common freedom necessarily perishes" (TP 10/8). But, unfortunately, he does not elaborate on why inequality erodes liberty, nor does his use this claim to much effect.

[47] The closest claim is that we retain rights of consultation (TTP 16.36, iii.195, above).

[48] My conjecture is that these chapters were written at quite different times. As the TTP was in progress from 1665 but was not published until 1670, it would not be surprising to find vestiges of earlier views in the text.

We can appreciate Spinoza's break with orthodox republicanism by considering his unique treatment of the Roman law concept of being *sui iuris*. Roman republicans and their early-modern successors conceived of liberty in terms of being *sui iuris*, or retaining right over oneself, rather than placing oneself under the rights of another (*in potestate, sub potestate,* or *sub alterius iure*). While the terms shifted somewhat from ancient to early-modern times, the distinction between being the author of one's own action and being subject to another's will remained salient. Algernon Sidney, for example, construes "liberty" as "independency upon the will of another, and by the name of slave we understand a man, who can neither dispose of his person nor goods, but enjoys all at the will of his master."[49]

Spinoza, however, does not conceive of standing under the authority of another as a form of servitude. To the contrary, he thinks that the kind of dependency that one enters into when one puts oneself under the right of the sovereign is assuredly a good thing. The more firmly we depend on the will of the sovereign, the more absolute the state will be, and the better off we will be in turn. Given the ideal of absolutism, in the best state the citizen will resolve "wholeheartedly to obey all the other's commands" and will thus be "most under another's control [*maxime sub alterius imperio est*]" (TTP 17.8, iii.202). Far from limiting one's freedom, this form of dependency actually enhances it. To be free, one must sacrifice the natural condition (natural liberty) of being *sui iuris*: "sound reason cannot dictate that each person remains *sui iuris*" (TP 3/6).

Elsewhere, Spinoza makes it clear that what determines whether or not one is free is not the source of the legislation, but the quality of the legislation[50]:

[Obedience] isn't what makes the slave. It's the reason for the action. If the end of the action is not the advantage of the agent himself, but of the person who issues the command, then the agent is a slave, useless to himself. But in a Republic, and a state where the supreme law is the well-being of the whole people, not that of the ruler, someone who obeys the supreme power in everything should not be called a slave, useless to himself, but a subject. So that Republic is most free whose laws are founded on sound reason. For there each person, when he wishes, can be free, i.e., live wholeheartedly according to the guidance of reason (TTP 16.33–4, iii.194–5).

Spinoza allows that, since freedom consists in rational activity or power, rather than in independence from the will of another, "a multitude can preserve a full enough freedom under a King" (TP 7/31). While Spinoza's sympathies are republican, even democratic, in terms of the conceptual trichotomy between freedom from interference (negative liberty), freedom from domination

---

[49] Sidney DCG, p. 17.
[50] See J. Steinberg 2008.

(republican liberty), and freedom as self-realization (positive liberty), the free-dom that Spinoza prizes in itself is, as we would expect (Section 3.2), the freedom of self-realization, empowerment, or rational self-control: "the only free person is the one who lives wholeheartedly according to the guidance of reason alone" (TTP 16.32, iii.194; cf. TP 2/7; TP 3/6). By severing the puta-tively connection between living in a republic and being free, he distances himself from orthodox republicans and principled democrats.

Spinoza's defense of equality is also more complex than the passages cited above might seem to suggest. While Israel points to these passages to support his portrayal of Spinoza as a principled egalitarian, for whom "the pristine equality of the state of nature is our ultimate guide and criterion, not just in determining the character and legitimacy of any society's political arrange-ments but also in shaping the common good,"[51] a deeper investigation into Spinoza's egalitarianism reveals that civic equality is a good primarily because of its consequences. Indeed, the thrust of Spinoza's case for equality is better framed as a case *against civic inequality*, as it focuses on the deleterious effects of power imbalances.[52]

Consider his claim that democracies are good because in them "nobody is bound to be subject to his equal" (TTP 5.23, iii.74). Spinoza does not simply leave it at this, as if subordination in itself were bad simply because it is an affront to human dignity or autonomy; rather, he suggests that subordination is unstable, since the "hardest thing for [people] to endure is being subservient to their equals, and being governed by them" (TTP 5.22, iii.74). He repeats this point in the TP: "it's certain that everyone prefers ruling to being ruled. 'For no one willingly grants another the right to command,' as Sallust observes in the first speech to Caesar" (TP 7/5; cf. TP 8/12). Just as we resist illiberal governance, we resist arbitrary subordination – both of which are perceived as oppressive.

Here, once again, natural ambition and ideological preservationism (Section 6.2) figure prominently in Spinoza's analysis. Because humans strive to have others conform to their *ingenia* rather than the other way around, static hierarchi-cal relations breed envy, hatred and resistance.[53] Consider his account of the

---

[51] Israel 2001, p. 274.

[52] Beth Lord has challenged egalitarian readings in a somewhat different way in a couple of ar-ticles: Lord 2014; 2016. While I sympathize with her critique in general, I think she saddles advocates of the egalitarian reading with unnecessary commitments, like the commitment to equality of capacities. Egalitarianism need only imply (relative) equality of political power or status, not equality of *total* causal power.

[53] Matheron, "Une fois que l'ambition de domination entre en jeu, elle se crée à elle-même un nouvel objet: le pouvoir sur nos semblable, qui, dans l'état civil, devient pouvoir politique. Et ce nouvel objet, lui aussi, peut on non être monopolisé. Si les dirigeants sont en nombre trop restre-int, s'ils forment une caste trop fermée, l'homme ordinaire ne peut guère espérer accéder aux postes de commande; il envie donc ses supérieurs, même si son tempérament et son histoire ne le

role of ambition – and its kindred affects, pride and envy – in his analysis of the causes of disharmony that a state must anticipate and guard against in TTP 17:

Everyone thinks that he alone knows everything, and wants everything to be done according to his *ingenium*. He thinks a thing fair or unfair, permissible or impermissible, just to the extent that he judges it brings him profit or loss. From love of esteem, he disdains equals, and *will not put up with being ruled by them*. From envy for the greater praise or better fortune someone else receives – these things are never equal – he wishes the other person ill, and is delighted when bad things happen to him (TTP 17.15, iii.203 – my emphasis).

Because we are naturally ambitious and envious, hierarchical regimes that make political power an exclusive good provoke pervasive envy and hatred. Spinoza explicitly makes this point in the TP when opposing lifetime appointments for counselors in a monarchy: "If they were chosen for life, there would be a number of bad consequences: most citizens could hardly conceive any hope of achieving that honor. This would lead to great inequality among the citizens, and so to envy, constant grumbling, and finally, to rebellions" (TP 7/13). Where there is inequality between apparent equals there will be envy, resentment, and resistance.

Even those passages in which Spinoza looks most like a principled democrat get their justificatory traction from his psychology. Democracies are most "natural" in that in them one acts most in accordance with one's own *ingenium*, one acts more from one's own bent (*sponte*) and feels freer (see Section 4.3). *Securitas* prevails over fear and envy; and harmony prevails over discord, resulting in a more absolute state. So, while all forms of governance entail to some degree the curtailment of one's natural authority, by allowing broad participation in the formation of the sovereign will and rendering political posts available to all, democracies foster greater political buy-in or a stronger sense of authorship (Sections 4.3–4.4). The result will be a more stable state (TP 7/2), marked by a more willing, more *secure* citizenry.

This psychological analysis of the dynamics of equality, participation, and political buy-in underlies Spinoza's rather idealized account of the history of Jews in late fifteenth-century Spain and Portugal (TTP 3.54, iii.56–7). On his account, though Spanish Jews were either forced to convert to Catholicism or leave the country, those who converted were granted full and equal civil status, leading them to integrate. However, Jews who were forced to convert to Catholicism in Portugal were still treated as second-class citizens,

---

prédisposaient nullement à l'ambition: il leur veut du mal et se réjouit de leurs infortunes...si, par contre, le recrutement des élites est démocratique, ou du moins largement ouvert, l' *invidia* sera privée de son aliment essentiel" (Matheron 1969, pp. 178–9).

resulting in estrangement and resentment. While the contrast is surely too starkly drawn, it highlights the connection that Spinoza makes between relative equality and *securitas*, a connection that is drawn at several other points, including when he writes: "if the Republic had been constituted in accordance with [God's] first intention, the right and honor would always have been equal among all the tribes, and everything would have been arranged most securely [*securissime*]" (TTP 17.101, iii.218). Since some degree of political buy-in can be achieved by securing basic civil rights, it is not at all surprising that Spinoza thinks that significantly greater commitment to the state can be achieved by granting people equal rights to participate in sovereignty.

We see from this how Spinoza's democratism reflects his dynamic realism. Taking people as they are actually constituted, relative equality must be maintained lest society be riven by envy, jealousy, and hate.[54] The more participatory and inclusive a state is, the more hopeful and willing the citizens will be. This is what ultimately grounds Spinoza's appeals to natural equality and liberty. By distributing political power more equitably, democratic governance also helps to limit the expression of ambition and pride, thereby diminishing one of the chief sources of intolerance (Section 6.2). Democratism thus entails a train of affective benefits.

7.3 Spinoza's Psychological Defense of Democracy: The Epistemic Dimension

The affective case for democratism is pretty straightforward: the more dispersed political power is, the more hopeful or secure the people will be, and consequently the more unified and absolute the state will be. However, a full vindication of democratism requires an epistemic justification as well, since if affective and epistemic measures of civic success come apart, one might prefer a rational, disharmonious state to an irrational, harmonious one. This section will explore Spinoza's epistemic case for the superiority of democracies, concluding with some observations about how the affective and epistemic components hang together.

The claim that Spinoza advances an epistemic defense of democracy might surprise some. How could the same person who discouraged common people from reading the TTP on account of their obstinacy and irrationality (TTP preface.33, ii.12) also be a defender of the wisdom of crowds? Such expressions of elitism lend support to Steven Smith's characterization of Spinoza as a "begrudging" democrat, who "did not hold any great confidence in the

---

[54] Contrast with del Lucchese's conflictualism (del Lucchese 2009).

wisdom, actual or potential, of the people as a whole,"[55] and who denied "the superior wisdom of popular assemblies" and "virtues of deliberation."[56]

This portrayal is quite mistaken, in my view. Spinoza offers a host of reasons for thinking that democratized regimes will tend to make better collective judgments than non-democratized regimes.[57] One class of argument that Spinoza puts forward stresses the deliberative or educative advantages of democracy. Democratic deliberation is a powerful tool for bringing new information and new perspectives to light, and for improving grounds for belief in general. In one particularly inspired, if somewhat overblown, passage, Spinoza writes that "human wits are too sluggish to penetrate everything right away. But by asking advice, listening, and arguing, they're sharpened. When people try all means, in the end they find ways to the things they want which everyone approves, and no one had ever thought of before" (TP 9/14).[58] Even if deliberative decision-making bodies are somewhat inefficient, this downside is more than offset by the improvement in the quality of decisions that follow vigorous debate.

The epistemic benefit is especially pronounced when the deliberating body is sizable. While small councils cannot be trusted because "everyone there tries to have dull colleagues, who will hang on his every word" (TP 7/4), when a council is sufficiently large, like the council of patricians that Spinoza recommends in his model aristocracy, its will is governed by reason rather than excessive desire (TP 8/6). This echoes Spinoza's claim in the TTP that in a democracy "absurdities are less to be feared. If the assembly is large, it's almost impossible that the majority of its members should agree on one absurd action" (TTP 16.30, iii.194).[59] The guiding assumption in these passages is that

[55] Smith 1997, p. 121.
[56] Smith 2003, p. 132.
[57] He adopts the following three assumptions on which epistemic defenses of democracy depend: (i) for at least *some* political choices there are objectively better or worse decisions; (ii) good outcomes are defined independently of any procedure (see Cohen 1986, p. 29); and (iii) democratic decision procedures are better than alternatives at producing just or good results. See J. Steinberg 2010a.
[58] Compare this remark with that of the Cartesian philosopher of logic (at Leiden in the 1650s), Adriaan Heereboord: "Disputation is the sieve and, as it were, the whetstone of truth; it enhances the mind, it sharpens judgement, it arouses both; it improves memory and furthers the freedom of speech. And as fire comes from the contact of two flints, truth arises from disputations" (quoted in Van Bunge 2001).
[59] The potential epistemic advantages of sizeable deliberative bodies have been duly noted in the contemporary work on democracy. Some have claimed that the extent of participation in a democracy is a decisive mark in its favor because of the so-called Condorcet Jury Theorem (see Grofman and Feld 1988; Barry 1965). The Jury Theorem states that if individuals are competent (defined here as being more likely than not to choose correctly between two options), then the reliability of the group is increased as it is made larger. Still, invoking the Condorcet Jury Theorem to support real world deliberative democracies may be naïve, especially in light of further work that has shown just how susceptible deliberative bodies are to group-think, information cascades, suppressed profiles, and ideological amplification (see Sunstein 2002; 2003; Sunstein, Schkade, and Hastie 2007). These studies show how reputational pressures or

after exposure to a wide range of views, members of a large deliberative group are likely to avoid very bad decisions, and may well converge on good ones.[60]

At least as important as the way that deliberation "sharpens the wits" of interlocutors is the way that democratically organized governing bodies rein in private interest, ensuring that the will of the sovereign serves the *salus populi*. In regimes where the power of governing agents is unchecked, the ruling class will tend to legislate self-servingly, at the cost of the general good: "when the few decide everything, simply on the basis of their own affects, freedom and the common good are lost" (TP 9/14).[61] Democratic accountability helps to keep in check what he calls in the TTP the "absurdities of appetite" [*absurda appetitus*] (TTP 16.30, iii.194), desires that are damaging to one's long-term welfare.

One reason why large deliberative bodies protect against the "absurdities of appetite" is that in them one must invoke broad civic reasons for one's position: "the will of a Council so large cannot be determined so much by immoderate desire as by reason. Indeed, evil affects pull men in different directions. They can't be led as if by one mind except insofar as what they desire is honorable, or at least has the appearance of being honorable" (TP 8/6). Of course, public justification does not necessarily prevent one from acting in self-serving ways; it just requires that one invoke publicly accessible reasons for pursuing these goals, leaving plenty of room for chicanery and rationalization, since clever people can find intellectual cover for even the most repugnant measures. Nevertheless, the demand of public justification acts as at least a mild constraint.[62]

More importantly, democratized institutions promote the "balancing of interests,"[63] aligning individual desires with public goods: "to establish things so that everyone, whatever his *ingenium*, prefers the public right to private advantage, this is the task, this is our concern" (TTP 17.16, iii.203; cf. TP 6/3; TP 7/2). This requires that political power be broadly distributed. In a democratized, balanced monarchy, the monarch will be compelled to make judgments based on the advice of a large, incorruptible body of citizen counselors (TP 7/3; TP 7/9; TP 8/38), whose "personal situation and advantage" are made to "depend on peace

---

biases can compromise judgment in certain deliberative contexts. While Spinoza might not have anticipated these problems, he was certainly aware that not all deliberating bodies are equally conducive to knowledge.
[60] For more on the epistemic benefits of deliberation, see Matheron 1969, p. 169; James 2011, p. 190.
[61] See TP 6/8.
[62] See Jon Elster's assertion that "in a political debate it is pragmatically impossible to argue that a given solution should be chosen just because it is good for oneself. By the very act of engaging in a public debate – by arguing rather than bargaining – one has ruled out the possibility of invoking such reasons" (Elster 1997, p. 12).
[63] Cf. McShea 1968, p. 109. Balancing interests was also a central feature of De la Court's writings. For a thorough discussion, see Haitsma Mulier 1980.

and the common well-being of everyone" (TP 7/4). In such a well-structured monarchy, "whether the King is led by a fear of the multitude, perhaps to bind the greater part of the armed multitude to himself, or led by a nobility of spirit, to consult the public advantage, either he'll always endorse the opinion which has the most votes ... or he'll be anxious to reconcile, if possible, the inconsistent opinions brought to him, so that he draws everyone to himself" (TP 7/11). Such accountability mechanisms are more formalized and more effective in aristocracies, where periodic elections, term limits, the rotation of offices, and the adoption of regulatory councils help to limit individual power and ensure that narrow – individual or factional[64] – interests are not advanced at the expense of the general good. But defective aristocracies that lack these institutions and concentrate power too narrowly are easily toppled. This is how Spinoza explains the fall of de Witt's republic (e.g., TP 8/44; TP 9/14), which was content to retain the old institutions save for the stadtholder, creating a situation in which "those who really had the authority were *far too few* to be able to govern the multitude and overcome powerful opponents" (TP 9/14 – my emphasis).

At this point, one might wonder what accountability mechanisms and the balancing of interests have to do with an *epistemic* defense. Here, we must bear in mind, once again, that evaluative judgments are constituted by affects (Section 1.1). So, the extent to which one's evaluative judgments are rational is a function of the affective power of adequate ideas relative to the affective power of competing passions. Reliable appetitive control is thus evidence of rationality; and the lack of appetitive control is evidence of irrationality. As a slogan: the conative expresses the cognitive.

The same reasoning applies at the state level. To the extent that the state is moved to act by desires that undermine its own ability to exist and act (i.e., its own power), it is irrational. So, when some part of the body politic advances a private interest at the expense of the general good, even if its members in some sense know what would be good for the state as a whole, the state is acting irrationally. Spinoza points precisely to what might be dubbed collective *akrasia* to show why, "in actual life," aristocracies are typically less rationally governed than democracies:

[I]f Patricians were the kind of people who, in choosing colleagues, were free of every affect, and guided only by zeal for the public well-being, there would be no state to compare with an Aristocracy. But experience has shown abundantly that things don't

[64] Spinoza thinks that the diffusion of power into the hands of many will have the effect of reducing the power of factions. In a passage that anticipates Madison's argument in *Federalist* #10, Spinoza writes: "if only two Patricians have been selected, each will strive to be more powerful than the other, and because each one has too much power [for the other to conquer easily], the state will easily be divided into two factions – and into three, or four, or five factions, if three or four or five [Patricians] have power. But the factions will be weaker the more the rule has been conferred on many people" (TP 8/1).

work that way – especially in oligarchies, where the will of the Patricians is least bound by the law, because they lack rivals. For there the Patricians, in a partisan spirit, keep the best men off the Council, and seek comrades on it who will hang on their every word. In such a state things go much less fortunately [than they do in a Democracy], because the Selection of the Patricians depends on the absolute free will of certain men, or a will unconstrained by any law (TP 11/2).

A knowledgeable, but unconstrained elite will generally exhibit worse collective judgment than a democracy because the former is more susceptible to the absurdities of appetite. In this way, Spinoza upends the Platonic order, treating democracies as most likely to exhibit control over its own appetites.

Spinoza's realist analysis here yields a line of defense that has been neglected by contemporary epistemic democrats, who tend toward ideal theory.[65] For instance, Joshua Cohen rests his epistemic defense on the assumption that "voting expresses beliefs about what the correct policies are...not personal preferences for policies,"[66] a condition that quite evidently does not widely obtain in real-world democracies. Spinoza, by contrast, suggests that democracies in fact have epistemic advantages over other regimes in part because of the pervasiveness of self-interest. His insights thus may fortify the epistemic defense, revealing how an apparent weakness of democracies – namely, the graspingness of individuals – might actually be a strength.

Democratism and Epistemic Conditions

This leads us to an important qualification. We would expect that, as a psychological realist, Spinoza would be attentive to the ways in which the epistemic advantages of a democracy depend on the safeguarding of certain conditions. For instance, in order for deliberation to "sharpen the wits" of the participants and converge on rational decisions, deliberative bodies must be free from the influence of fear-mongering, superstitious clerics. We saw in Chapter 6 how attuned Spinoza is to this threat to collective rationality, organizing the TTP around the goal of preventing or counteracting this form of corruption. And the threat of mob mentality – a particularly noxious form of group-think and *aemulatio* – would have impressed itself upon Spinoza in brutal slayings of the de Witts in 1672. So, when Spinoza claims that in a large, deliberative body, the majority is unlikely to make irrational judgments, I think that we should understand this as conditional on the establishment of reasonably good epistemic conditions. This explains, once again, the methodological pride of place of the TTP.

---

[65] See for instance Estlund 1997; Cohen 1986. A notable exception is Anderson 2006.
[66] Cohen 1986, p. 34.

Spinoza stresses the importance of good epistemic conditions forcefully near the end of TP 7 where he attempts to rebut those who claim that common people are too stupid and tempestuous to participate in governance. Spinoza is at his most fiercely anti-elitist in these remarkable passages (TP 7/27–7/29) which contain one of his clearest expressions of the view that human nature is homogeneous: "everyone shares a common nature –we're just deceived by power and refinement [*cultu*]" (TP 7/27).[67] Widespread differences between people's capacities can be ultimately traced back to divergent civil structures and practices (Section 1.3), and one particularly important factor here concerns access to information. The primary reason that most people are poor judges in political matters is that governors tend to be obscurantist:

[I]t's no surprise that "there's neither truth nor judgment in the plebeians" when the rulers manage the chief business of the state secretly, and the plebeians are only making a guess from the few things the rulers can't conceal...So it's sheer stupidity to want to do everything in secrecy, and then expect the citizens not to judge the government's actions wrongly, and not to interpret everything perversely (TP 7/27).

This is a striking rebuke of the conception of Spinoza as an anti-populist. If he is distrustful of the multitude, it is because he is distrustful of the structures of power that facilitate mass ignorance.

Spinoza follows this observation with a plea for political transparency: "it's much better for the state's proper and true plans to be open to its enemies than for a tyrant's wicked secrets to be kept from his citizens" (TP 7/29). Without adequate access to information, the people cannot effectively deliberate or hold their leaders accountable, and the epistemic advantage of popular participation in governance will be lost. But if the state promotes broad political engagement and governs transparently, we can reasonably expect widespread competency, since all people are "shrewd and clever enough in matters [one] has long been passionately involved in" (TP 7/4).

There are, thus, at least two sets of conditions that must obtain in order for democracies to function well: the state must be free from ideological contamination and it must be governed openly, before the vigilant eyes of an engaged citizenry. In light of these observations about the need for good epistemic conditions, we see that Spinoza's arguments point to the potential virtues of democracies while also indicating how vulnerable they are to corruption. His democratism is at once promising and sobering. Large, deliberative bodies that govern transparently and are not under the spell of clerical zealots are likely to make better judgments than other governing bodies. However, in the

---

[67] Curley's translation of "*cultu*" as "refinement" misses the religious connotation. I take it that Spinoza is here referring to the effects of culture and civilization as well as "worship," specifically in the form of superstition.

absence of such good cognitive conditions, the masses may well be reduced to a muddled mob.

The Affective and the Epistemic

Let me conclude this section with a brief observation about how the affective and epistemic defenses of democracy fit together. I have treated these aspects as if they constituted distinct bases for evaluating civic success. This seems reasonable, since we can certainly conceive of states that seem to succeed in one respect and not the other – states that are cohesive but not especially rational, or vice versa. Nevertheless, there is reason to think that, ultimately, Spinoza believes that affective welfare and epistemic welfare co-vary, since as one becomes more joyful, one's power of thinking (one's power of acting considered under the attribute of thought) increases; and, conversely, as one's power of thinking increases, one becomes more joyful (3p11). Moreover, the political ideals to which Spinoza refers – peace, harmony, *securitas* – seem to be at once affective *and* epistemic conditions.

Consider, once again, absolutism, or the condition in which a people are guided as if by a single mind. What he is describing here looks primarily like an affective condition in which coordination is enabled by civic trust or commitment. But such unity also bespeaks rationality, as a people cannot be "led as if by one mind … unless the state has laws established according to the prescription of reason" (TP 2/21; cf. TP 3/6; TP 3/7; TTP 16.30, iii.194). An absolute state is not only cohesive, it is also rational. This point is stressed in Spinoza's analysis of aristocracy, where he claims that aristocracies are "more secure" (*magis securum*) than monarchies because they are more absolute; and the more absolute the right of the sovereign, "the more the form of the state agrees with the dictate of reason [*cum rationis dictamine magis convenit*]" (TP 8/7).

The ideal of harmony or civic agreement, to which Spinoza thinks the state should aspire, can be achieved only to the extent that individuals are epistemically well off. Peace arises from "from strength of mind" (*animi fortitudine*) (TP 5/4); and even if full-fledged, widespread rationality or *fortitudo* is too much to expect, a pretty decent approximation – namely, *securitas,* or the well-founded confidence that arises from the recognition that one benefits from civic cooperation – is not.

7.4   *Ingenia*-relativity Conservatism, and Exclusion

As I noted above, Spinoza does not advocate the universal adoption of democratic governance, even while he does advocate the *democratization* of governance. As a realist, he takes very seriously the view that states have a certain "nature" (*natura*), "condition" (*conditio*), or *ingenium* that must be respected.[68] His reverence for the nature or *ingenium* of a state – which mirrors his respect for the individual *ingenium* – leads him to recommend different institutions for different regime forms.[69] It also leads him to adopt a path-dependent, custom-respecting approach to reform. Here Spinoza's realism bends toward conservatism.

Consider again his analysis of the United Provinces in the stadtholderless period (1650–72):

> [T]he Hollanders thought that to maintain their freedom it was enough to renounce their Count and cut the head off the body of the state. They didn't think about reforming it, but left all its members as they'd been set up before, so that Holland remained a county without a Count, or a body without a head, and the state itself remained without a name (9/14).

Taken on its, this passage is not especially conservative. Indeed, some see it as evidence of Spinoza revolutionary tendencies, reading the passage as implying that Dutch freedom required razing the institutions of the *Ancien Régime* to the ground. But remarks elsewhere in the work militate against a revolutionary reading. In TP 7, for instance, he proclaims that "the form of the state should be kept one and the same" (TP 7/25), maintaining that "one who has become accustomed to another form of state won't be able to uproot the foundations they've received without a great danger of overthrowing the whole state and changing its structure" (TP 7/26). And he advocates maturity conditions among councilors in a monarchy and syndics in an aristocracy, because those who are older tend to "prefer the old and safe to the new and dangerous" (TP 7/17; cf. TP 10/2). Hardly the remarks of a revolutionary.

While, ultimately, Spinoza may be unduly cautious and conservative with respect to institutional reform, one can at least see how he derives these views from his political psychology. And the basic insight that governance must suited to the "nature of the place and the *ingenia* of the people" (TP 10/7) is, I think, a welcome one. It recognizes the need for normative political theory to vigilantly track and respect real-world conditions (Section 5.3).

A more troubling deployment of psychological realism is to be found in Spinoza's exclusion of women from democratic participation in the fragmentary final sections of the *Political Treatise*. Here he puts forth two main arguments for denying women participatory rights, the second of which raises a challenge for realism in general. According to this argument, rooted in an

---

[68] See TP 7/26; TP 8/37; TP 9/4; TP 9/14.
[69] To cite just two examples: (1) A national church will help aristocracies to flourish (TP 8/46), but it has no place in a monarchy (TP 6/40); (2) Housing and land should be public property in a monarchy (TP 6/12), but private property in an aristocracy (TP 8/10).

analysis of "human affects," if women were permitted to participate in governance, men would be distracted by passions, jealousies, and sexual competition, which would thereby disrupt the peace.[70] Moira Gatens, who describes Spinoza's exclusionism as a scar that "'disfigures' Spinoza's Philosophy,"[71] criticizes this argument on the following ground: "Men have all sorts of passions about all sorts of things that the body politic is not obliged to consider. Men may be greedy, querulous, ambitious, and so on, all of which may lead to upsetting the peace. However, in none of these cases does Spinoza consider it appropriate for the political realm to accommodate such passions."[72] While Gatens is right to emphasize the extent to which this is a blight on his philosophy, I don't subscribe to her characterization of his method. Spinoza consistently *does* accommodate passions like greed and ambition, and the form of this argument is entirely compatible with his psychological realism. The problems are: (1) it relies on a parodically shallow psychological analysis; and (2) even if it were good psychology, it would concede too much to prevailing opinions and affects.

The danger of yielding too much haunts all forms of political realism. Consider, for instance, Abraham Lincoln's Peoria Speech from 1854, a response to the Kansas-Nebraska act, which would allow Western states to permit slavery. In this oration, Lincoln considers various solutions to the problem of slavery, rejecting the option of liberating all slaves and living with them as social equals on the grounds that this approach provokes revulsion in whites. Lincoln claims that we should accommodate this sentiment, for "whether this feeling accords with justice and sound judgment, is not the sole question, if indeed, it is any part of it. A universal feeling, whether well or ill-founded, cannot be safely disregarded." Leaving aside the astonishing disregard for the feelings of blacks in this calculus, the point that I want to stress about this example is that it illustrates that yielding to popular opinion can obviously obstruct social progress. While dynamic realists ought to be sensitive to how such pandering undermines the transformative aims of *ingenia* reform, Spinoza's "realist" exclusion of women is, like Lincoln's accommodation of racist sentiments, a condemnable expression of quiescence.

In the other argument for exclusion, Spinoza abandons his realism altogether. Here he acknowledges that if the subjugation of women "happened only by custom, then no reason compels us to exclude women from rule"

---

[70] Biochemist Tim Hunt trotted out a tired version of this sexist argument when he explained why women should not be permitted to work in science labs with men: "Let me tell you about my trouble with girls...three things happen when they are in the lab... You fall in love with them, they fall in love with you and when you criticise them, they cry" (See www.theguardian.com/uk-news/2015/jun/10/nobel-scientist-tim-hunt-female-scientists-cause-trouble-for-men-in-labs).

[71] Gatens 1995, p. 134.

[72] Ibid.

(TP 11/4), but proceeds to argue that the subordination of women is natural, taking as evidence for this the historical pervasiveness of patriarchy. The argument hinges on an unreflective set of assumptions about how power is obtained and perpetuated. The analysis is particularly disappointing given that elsewhere Spinoza evinces an appreciation of the dynamics of power and submission and is typically careful not to regard historical contingencies and artifacts as universal principles of nature. Had his biases not disabled further inquiry, he might have seen that if women "necessarily submit to men" (TP 11/4), this is only because institutions of power left them with no hope for achieving genuine equality – for, on his own analysis, where there is hope and inequality there is resistance. Why not treat the despairing subordination of women like he treats the condition of subjects in the Ottoman Empire? When half of the population must resign to their own subordination, having forsaken all hope for equal standing, the condition is better described as a "wasteland," a limp and languishing condition, rather than a flourishing body politic.

This argument also raises questions about Spinoza's plastic essentialism. Throughout his works, Spinoza claims that all humans share one and the same nature, and where we find variation, it is due primarily to political institutions (Section 1.3). His argument for the natural subordination of women in TP 11/4 invites the perennial question of whether this is a misapplication of his universalist principles or evidence that his principles were not truly universal to begin with.[73] While I won't try to settle this extremely thorny matter here, I will note that I don't think either of these two options on their own captures the complexity of the situation. As Hasana Sharp has effectively argued, in the *Ethics*, Spinoza conceives of the possibility of female equality not only in his remarks about a marriage grounded in a love born from "freedom of mind" (4 app. XX), but even more strikingly in his account of the "first man" where he presents Eve as "agree[ing] completely" with Adam's nature (4p68s).[74] To suppose that the "human nature" that is everywhere the same was intended to be restricted to biological males is to suppose that Spinoza is more consistent than he actually is. And to suppose that this is a mere misapplication of universalist principles is to downplay the efforts of TP 11/4 to maintain consistency through rationalization.[75]

However, exactly, one tries to square these passages with the rest of Spinoza's philosophy, this much is clear: Spinoza's own analysis is marred by prejudice, leading him to advocate a version of "democracy" that is so exclusionary[76] that

---

[73] Sharp raised a version of this question in her commentary on an earlier draft of this manuscript.
[74] See Sharp 2012.
[75] For a rich and thought-provoking analysis along these lines in response to a formally similar problem, see Allais 2016.
[76] It also excludes others who are not *sui iuris*, including foreigners and servants (TP 11/3).

it does not warrant the designation and certainly does not qualify, *pace* Israel, as radically egalitarian. Fortunately, we can learn from past thinkers without canonizing them. And sometimes we learn most from their missteps. One general lesson to glean from Spinoza's exclusionism is that biases are bound to endure as long the targets of this bias are deprived of a voice. The remedy, by my lights, is clear: more democratization.

8   Salvation, Eternity, and the State

> How is it that we who possess in ourselves such great things are not aware
> of them, that some of us often, and some of us always, fail to actualize these
> capacities ... To grasp what is within us we must turn our perceptive faculties
> inward, focusing their whole attention there. Just as the person who wants to
> hear a cherished sound must neglect all others and keep his ears attuned to the
> approach of the sound he prefers to those he hears about him, so we too must
> here close our senses to all the noises that assail us (if they are not necessary)
> and preserve the perceptive power of the soul pure and ready to attend to
> tones that come from above.
>   – Plotinus, "The Three Primal Hypostases"[1]

We have seen in the preceding chapters that, according to Spinoza, the state
plays an important role in affectively re-orienting its citizens. It does not follow from this, however, that the state contributes to the highest forms of human
liberty: salvation (*salus*) and blessedness (*beatitudo*). It might be that civil
mechanisms and philosophical teachings produce effects on a single scale, but
in wholly different registers (Section 3.2). One might even think that the state
could not contribute to the upper register of human liberty, since this concerns
the perfection of the intellect, or the part of the mind that is eternal, while politics deals only with determinate, durational things, and directly involves only
the imagination, the part of the mind that dies with the body.

I will begin this concluding chapter by further motivating the reasons for
thinking that the state could not contribute to beatitude or salvation (Section 8.1).
I then advance an interpretation of cognitive achievement that enables us to see
how the imagination can contribute to intellectual perfection (Sections 8.2–
8.4) and how the state may facilitate this (Section 8.5). I close by confronting
an unresolved problem that haunts Spinoza's mature philosophy: why does
someone who privileges the eternal order write two, or the better part of two,
political treatises, which are chiefly concerned with things in the diminished
durational or historical order? My proposal is that Spinoza thinks that even
if the historical order is less intelligible and less real than the eternal order,

---

[1] Plotinus 1964, pp. 103–4.

one's determinate existence is the only condition about which it makes sense to care (Section 8.6). While it would be foolhardy to suppose that in a single chapter I could offer a decisive interpretation of all the abstruse matters that are addressed here, I aim to offer a well-grounded and plausible reading that highlights the overall coherence of Spinoza's philosophy.

8.1   Two Challenges to Civic Salvation

First Challenge: The Imagination/Intellect Gap

Near the end of the *Ethics*, Spinoza analyzes the intellectual love of God that arises from *scientia intuitiva*, or the third kind of knowledge, claiming that it is the source of our "salvation, or [*seu*] blessedness, or [*seu*] freedom" (5p36s). Perfecting the intellect in this way yields the greatest satisfaction of mind (*mentis acquiescentia*) (5p27). The tools of the state seem to be poorly suited to contributing to this end. Laws, institutions, political symbols, and so forth, act only on our imagination and our passions, without directly promoting adequate knowledge or salvation. As Spinoza baldly puts it in the TTP, "absolutely no one can be compelled by force or by laws to become blessed [*beatus*]" (TTP 7.90, iii.116). This also accords with his analysis of the function of the rites and ceremonies of Judaism, where he maintains that such outward matters promise only "corporeal advantages," but "contribute nothing to blessedness [*beatitudinem*]" (TP 5.31, iii.76).

Indeed, there seems to be an unbridgeable gap between the imagination and the intellect that precludes the state from contributing to blessedness by acting on the imagination. There are at least three reasons why one might think that ideas of the imagination are fundamentally disconnected from ideas of the intellect: they have distinct origins, follow distinct orders, and take distinct objects. We will consider these points successively. But first, a caveat: "the imagination" and "the intellect" are not faculties. Rather, "the imagination" refers to the first kind of cognition, which includes sensory perception, hearsay, and symbolic association (2p40s2). "The intellect," by contrast, encompasses ideas that arise from second and third kinds of knowledge – ideas that one has insofar as one grasps things adequately (2p40s2; 5p10d). The imagination comprises all, and only, inadequate ideas, while the intellect comprises all, and only, adequate ideas.

According to Spinoza's definitions of inadequate and adequate ideas in 2p11c, the former are in God's infinite intellect insofar as he has the idea of some external thing together with an idea of the individual, while the latter are in God's infinite intellect insofar as he constitutes the essence of the individual mind (2p11c). Inadequate ideas arise only insofar as one is affected by external things (2p25; 2p16) – they have a partially exogenous source. By contrast,

192 Spinoza's Political Psychology

adequate ideas follow from the very nature of the mind – they have a wholly endogenous origin.[2] I will have more to say about this etiological distinction in a moment.

The imagination and the intellect operate according to different principles, resulting in fundamentally different orders of ideas. This view is advanced in the early *Treatise on the Emendation of the Intellect*: "those activities by which imaginations are produced happen according to other laws, wholly different from the laws of the intellect" (TdIE, Section 88; cf. Ep. 37). And Spinoza remains firmly committed to this very distinction in the *Ethics* where he claims that ideas of the imagination follow the "common order of Nature" (2p29s) or "the order and connection of the affections of the human body" (2p18s), according to which one represents things on the basis of happenstance encounters and associations that are specific to one's experiences (Section 1.2). This is distinguished from "the order of the intellect, by which the mind perceives things through their first causes, and which is the same in all men" (2p18s; cf. 2p40s2, 5p10, 5p40s) since it tracks the real conceptual and causal relations between things. While much more would need to be said to make this account of these two orders precise, one thing is clear: one cannot derive adequate ideas from inadequate ideas:

For whatever we understand clearly and distinctly, we understand either through itself, or through something else which is conceived through itself; that is, the ideas which are clear and distinct in us ... cannot follow from mutilated and confused ideas, which (by IIP40S2) are related to the first kind of knowledge; but they can follow from adequate ideas, *or* (by IIP40S2) from the second and third kind of knowledge (5p28d).

There is no inferential connection from the "common order of Nature," the order of the imagination, to the "order of the intellect."

Finally, the objects of the imagination and the objects of the intellect are distinct. The object of the imagination is the *actually existing* human body (2p13) – that is, the body insofar as it has a finite, determinate existence or duration (1p21d; cf. 1p24c; 2D5; 5p23d). Consequently, one imagines things only as long as the body endures, since the imagination is the part of the mind that is destroyed with the destruction of the actually existing body (5p21). However, Spinoza notoriously maintains that there is a part of the mind that exists without the enduring body; this "eternal part of the mind" is the intellect (5p40c; 5p40s). The object of the eternal part of the mind is the "body's essence under a species of eternity" (5p29; cf. 5p22, 5p23d, 5p29, 5p31). I will reinforce this

---

[2] The genealogical distinction between inadequate ideas (imagination) and adequate ideas (intellect) has led many commentators to regard with suspicion Spinoza's claim that we can form adequate ideas of affections of the body (5p4). For, how can something that is exogenous become endogenous? (see Bennett 1984, p. 336).

distinction between the object of the imagination and the object of the intellect when I turn to the second challenge.

On the basis of these three considerations, it would seem that there is a gulf between the imagination and the intellect, such that the state's influence on the imagination could not contribute to the intellectual perfection required for salvation, beatitude, or freedom. So, even if one grants that the state can reorient *ingenia* in the ways described in the previous two chapters, one might doubt whether it could contribute directly to one's salvation.

Second Challenge: Eternalism and the Diminished Reality of Civil Life

The second challenge to the view that the state could contribute to our salvation concerns what I will call Spinoza's Eternalism, by which I mean his privileging of the eternal order of things over the historical or temporal order of things. By privileging the eternal perspective – something like the Boethian *nunc stans* – Spinoza would seem to fit more naturally alongside Platonists and Augustinians, who see the world of corruptible things in time as a mere simulacrum of reality and who take our salvation to lie decidedly beyond the temporal realm, than he does alongside those who prioritize the *saeculum*, the historical order of things, and who emphasize the cultivation of virtue and happiness in the here and now.[3]

This raises a problem for the coherence of Spinoza's mature philosophy. Why would an Eternalist whose goal is salvation spend much of the last decade of his life working on political treatises that are precisely concerned with destructible, ephemeral things in the diminished temporal order? Those who work on Spinoza's metaphysics often attribute to him some version of Eternalism, but offer no explanation as to why he remained so deeply invested in political theory. Conversely, those who work on Spinoza's politics start from a recognition of his concern with determinate existence without satisfactorily explaining how this preoccupation is to be squared with the account of the eternal mind in the concluding part of the *Ethics*. And yet, Spinoza's mature normative thought cannot be made coherent unless we reconcile these two features.

Spinoza quite clearly privileges the eternal to the durational. In a range of texts, Spinoza affirms that to exist finitely, determinately, in time, is to be limited in a way that eternal things are not:

[B]eing finite is really, in part, a negation (1p8s1).

Since being finite is really, in part, a negation, and being infinite is an absolute affirmation of the existence of some nature, it follows from P7 alone that every substance must be infinite (Ep. 50 to Jelles).

---

[3] For a discussion of this dialectic see Pocock 1975.

[T]he limited [*determinatum*] denotes nothing positive, but only the privation of the existence of the same nature which is conceived as limited (Ep. 36 to Hudde).

While even infinite, eternal modes involve some degree of negation, since they too are determined (e.g., 5p40s) and have a certain definition, finite modes also involve a temporal limit: they have only a determinate existence or duration (1p21d).[4] Things that have only a finite and determinate existence have less reality than things that exist eternally.

Indeed, several passages seem to suggest that when we conceive of things as having a spatio-temporally determinate existence, as parts of a larger whole, we conceive of them only abstractly, superficially, and confusedly (1p15s; 2p45s). The contrast between conceiving of things existing in time – the durational or historical perspective – and conceiving of things under an aspect of eternity (*sub specie aeternitatis*), is perhaps most sharply drawn in 5p29s:

> We conceive things as actual in two ways: either insofar as we conceive them to exist in relation to a certain time and place, or insofar as we conceive them to be contained in God and to follow from the necessity of the divine nature. But the things we conceive in this second way as true, *or* real, we conceive under a species of eternity, and their ideas involve the eternal and infinite essence of God (as we have shown in IIP45 and P45S).

It is tempting to read this passage as entailing that the difference between these "orders" is *merely* epistemic[5]: when we conceive of things *sub specie durationis*, we grasp them abstractly and confusedly; but when we conceive of the same things *sub specie aeternitatis,* we grasp them adequately, as they really are. However, the passage itself does not settle whether eternity and duration are *merely* distinct ways of conceiving, or whether they also reflect distinct ways of existing. What is clear, however, is that the perspective of the eternal is privileged over the perspective of the durational.

I want further to propose that the distinction between eternity and duration should be understood as ontological and not merely epistemical. To see why, consider the case of finite things. Finite things depend on God for both their essence *and* their existence, but the essence and the existence of finite things depend on God in different ways, as "a man is the cause of the existence of another man, but not of his essence, for the latter is an eternal truth" (1p17s; 1p24c). God can cause the essence of a finite thing without causing its existence, since existence is not part of a finite thing's essence (1p17s; 1p24; 1p24c; 2a1; Ep. 12; TP 2/2). Simply put, finite things and their essences are not coextensive: the essence of a finite thing is eternal, while its actual existence is not.

---

4   Thanks to Don Garrett, John Grey, and Valtteri Viljanen for pressing this point.
5   Epistemic readings may claim either that our "eternity" is just a being of reason, not an actual form of existence, or that conceiving of things in time is just a confused way of apprehending real (eternal) existence. The former denies the independent existence of eternal essences of singular things; the latter denies the independent existence of durational beings. I reject both readings.

At first blush, this looks like a violation of Spinoza's definition of essence, according to which existing things stand in a one-to-one relation with their essences:

I say that to the essence of any thing belongs that which, being given, the thing is [NS: also] necessarily posited and which, being taken away, the thing is necessarily [NS: also] taken away; or that without which the thing can neither be nor be conceived, and which can neither be nor be conceived without the thing (2D2).

To reconcile the separability of the essence and existence of finite modes with this definition of essence, we must return to the distinction between formal and actual essences (Section 1.1). The former are essences insofar as they are contained in God's attributes, while the latter are these very essences insofar as they are realized in time. While the formal essence of a finite thing does not entail its determinate existence – that is, its existence in time (1p28d) – a thing's *actual* essence, or striving, does. A thing's actual essence stands in a one-to-one relation with its actual existence. And a thing's eternal formal essence stands in a one-to-one relation with its eternal existence.

| Actual essence | ← → | Actual existence |
| Formal essence | ← → | Eternal existence |

The claim that formal essences exist eternally is supported by 2p8c. The proposition itself reads: "The ideas of singular things, or of modes, that do not exist must be comprehended in God's infinite idea in the same way as the formal essences of the singular things, or modes, are contained in God's attributes" (2p8). In the corollary, he makes it clear that when he refers to things that "do not exist," he means things that do not exist *in time*, things that do not *actually* exist in Spinoza's technical sense of having duration[6]:

From this it follows that so long as singular things do not exist, *except insofar as they are comprehended in God's attributes,* their objective being, or ideas, do not exist except insofar as God's infinite idea exists. And when singular things are said to exist, *not only insofar as they are comprehended in God's attributes, but insofar also as they are said to have duration*, their ideas also involve the existence through which they are said to have duration (2p8c – my emphasis).

While 2p8 underscores the distinction between the formal essence and actual existence of a singular thing, 2p8c indicates that a thing's formal essence – and the corresponding divine idea thereof – has its own form of existence. Unlike the *actual* existence of a singular thing, the existence corresponding

---

[6] D. Garrett 2009, p. 287.

to a singular thing's formal essence is eternal. And in 2p45s, Spinoza makes it clear that the eternal existence of singular things "insofar as they are in God" – that is, the (formal) essences of things themselves (cf. 1p24c) – is the privileged form of existence. This form of existence is utterly distinct from existence in time. From the fact that a formal essence of a thing exists eternally, we cannot infer how many or even whether any such modes exist in time (see Ep 12, 1p17s, and 1p8s2).

This dual existence reading is also supported by the discussion of the eternity of the mind in *Ethics* 5. The demonstration of the proposition that "the human mind cannot be absolutely destroyed with the body, but something of it remains which is eternal" (5p23) invokes two forms of existence:

> In God there is necessarily a concept, *or* idea, which expresses the essence of the human body (by P22), an idea, therefore, which is necessarily something that pertains to the essence of the human mind (by IIP13). But we do not attribute to the human mind any duration that can be defined by time, except insofar as it expresses the actual existence of the body, which is explained by duration, and can be defined by time, that is (by IIP8C), we do not attribute duration to it except while the body endures. However, since what is conceived, with a certain eternal necessity, through God's essence itself (by P22) is *nevertheless something*, this *something that pertains to the essence of the mind* will necessarily be eternal (5p23d – my emphasis).

Even when the determinate existence of the body comes to an end, one still exists in some sense because one's formal essence is inscribed in God's attributes.[7] And the corresponding idea of this formal essence in God's intellect is one's eternal mind.

So, while some have represented Spinoza's view of our eternity as a fiction[8] and others have treated it as merely a distinct way of representing determinate existence,[9] I think that the text favors the view that one's eternal essence exists distinctly from one's determinate existence. Formal essences exist eternally in God's attributes, while determinate things exist in time. But while both forms of existence are real, Spinoza is committed to the view that determinately existing things enjoy only a diminished degree of reality.[10] This leaves us with

---

[7] Since God's idea of our formal essence is an "eternal mode of thinking" (5p40s), and since eternal modes of thought are not temporally limited, and so are not finite, I am prepared to agree with Don Garrett's somewhat controversial claim that the eternal part of our mind is an infinite mode (D. Garrett 2009).

[8] See Gatens and Lloyd 1999, p. 33; Lord 2011, p. 44.

[9] See Allison 1975, p. 157; Parchment 2000, p. 378; Klein 2014.

[10] Spinoza is not, as Hegel charged, an acosmist. In several works, including Melamed 2013a, Yitzhak Melamed has built a compelling case for Spinoza's commitment to the reality of modes. This leaves open the possibility that certain core metaphysical commitments cut against the reality of modes so completely that Spinoza *should* have denied their reality. For more on this, see Hübner 2015.

the coherence problem noted above: why would someone who privileges the reality of the eternal order occupy himself to such an extent with political theory, which concerns only the diminished historical order of things?

8.2   Nativism of Adequate Ideas

I will begin to build the case for the civil contribution to blessedness in a counterintuitive fashion, by apparently strengthening the basis for one of the challenges. Specifically, I will uphold the genealogical distinction between adequate and inadequate ideas noted above: the former are innate, while the latter are adventitious. Acknowledging that Spinoza is a nativist about adequate ideas will force us to reconceive of cognitive achievement and intellectual perfection. And the way that I propose that we understand cognitive achievement will enable us to overcome the first challenge delineated above.

The first indication that Spinoza is a nativist comes in the passage in which he first introduces the concepts of adequate and inadequate ideas in 2p11c:

From this it follows that the human mind is a part of the infinite intellect of God. Therefore, when we say that the human mind perceives this or that, we are saying nothing but that God, not insofar as he is infinite, but insofar as he is explained through the nature of the human mind, *or* insofar as he constitutes the essence of the human mind, has this or that idea; and when we say that God has this or that idea, not only insofar as he constitutes the nature of the human mind, but insofar as he also has the idea of another thing together with the human mind, then we say that the human mind perceives the thing only partially, *or* inadequately (2p11c).

Bearing in mind that "God ... insofar as he constitutes the essence of the human mind" is just an oblique way of expressing "the essence of the human mind" (5p23d), we may factor "God's mind" out of this analysis and reformulate the definition of adequacy in something like the following way: ideas are adequate in a mind if and only if they are explained through the nature or essence of that mind alone.[11]

This is precisely what Spinoza maintains in the early propositions of *Ethics* 3. Here, Spinoza claims that one acts, under the attribute of thought, if and only

---

[11] The case for the nativism of adequate ideas has been forcefully advanced recently by Marshall 2008 and 2013. Marshall takes 2p11c as expressing what he calls the "containment" criterion of adequacy: "Idea x as it exists in God's mind is adequate in human mind y, itself a complex idea, iff x as a whole is a part of y" (Marshall 2013, p. 26). Ideas are adequate when they are (entirely) a part of the human mind. While I'm not sure that we should think of adequate ideas as constituent parts of the mind, I am otherwise very sympathetic to Marshall's analysis.

if one has adequate ideas. This turns on his rather technical definitions of adequate causation and action in 3D1 and 3D2:

"I call that cause adequate whose effect can be clearly and distinctly perceived through it. But I call it partial, *or* inadequate, if its effect cannot be understood through it alone" (3D1).

"I say that we act when something happens, in us or outside us, of which we are the adequate cause, that is (by D1), when something in us or outside us *follows from our nature*, which can be clearly and distinctly understood through it alone. On the other hand, I say that we are acted on when something happens in us, or something follows from our nature, of which we are only a partial cause" (3D2 – my emphasis).

These definitions entail that one acts if and only if some effect can be clearly and distinctly perceived through one's nature alone. On the basis of these definitions, Spinoza proceeds to argue in 3p1 that we act (under the attribute of thought) if and only if we have adequate ideas. He invokes the definitions of adequate and inadequate ideas from 2p11c in order to establish that adequate ideas produce effects that can be clearly and distinctly perceived through the nature of one's mind alone, while inadequate ideas do not. This is because, once again, adequate ideas themselves, unlike inadequate ideas, follow from and are perceived through the essence of the mind alone.[12]

This same reasoning lies behind the later claim that "the third kind of knowledge depends on the mind, as on a formal cause, insofar as the mind itself is eternal" (5p31). The third kind of knowledge – which "proceeds from an adequate idea of the formal essence of certain attributes of God to the adequate knowledge of the [NS: formal] essence of things" (2p40s2) – has the eternal essence of the mind as its "adequate, *or* [*sive*] formal, cause" (5p31d), because it consists of adequate ideas, which follow from the essence of the mind alone. The third kind of knowledge, like *all* adequate knowledge, follows from the eternal essence of the mind. Spinoza makes this point explicit in a letter on method to Bouwmeester: "all the clear and distinct perceptions we form can arise only from other clear and distinct perceptions in us, and *cannot have any other cause outside us*. From this it follows that the clear and distinct perceptions we form depend only on our nature" (Ep. 37, 10 June 1666).

The reasoning behind the thesis that adequate ideas are innate can be neatly captured by the following *reductio*:

1. Assume that there are adequate ideas that are not innate in the mind.
2. All ideas are innate or adventitious[13] (Def).
3. Consequently, there are adequate ideas that are adventitious (by 1 and 2).

---

[12] See Marshall 2013, p. 52.
[13] "Adventitious" here simply means arising from some nonnative source.

4. If an idea is adventitious, it must be partially understood through something other than one's own nature (by 1a4).
5. There are adequate ideas that are not conceivable through one's nature alone (by 3 and 4).
6. But this is contrary to the very definition of adequate ideas (2p11c).
∴. All adequate ideas are innate in the mind.

Adequate ideas follow from the nature of the mind alone; they admit of no extrinsic cause or explanation.

But even if one admits that adequate ideas are innate in the sense that they follow from the nature of the mind alone, one might deny that these ideas are always fully actualized in the mind.[14] One might think that just because adequate ideas *can* follow from the nature of the mind alone, this does not mean that they necessarily do. Perhaps adequate ideas are innate in a Leibnizian, dispositional sense: natively sourced, but actualized by experience.

As I see it, this scenario is incompatible with Spinoza's metaphysics, which does not admit non-actualized powers or mere dispositions. If the mind really has sufficient causal power to produce adequate ideas, it *will* produce these ideas unless prevented by some opposing force. As there is nothing internal to the mind that could prevent the production of these adequate ideas, then when we attend to the essence mind alone, these adequate ideas necessary follow. To posit the essence of the mind is to posit those ideas or affections that follow from it.

We can make this same point in a slightly different way. If adequate ideas were only dispositionally innate, something would need to explain the conversion from non-actualized to actualized.[15] That something cannot be extrinsic to one's nature, as that would violate the very definition of adequate ideas as explicable through one's nature alone (see *reductio* above). Nor could it be internal to one's nature, since, once again, when one attends to one's nature alone, one finds all and only those things that are posited by the nature itself.

---

[14] Don Garrett raised this possibility in response to an earlier draft.
[15] In her comments on this section, Karolina Hübner suggested that the transition from non-actualized to actualized might be explained by the logical sequencing of adequate ideas themselves: some adequate ideas follow from others. It is certainly true that there are asymmetric entailment relations to the "order of the intellect" such that some ideas are prior to others; but this does not imply a temporal ordering. If one's nature entails x, and x entails y, when one's nature is posited, x and y will *both* be posited, unless something could block the positing of these entailments. The preventing cause is not, and could not be, internal the nature of the thing; nor can it be external, as that would entail that the possession of an adequate idea would depend on the nature of the thing *and* the absence of external preventing causes, in which case adequate ideas – contrary to their very definition – would not be explicable through the nature of a thing *alone*. Nevertheless, as I shall argue, there is a sense in which external things can prevent the overt expression, though not the existence, of adequate ideas, since they can offset or overpower them.

It seems to me, then, that Spinoza would have to admit that those things that are deducible from, or conceivable through, one's nature alone are posited wherever one's nature is posited.[16] Those ideas that are explicable through the essence of the mind alone are the "innate" affections to which he refers in the appendix to *Ethics* 3 (3 DA, iii.190).

This account does, however, raise a couple of problems. The first is what we might call the *Problem of Ignorance*: how can one fail to know things that are innate to the mind? This problem is intensified by his claim that "he who has adequate ideas, *or* (by P34) who knows a thing truly, must at the same time have an adequate idea, *or* true knowledge, of his knowledge. That is (as is manifest through itself), he must at the same time be certain" (2p43d). If all of one's adequate ideas are already in one's mind, and if one is certain of all of one's adequate ideas, how is it that one can be utterly unaware of so many of these ideas?[17] There is also the *Problem of Acquisition*: if adequate ideas are innate, how is it that we can (adequately) learn new things? The analysis of intellectual perfection in Ethics 5 seems to depend on the capacity to gain new adequate ideas – a capacity that is incompatible with the nativist account proposed above. Spinoza cannot respond to the problems of ignorance and acquisition by relying on a distinction between potentiality and actuality, for the reasons noted above.

Fortunately, though, I think that Spinoza can answer the problems of ignorance and acquisition in one fell swoop, while maintaining that adequate ideas are actual in our minds. To see how, we must investigate some of the opaque claims that Spinoza makes about cognitive achievement in *Ethics* 5.

8.3   Cognitive Achievement

Ethics 5 is shot through with the language of cognitive achievement. Here, Spinoza writes that we can form adequate ideas of affections of the body (5p4), that "the more we understand singular things, the more we understand God" (5p24), and that "the more anyone can achieve in this [third] kind of

---

[16] This fits with the suggestion in the TTP that things that are deduced from one's nature alone are innate: "We have deduced [divine law] from human nature in such a way that we must think that it itself is innate to, and as it were, written in the human mind" (TTP 5.1, iii.69). Since the context does not give us any reason to think that "in such a way" is doing any real qualifying work here, Spinoza seems to take the deduction itself as evidence of nativism.

[17] It is worth noting here that this problem exists in some form – though not to the same extent – for any interpretation, since Spinoza argues that humans have adequate knowledge of God's eternal and infinite essence, even while most people make terribly confused claims about God's nature. Spinoza's cursory explanation in 2p47s – that people "have joined the name *God* to the images of things which they are used to seeing" – does not satisfactorily explain why people seem to be ignorant about an idea that they know that they adequately know.

knowledge, the more he is conscious of himself and of God" (5p31s).[18] To over-come the *Problem of Acquisition* I must show how the language of cognitive achievement is consistent with nativism.

I propose that we take cognitive achievement to consist in the intensification, or potentiation (i.e., power-enhancement), rather than the acquisition of, ade-quate ideas. The importance of the potency or intensity of ideas is stressed in the early propositions of *Ethics* 4, where Spinoza claims that: "imaginations do not disappear through the presence of the true insofar as it is true, but because there occur others, *stronger than them* (*iis fortiores*), which exclude (*secludunt*) the present existence of things we imagine" (4p1s – my emphasis). The striving for understanding is ultimately a striving for the intellect to predominate over the imagination, or for our adequate ideas to overpower or restrain (*coercere*) the passions. It is not enough to *have* adequate ideas; they must be powerful.[19] This explains why large swathes of *Ethics* 4 and 5 are devoted to analyzing the determinants of the intensity of ideas (4p5–4p16; 5p5–5p13).

The view of achievement as potentiation is reflected in several passages in *Ethics* 5, including 5p36s:

[F]or although I have shown generally in Part I that all things (and consequently the human mind also) depend on God both for their essence and their existence, neverthe-less, that demonstration, though legitimate and put beyond all chance of doubt, still does not affect [*afficit*] our mind as much as when this is inferred from the very essence of any singular thing which we say depends on God.

Spinoza's point here is that third kind of knowledge is superior to the second in part because it is more powerful – it "affects the mind" more. To know things in this way is to have a *powerful* intellect, so that adequate ideas and the joy that follows from them affect or engage [*occupare*] the mind more than the passions and the imagination.[20]

Some evidence for the achievement as potentiation or intensification read-ing comes from Spinoza's claims about the eternity of the mind. Near the end of the *Ethics*, Spinoza claims that "the more the mind understands things by the second and third kind of knowledge, the greater part [*maxima pars*] of it remains [after the destruction of the actually existing body]" (5P38d). This is sometimes glossed as the claim that through gaining adequate knowledge we "make our minds more eternal."[21] This way of posing things seems wantonly

[18] See LeBuffe 2010b, p. 376 for an enumeration of further passages.
[19] See, for instance, his claim in the TP that while "everyone is persuaded that Religion teaches each person to love his neighbor as himself...this persuasion has little power against the affects" (TP 1/5). Cf. 4p14–17.
[20] See 5p11, 5p16, 5p20s, 5p39d. In these passages potency is represented in terms of an idea's capacity to "engage the mind" or "flourish" (*viget*) (5p11).
[21] Della Rocca 2008a, p. 258.

202   Spinoza's Political Psychology

paradoxical, as if what is eternal is itself subject to alteration. However, the paradox disappears if we understand enhancing the eternal part of the mind not as a change in eternal ideas themselves, but rather as a change in the relative potency of eternal, adequate ideas vis-à-vis one's actual (determinate) mind.

Consider Spinoza's claim in 5p20s that one who has a mind "of which adequate ideas constitute the greatest part ... may have as many inadequate ideas as [one whose inadequate ideas constitute the greatest part]," but he is "distinguished more," guided more, by his adequate than by his inadequate ideas. The claim that one's mind is "distinguished" [*dignoscatur*] more or "occup[ied]" more (5p20s) by adequate rather than inadequate ideas is a claim not about the relative quantity of these ideas, but rather about their relative intensity.[22]

Later propositions suggest that increasing the power of the eternal part of the mind consists in becoming more conscious of adequate ideas. Spinoza writes: "the more each of us is able to achieve in this [third] kind of knowledge, the more he is conscious of himself and of God" (5p31s). The connection between intellectual capability and consciousness is reinforced a few propositions later:

[W]e must note here that we live in continuous change, and that as we change for the better or worse, we are called happy or unhappy ... he who, like an infant or child, has a body capable of very few things, and very heavily dependent on external causes, has a mind which considered solely in itself is *conscious of almost nothing of itself*, or of God, or of things. On the other hand, he who has a body capable of a great many things, has a mind which considered only in itself *is very much conscious of itself, and of God, and of things* (5p39s – my emphasis).

Don Garrett reads such passages as revealing that "the intellectual life of a human being is a struggle to actualize within that human being's mind, as consciously as possible, as much adequate cognition as possible of the formal essence of his or her body and of other things as they relate to, and are involved in, that formal essence."[23] Eugene Marshall proposes that we understand consciousness in terms of "affectivity": the more affectively powerful ideas are, the more conscious we are of them. While there are differences between Garrett's interpretation of consciousness and Marshall's,[24]

---

[22] Michael LeBuffe claims that bringing it about that a greater part of mind is eternal consists simply in increasing the *proportion* of adequate to inadequate ideas, which can be achieved not, *per impossibile*, by gaining adequate ideas, but by diminishing the number of inadequate ideas (2010b, p. 370). We must be careful here not to understand "proportionality" as a numerical ratio, but rather as ratio of relative power or intensity. LeBuffe affirms this (p. 374), though his initial presentation invites us to think of the ratio as quantitative (p. 371).

[23] D. Garrett 2009, p. 300.

[24] For Marshall's critique of Garrett, see Marshall 2013, pp. 114–17. I'm not entirely persuaded that Marshall's objections pose a problem for Garrett's interpretation, though they do expose its incompleteness. I agree with Garrett, against Marshall, that every idea has a degree of consciousness.

they agree that perfecting one's intellect consists in becoming more conscious of one's adequate ideas and that consciousness is an expression of
ideational potency. I think they are right about this. Intellectual achievement should be understood in terms of becoming more conscious of one's
adequate ideas, which requires the potentiation, or intensification, of
adequate ideas.

This way of understanding cognitive achievement sheds light on certain
otherwise puzzling passages about the eternal part of the mind in the latter
half of *Ethics* 5. For instance, after claiming that "achiev[ing]" the third kind
of knowledge entails becoming more "conscious" of oneself and of God,
Spinoza writes: "although we are already certain that the mind is eternal,
insofar as it conceives things under the species of eternity, nevertheless for
an easier explanation and better understanding of the things we wish to show,
we shall consider it as if it were now beginning to be, and were now beginning to understand things under a species of eternity" (5p31s). Spinoza reinforces this point a couple of propositions later, claiming that the notion that
one's intellectual love of God could "come to be" is a fiction, since this love
is eternal (5p33s). One reason why he might permit "feigning" the generation
of adequate ideas is that this way of speaking captures the experience of cognitive achievement. Adequate ideas are initially so weak that one is hardly
conscious of them at all; as one becomes more conscious of these ideas, they
seem to arise in the mind.[25]

This account yields straightforward resolutions to the *Problem of Ignorance*
and the *Problem of Acquisition*. We can fail to be aware of what we certainly
and adequately know because awareness requires that ideas acquire a certain
intensity or potency. And when one becomes aware of an adequate idea, it feels
as though it has been acquired, despite the fact that the adequate ideas that
follow from our eternal essence neither come nor cease to be.

This reading also helps to explain Spinoza's odd claim that we "feel"
(*sentimus*) that we are eternal (5p23s). We necessarily and innately have an
adequate idea of our eternity, and this idea necessarily affects us with some
degree of joy, "for the mind feels those things that it conceives in understanding no less than those it has in the memory" (5p23s). But one's idea of
eternity is often too muted, too anemic for one to be very consciously aware
of it. Consequently, most people, including many readers of the *Ethics*, find
the suggestion that we feel that we are eternal to be deeply implausible. The
mistake lies in assuming that feelings must be highly conscious. In order for
us to consciously register this knowledge, we must find ways to ramp up the
power of these ideas.

---

[25] See LeBuffe 2010b, p. 380.

8.4   Affective Power and the Network of Ideas

Before exploring what the state can do to potentiate adequate ideas, we must better understand the determinants of ideational power. I have argued elsewhere that the "power of ideas" is an ambiguous concept for Spinoza.[26] It may refer to the *doxastic* or purely affirmative power of an idea or to the *affective* power of an idea, of which the doxastic power is but a part. When Spinoza confronts the extent to which ideas "engage the mind" in *Ethics* 5, he seems to have in mind the affective power of the ideas. As I see it, there are four major categories of determinants of the affective power of ideas: (1) the power of eliciting causes; (2) steadiness of affirmation; (3) purity of valence; and (4) connectivity.[27]

Part of what determines the intensity of an idea is the strength of the eliciting causes (4p5; cf. 5a2). When it comes to passions, the greater the power of the affecting thing, the greater the affect. So, for instance, the more intense a thunderstorm is, the more intense one's affective response will be, *ceteris paribus*. Of course, it is not the overall power of the eliciting cause *tout court* that determines the strength of the affect, but the power in some particular respect implicated in the causal interaction.

Another determinant of affective intensity is the steadiness with which one affirms the things represented. Just as vacillation and unsteadiness constitute doubt (2p44s), steadiness of affirmation constitutes confidence. The more steadily one affirms something, the more confident one is. Steadiness of affirmation varies according to both modal and temporal features of representation. Affects directed toward things that are represented as necessary will be more intense (*intensior*) than affects directed toward things that are represented as merely possible or contingent because the former are firm and unopposed, while the latter involve representations of excluding causes or alternate effects (4p11; 5p6). And the more temporally distant a thing is, the more potentially excluding causes must be posited in order to represent it (4p10). The upshot is that the more steadily one affirms that something will happen, is happening, or will continue to happen, the more powerful one's affective attitude toward it will be.

A third determinant is the purity of affective valence. Ideas of things whose valence is unalloyed (whether negatively or positively) will be more affectively charged than ideas of things toward which we are ambivalent, since

---

26   See J. Steinberg 2018a.
27   Others have carved up the territory somewhat differently. For instance, Ben Ze'ev identifies "six basic intensity variables: (a) the strength of the eliciting event, (b) the event's degree of reality, (c) the event's relevance, (d) our accountability concerning the eliciting event, (e) our readiness for the eliciting event, (f) our deservingness for the eliciting event" (Ben Ze'ev 1999, p. 143). See also Frijda 1999.

ambivalence toward an object, which Spinoza calls a "vacillation of mind" (*fluctuatio animi*) (3p17s), results in the attenuation, or partial neutralization, of the affective power. Such vacillations of mind are a distinct species of unsteadiness of affirmation, "related to the affect as doubt is to the imagination (IIP44S)" (3p17s).

Finally, there is connectivity. In *Ethics* 5, Spinoza claims that an "image or affect [*imago sive affectus*]" will flourish (or be encouraged) to the extent that it is connected with other images or affects (5p11 and 5p13). The more an image or affect is joined to other images or affects, the more likely it is to be aroused, making it a more potent mode of thought.

In light of these four determinants – the power of eliciting cause, the degree of confidence or steadiness of affirmation, the purity of valence, and the connectivity – it is not surprising that Spinoza should conclude that the "love toward God must engage the mind the most" (5p16). We all have an adequate idea of God (2p47), which gives rise to an intellectual love of God (5p32c). This love is in some sense caused by, and directed at, the most powerful thing conceivable (*Power of Eliciting Cause*), a thing that necessarily exists and whose existence, insofar as it is known, admits of no doubt (2p43s) (*Steadiness of Affirmation*). It is entirely pure, "untainted" (*inquinari*) with any forms of sadness or hate (5p18; cf. 5p37) (*Purity of Valence*). And, one's knowledge and love of God is "joined to all affections [JS: or images] of the body" (5p16d) (*Connectivity*).

However, it should be apparent that something is still missing from the preceding analysis, since as a matter of fact this eternal, certain, pure, well-connected love does *not* actually dominate the minds of most people. I take it that when Spinoza claims that the love of God "must engage the mind the most" (5p16), there is a tacit condition built in: this love must engage the mind the most if it is stimulated in the right way. The idea of God is maximally connected, but the *strength* of these connections may be too weak for it to "flourish" [*viget*] (5p11). Here I think we must amend our understanding "connectivity" to encompass both the scope *and strength* of connections.

Spinoza's cognitive therapy provides some support for this reading. In the first half of *Ethics* 5, he claims that "there is no affection of the body of which we cannot form a clear and distinct concept" (5p4) and that we can direct our affects in accordance with the order of the intellect (5p10; 5p20s). These assertions hinge on the premise that particular affections involve common properties, features of bodies that are common to all (2p38) or some subset (2p39) of bodies and which are necessarily adequately understood (2p38). The demonstration for 5p4 reads: "Those things which are common to all can only be conceived adequately (by IIP38) and so (by IIP12 and L2 [II/98]) there is no affection of the body of which we cannot form some clear and distinct concept" (5p4d). While the demonstration is opaque and frustratingly brief, the suggestion is that we can form adequate ideas of any particular affection because particular affections involve common properties.

We get a better understanding of the nature of the relationship between particular affections and common properties, by considering the relationship between ideas of particular affections and the idea of God (2p45–2p47). Spinoza claims that "each idea of each body, or of each singular thing which actually exists necessarily involves an eternal and infinite essence of God" (2p45). From the fact that ideas of affections involve (*involvere*) an eternal essence of God, Spinoza infers that the human mind has (*habere*) an adequate idea of God (2p47 and 2p47d). To see what licenses this inference, we must consider what it means for one idea to involve another for Spinoza. Don Garrett and Alan Gabbey have plausibly suggested that the verb *involvere* should be understood to mean something like "implicate,"[28] as when he claims in 2p16–17 that the idea of an affection of the human body *involves* both the nature of the human body and the nature of the affecting body. We see this also in his treatment of ideas in 2p49, where he writes that "in the mind there is no volition, or affirmation and negation, except that which the idea involves [*involvit*] insofar as it is an idea," explaining in the demonstration that ideas "can neither be nor be conceived" without such affirmation (or negation). X involves Y just in case X can't be conceived without also conceiving of Y – representing X is sufficient for representing Y.[29] This explains the inference from 2p45 to 2p47: one cannot represent any modification of extension (say, a particular triangle) without representing extension as such – the latter is a *sine qua non* of the former. The relationship between particular affections and common properties should be understood in just this way: an affection implicates common properties without which the former could not exist. On this interpretation, when my body is affected in a particular way, as when I taste something unpleasantly sour, I have only a confused understanding of the particular bodily affection and of the sour thing (2p25, 2p27); but this interaction involves an adequate idea of the common properties of body that make this interaction possible.

The thesis that particular affections implicate common properties also underwrites 5p12, which reads: "The images of things are more easily joined to images related to things we understand clearly and distinctly than to other images" (5p12). The main idea here is rather simple, even if it is expressed somewhat obscurely: because the things that we clearly and distinctly understand are common properties,[30] or (relatively) pervasive features of body, they are "related to more things" (5p11) and so are more easily aroused in us than

---

[28] See Gabbey 2008; D. Garrett 2017.
[29] As Don Garrett rightly noted in his comments on this section, implication here should not be confused with the causal entailment. In fact, in most of the cases that Spinoza discusses, it is effects that involve or implicate causes – we reason from the effects to the cause *sine qua non*.
[30] Here he is restricting his analysis to the second kind of knowledge.

other singular bodily affections (5p12d). Singular bodily affections may come to be joined to other singular affections by association (2p18); but many more affections will be joined to common properties by implicative links.[31] This proposition plays a central role in Spinoza's analysis of how we can bring it about that our affections follow the order of the intellect (5p20s; 5p14).

It is crucial to recognize at this point that the extensive connectivity of common properties is not enough to ensure that they are especially powerful. The implicative links between affections and common properties are fixed by the character of the affections themselves. So when Spinoza indicates that we can gain greater control over the affects, he must not mean, *per impossibile*, forging *new* connections between affections and common properties. These relations are invariant. What is alterable, however, is the *relative strength of the connections* between affections and common properties. A swig of sour Kombucha tea can be an occasion for me to attend to my unpleasant experience and how it relates to other associated unpleasant experiences; but it can also be an occasion to attend to the common properties (laws of motion and rest) implicated by this affection. The strength of connections will determine to a large degree which of these ideas most engages the mind.

We may transfer this analysis to one's idea, and love, of God. When Spinoza claims that "the mind can bring it about that all the body's affections, or images of things, are related [*referantur*] to the idea of God" (5p14; 5p16), he must not mean that we can establish links between affections and the idea of God, since such implicative links are already there. Rather, he must mean that one can *strengthen* the connections that necessarily exist between the ideas of particular affections and the idea of God. While the "love [of God] is joined to all the affections of the body" (5p16d), the connection between the idea of these affections and the idea of God is typically too weak to potentiate the love of God to any significant degree. In order to become more conscious of one's (innate) adequate ideas, one must strengthen the connection between them and the inadequate ideas that are frequently stimulated in one's everyday experience. One must make the imagination serve the intellect.

This analysis enables us to see what is mistaken about the putative imagination/intellect gap (Section 8.1). While one cannot derive the content of adequate ideas from the content of inadequate ideas, inadequate ideas are connected to adequate ideas through implicative links, such that the former may prompt the latter.[32] Spinoza's cognitive therapy relies on the connection

---

[31] Margaret Wilson appeals to what I call here "implicative links" in her discussion how inadequate ideas give rise to adequate ideas (M. Wilson 1999, p. 148).

[32] Particular affections (and the ideas of these affections) are tied to other particular affections (and the ideas of these affections) by links of association, while particular affection (and the ideas of these affections) are tied to common properties (and the ideas of these properties) by links of implication.

of inadequate and adequate ideas, as we seek to foster the causes "by which affections [are] related to [*referuntur*] common properties or to God" (5p20s). By strengthening the connection between inadequate and adequate ideas, we potentiate the latter, so that one may switch attentional tracks, as it were, from the order of the imagination to the order of the intellect.

It may be helpful to think of the Spinozistic mind as a network, like an arrangement of bells strung together. Some of these bells are deep, others are shallow; some are well connected, and others are more isolated. On this picture, the idea (and necessary love) of God is the deepest, most well-connected bell – it is poised to make the most resonant sound. And yet it does not because the smaller bells are only weakly joined to this deep, resonant bell. Our inadequate ideas and passions are, by contrast, bound together tightly like jingle bells, making a collective din. Even the biggest, most extensively connected bells will not be heard unless they are tightly connected to the other bells that are ringing. In order to increase the affective power of adequate ideas, we must reconfigure the circuitry of the mind – by which I mean alter the relative strength of connections – so that the "shallow bells" of the imagination stimulate and amplify the "deep bells" of the intellect. The state plays a vital role in structuring this network.

8.5   Politics, the Imagination, and Intellectual Perfection

The idea of preparing the mind so that the imagination conduces to knowledge has a rich and interesting history. Francis Bacon's description of rhetoric as the "moral" art of "contract[ing] a confederacy between the Reason and Imagination against the affections" (cf. Section 5.5) captures this idea.[33] Spinoza provides an account of how creatures like us, who are subject to the passions and driven primarily by the imagination, contract a Baconian confederacy in 5p10s:

The best thing, then, that we can do, so long as we do not have perfect knowledge of our affects, is to conceive a correct principle of living [*ratio vivendi*], or sure maxims of life [*dogmata vitae*], to commit them to memory, and to apply them constantly to the particular cases frequently encountered in life. In this way our imagination will be extensively affected by them, and we shall always have them ready. For example, we have laid it down as a maxim of life (see IVP46 and P46S) that hate is to be conquered by love, or nobility, not by repaying it with hate in return. But in order that we may always have this rule ready when it is needed, we ought to think about and meditate frequently on the common wrongs of men, and how they may be warded off best by nobility. For if we join the image of a wrong to the imagination of this maxim, it will

---

[33] *The Advancement of Learning*, p. 239. For a partial account of "medicine of the mind" tradition in early modern philosophy of which Bacon's view is an example, see Corneau 2011.

always be ready for us (by IIP18) when a wrong is done to us. If we have ready also the principle of our own true advantage, and also of the good which follows from mutual friendship and common society, and keep in mind, moreover, that the highest satisfaction of mind stems from the right principle of living (by IVP52), and that men, like other things, act from the necessity of nature, then the wrong, or the hate usually arising from it, will occupy a very small part of the imagination, and will easily be overcome.

I have argued elsewhere that the "maxims of life" to which he refers in this passage are just the dictates of reason from *Ethics* 4.[34] We "commit [these principles] to memory" by joining images that are frequently elicited to representations of adequate ideas, reflecting on the proper application of these maxims in everyday encounters, thereby strengthening the connections between inadequate and adequate ideas.[35] Such techniques have their roots in the *ars memoriae* tradition, in which the imagination is trained to facilitate the uptake of rational principles through meditative conditioning and the distillation of rational teachings to memorable "emblems."[36] Spinoza is acutely aware of the role of memory in promoting virtue, having acknowledged that "we can do nothing from a *decision of the Mind* unless we recollect it" (3p2s – my emphasis). Through meditation and memorialization, the intellect colonizes the imagination, as it were, exploiting the resources of the latter in order to expand its dominion. When the metaphorical deep bells are tightly linked to the shallow bells, the latter transmit some of their intensity to the former.

But however effective such techniques are, their scope of efficacy will necessarily be confined, since they will only be deployed by those who already consciously apprehend rational truths and engage in metacognitive reflection

---

[34] J. Steinberg 2014.

[35] In a letter to Johannes Bouwmeester, Spinoza describes a "method which would enable us to proceed, without either obstruction or weariness, in thinking about the most excellent things" (Ep. 37). Here he claims that the successful implementation, "require[s] uninterrupted meditation [*assiduam meditationem*], and a constant mind and purpose. To acquire these it is necessary above all to decide upon a definite way and principle of living [*certum vivendi modum et rationem statuere*], and to prescribe a definite end for oneself" (Ep. 37). One can see connections here to the Stoic psychotherapeutic tradition. See for instance, Seneca 1917, Epistle 95, Section 4; Epistle 95, 36–40; Epistle 94, Section 26. This Stoic tradition also informed Descartes's views. See his letter to Elisabeth from September 15, 1645: "[H]abituation is also required for being always disposed to judge well. For since we cannot always be attentive to the same thing – even though we have been convinced of some truth by reason of some clear and evident perceptions – we will be able to be turned, afterward, to believing false appearances, if we do not, through a long and frequent meditation, imprint it sufficiently in our mind so that it turns into habit" (AT IV, CSMK, pp. 295–6; cf. *Passions of the Soul* in CSM I, pp. 403–4; AT XI, CSM I, pp. 487–8).

[36] For accounts of emblematizing in the ancient rhetorical tradition, see Cicero 1942, pp. 469–71. Versions of these techniques persisted into the medieval period [Aquinas, *Aristotelis libros De sensu et sensato, De memoria et reminiscentia commentarium*, ed, R.M. Spiazzi (Taurini: Marietti, 1949), p. 93; cited in Yates 1966, p. 71] and late-Renaissance and early-modern periods: Guicciardini 1965; Bacon's *The Advancement of Learning*, in *MW*, pp. 230 and 238. See Carruthers 2008.

on the sources of their own impotence. Such self-help is useful only for those who are on the road to virtue. If efforts to strengthen the confederacy between reason and the imagination are to have broader reach, they must target structural conditions, shaping the social environment in ways that promote better general habits of thought. This is the promise of Spinoza's political philosophy. The state can restructure social conditions and enable epistemic capacities. Much of what we've considered in the last two chapters under the guise of *ingenia*-reform may be cast in such epistemic terms.

Perhaps the most significant way in which the state can contribute to the intellectual perfection is by protecting against or dismantling the institutions that promote superstition and persecution. By identifying and countering the socio-psychological roots of harmful and mutually reinforcing clusters of passions and confused ideas, a well-structured state helps its citizens disengage these patterns of thought. In place of pride, envy and fear, a good state promotes humility, tolerance, and *securitas*. To see that this constitutes epistemic progress we must bear in mind that cognitive achievement consists in the potentiation of adequate ideas and the etiolation of networks of inadequate ideas. Antisocial affects like pride and fear are "obstacles to knowledge" in part because they keep us fixed to confused and enervating ideas. By contrast, one who is led by what Spinoza calls "true Humility" in the *Short Treatise,* is said to be on "the true stairway on which we climb to our highest salvation" (*KV* 2.8.9, i.69). And even in the *Ethics*, where he insists that "humility is not a virtue" and that it "does not arise from reason" (4p53),[37] Spinoza claims that "those who are subject to [humility] can be guided far more easily than others, *so that in the end they may live from the guidance of reason, that is, may be free and enjoy the life of the blessed*" (4p54s – my emphasis). There is a straightforward explanation for this: people who are humbler recognize the limits of their own minds and are less fixed in their incapacitating ways than the proud; they are in turn more capable of attending to the "deep bells" of the intellect.

When people are protected from persecution and accorded relatively equal standing, fear and envy give way to *securitas*, which is fostered by toleration, a civil religion, and democratic institutions. *Securitas*, as a stable form of hope, is itself an indicator of intellectual empowerment. It signifies the diminution of fear and superstition, and, as a form of joy, it tracks the enhancement of our power of thinking. Spinoza adverts to this in the demonstration to 4p59:

Insofar as joy is good, it agrees with reason (for it consists in this, that a man's power of acting is increased or aided), and is not a passion except insofar as the man's power of acting is not increased to the point where he conceives himself and his actions adequately. So if a man affected with Joy were led to such a great perfection that he

---

[37] Soyarslan (forthcoming).

conceived himself and his actions adequately, he would be capable – indeed more capable – of the same actions to which he is now determined from affects which are passions (4p59dem).

As joy increases, so does one's power of acting, or power of thinking. Rather than taking this to imply that one's emotions determine one's intellectual capacities, as if a boost of serotonin could induce knowledge, we should see it as a claim about the epistemic side of the affects: as one's power of thinking increases, one experiences this transition as joy. The stable joy of *securitas* (Section 4.3), which arises only when the sources of superstition are diminished and one has gained a sense of trust in the civic order, is a sign that one's epistemic powers have been enhanced. One cannot neatly separate the affective from the epistemic. One's affective condition betrays one's epistemic condition; so, a state can effectuate salutary *ingenia* reform only if it enhances people's epistemic capacities.

Furthermore, we may recall that Spinoza indicates that collective and individual epistemic capacities are enhanced in a well-functioning state (Section 7.3). Participation in deliberative bodies "sharpens wits" (TP 9/14) by requiring that participants justify their views to those with whom they may not agree and by exposing participants to a range of alternative views. And governmental transparency (TP 7/29) facilitates the dissemination of information, such that individuals can make more informed judgments. In these ways, the state creates propitious conditions for knowledge and security (Section 7.3).[38]

One particular area of knowledge is facilitated by a good state, namely, how one conceives of one's relationship to others. As we become more secure and more powerful through our engagement with others, adversarial and competitive stances give way to a more cooperative attitude whereby we recognize the extent to which our power and welfare is bound up with the power and welfare of others and with the success of the commonwealth as a whole. While the extent to which citizens in even the best state grasp this truth as an adequate idea may be quite limited, there is no doubt that the more the state can foster an ethos of fraternity – supported by the minimal moral religion whose central dictate is to love one's neighbor – the more it promotes agreement (*convenientia*) between citizens (see TP 2/13; TP 2/15; 4p18s),[39] who can affirm that man is a God to man (4p35s).

The preceding analysis enables us to cast affectability in a new light. We don't become wise by rendering ourselves insensate; the capacity to be affected plays a critical role in intellectual perfection. There are several indications that Spinoza recognizes the importance of having a lithe imagination in the *Ethics*.

---

[38] See James 2011.
[39] See J. Steinberg (forthcoming).

For instance, excessive forms of *titillatio* incapacitate in part because they pre-occupy and ossify the mind: "The power of this affect can be so great that it surpasses the other actions of the body (by P6), remains stubbornly fixed in the body, and so prevents the body from being capable of being affected in a great many other ways" (4p43d). He proceeds to treat such fixedness as a form of madness (4p44s). But perhaps the most striking claim about affectability comes a few propositions earlier: "Whatever so disposes the human body *that* it can be affected in a great many ways, or [*vel*] renders it capable of affecting external bodies in a great many ways, is useful to man" (4p38; cf. 2p14 and 2p14d). The capacity to be affected can, when properly tempered, enhance one's capacity to affect, to act.

This can be illustrated again through the bells analogy. While the shallow bells of the imagination can be, and often are, the source of auditory interference, they can also enhance the intensity of the deep bells when they are joined to the latter so tightly that they communicate their force. What we want, then, is a supple and expansive imagination that is harnessed to serve the intellect, potentiating and thereby rendering conscious one's adequate ideas.[40]

With this we have dispatched the first challenge to the thesis that the state can contribute to the intellectual perfection of its citizens. While in the previous section we saw why that it is a mistake to suppose that there is an unbridgeable gap between the imagination and the intellect, in this section we see more specifically how, by reorienting the *ingenia* of its subjects, the state can strengthen the confederacy between the imagination and the intellect.

8.6   Salvation and Eternity

This leaves us to confront the second problem with which we began: why would an Eternalist, who affirms the ontological primacy of the eternal order of things, dedicate so much attention to politics, which is concerned only with determinate, corruptible things? Even if the state can contribute to the health and security of determinate individuals in the *saeculum*, it can do nothing to contribute to one's eternal salvation.

The first point that I want to make in response to this challenge is that what holds of Spinoza's political philosophy also holds of his moral philosophy: it too is focused on the diminished historical order of things. To see this, we must distinguish between two senses of salvation and eternity of the mind in *Ethics* 5.[41] On the one hand, the mind is eternal insofar as there is an idea in God that "expresses the essence of this or that human body, under a species of eternity"

---

[40] For an account of the importance of affectability toward which I am broadly sympathetic, see Sharp 2011, p. 98.

[41] Nadler 2002b.

(5p22). The mind exists eternally as an idea of one's formal essence, from which the knowledge and intellectual love of God follows (see 5p31–5p33). This is not unique to humans: there is an idea in God of the essence of all things. Consequently, in this sense, all things know and love God eternally. Martha Kneale has dubbed this the doctrine of universal salvation.[42]

However, it is misleading to relate this form of salvation to determinate things. It is not really me *qua* determinate thing that exists eternally. As the dual existence reading above makes clear, the existence of one's essence in the attributes of God is a thing apart from the one's determinate existence. The eternal existence of one's (formal) essence is an utterly impersonal form of immortality.[43] Moreover, even setting aside the concerns about identity, it is evident that, *qua* determinate being, I can do nothing to alter this eternal salvation. There is no bridge from here to eternity.[44]

This remark is liable to generate confusion, since Spinoza allows that determinately existing things have a "part" of the mind that is eternal, which suggests that in some sense such things already straddle the durational/eternal divide.[45] This isn't quite right, though. In fact, the eternal part of the human mind is just the essence of the mind and the ideas, or modes, that necessarily follow from it – that is, one's adequate, innate ideas (Section 8.2). The essence of the mind and all of its adequate ideas are, as we've said, eternal modes in God's infinite intellect (5p40s). This essence is realized in time when a thing with this particular structure is brought about by a series of finite, determinate causes. In this case, the essence of the mind and its innate properties/ideas are manifest temporally, but this does not make the essence itself temporal. We might think of the relationship between an essence and its temporal realization as analogous to the relationship between a song and its performance. The performance of a song is temporally indexed; but the song itself is not bound by the duration of its performance. So too the actual existence of this essence and its properties are temporally indexed; but the essence itself is not bound in this way. While the content of my adequate ideas – the eternal properties and relations that I grasp – is the same as the content of the eternal modes in God's infinite intellect, my ideas are durational manifestations of these eternal ideas.

When Spinoza writes of the enhancing the eternal part of the mind, he is addressing determinately existing beings, who "live in continuous change" (5p39s). Only determinate things have variable powers of acting, and they

---

[42] Kneale 1969, p. 240.

[43] Steven Nadler stresses this in several publications: Nadler 2002a, pp. 110, 124–5; 2002b, pp. 226–8; 2005.

[44] For a compelling account of why eternal modes (*qua* eternal modes) can't interact with determinate modes (*qua* determinate modes) see Grey 2014. My interpretation is compatible with Grey's analysis, since it is not eternal modes *qua* eternal modes that have determinate effects.

[45] John Grey raised this worry in his comments on this chapter.

214 Spinoza's Political Psychology

alone can undergo a transition to a greater state of perfection or power. What it means, then, to enhance the eternal part of one's mind is just to potentiate the (adequate) ideas that follow from one's essence. "Gaining eternity" and "achieving salvation" are just ways of describing cognitive achievement or intellectual perfection described above (Section 8.3). As we come to know things more adequately, we more fully realize the power of our essence, and we grasp things more as God does, without relation to time.[46] We "participate" more in eternity just in the sense that we more fully realize our essence, apprehending things *sub specie aeternitatis*. But the benefits accrued through such participation belong entirely to determinately existing beings; whatever salvation or "enhanced eternity" one achieves in this lifetime expires along with one's determinate existence.[47]

On this reading, in the *Ethics*, no less than in the political treatises, Spinoza is concerned with the welfare of things in the *saeculum*. All of these works are guides to the salvation (*salus*), beatitude (*beatus*), and freedom (*libertas*) of determinate things. They promote intellectual perfection and empowerment *in this life*. So, when Spinoza claims that the *salus populi* is the highest law of the state (TTP 16.34, iii.195; TTP 19.24, iii.232; TP 7/5), he is at once calling to mind the republican resonances of this phrase[48] while trading on the ambiguity of "*salus*," which can mean not only health or safety, but also salvation. This was part of what outraged theologians of his time, like Regnerus van Mansvelt, a Cartesian professor at Utrecht, who declared:

Most intolerable of all is his final conclusion: "the good of the people is the highest law to which all laws both human and divine should be adapted" [*salute populi summam esse legem, cui omnes tan humane quam divinae accommodari debent*] ... the people ought [to] seek their salvation only in God and the observance of the divine laws, and all their human laws should be directed only to that goal whereby such observance should be promoted more and more in their lands and, finally, eternal salvation obtained by divine grace through Christ.[49]

What rankled van Mansvelt was precisely the suggestion that ethical or spiritual welfare falls within the bailiwick of politics.

In this respect, Spinoza sides decisively with civic humanists who emphasized the achievement of virtue and happiness in the *saeculum*, opposing

---

[46] See Nadler 2002a, p. 122; D. Garrett 2009, p. 301; Garber 2005, p. 108.
[47] Once again, I am in agreement with Nadler, who writes: "the acquisition of true and adequate ideas is beneficial to a person in this lifetime" (Nadler 2002a, p. 121). See also Genevieve Lloyd "On my interpretation, Spinoza's eternity of the mind is entirely a state which is to be attained during life" (Lloyd 1986, p. 214) and Étienne Balibar "Eternity is 'part of our actual existence' not some 'Future or a Promised Land'" (Balibar 1997, p. 35).
[48] James 2012, pp. 236–7. See also Curley's editor's notes (p.289n16).
[49] Cited in Israel 2010b, p. 88.

Eternalists who conceived of salvation as a reward that lies beyond the historical order.[50] Steven Nadler has proposed that we see the concluding chapters of the *Ethics* as an important contribution to Spinoza's theologico-political project precisely because it liberates the reader from worrying about the afterlife: "without a belief in [personal] immortality, we can focus on our happiness and well-being in this life."[51] I'm not convinced that Spinoza's primary intent in these passages is to demonstrate that there is no meaningful sense of personal immortality. If this were his main aim, why include all of this potentially misleading material about the eternity of the mind? Nevertheless, I think Nadler is right that these passages serve Spinoza's secular, republican ends, as they lead one to concern oneself with what can be achieved in this life. This helps to explain Spinoza's rather oddly placed admission in the penultimate proposition of the work: "Even if we did not know that our mind is eternal, we would still regard as of the first importance morality, religion, and absolutely all the things we have shown (in Part IV) to be related to tenacity and nobility" (5p41). We don't need a belief in the afterlife to underwrite the value of building strong moral communities in this life.

As for how we are to reconcile Spinoza's preoccupation with the well-being of determinate, historically situated beings with his brand of Eternalism, my proposal is simple: Spinoza believed in the ontological primacy of the eternal order of things and the ethical primacy of determinate things. The only salvation worthy of one's attention is the salvation that consists in the intellectual perfection, or *ingenia* reorientation, of determinate beings; and, as we've seen, this is an end to which the state can profoundly contribute. So, even if one's determinate existence has diminished reality, it is the only condition about which it makes sense to care.

Conclusion

With this, the case for seeing Spinoza's politics as an extension of his ethics is now complete. Despite the reasons that we explored in Chapter 3 for thinking that these domains are discontinuous, I have now shown that by promoting peace and *securitas* through the advancement of free, democratic institutions that limit the power of the clergy and assure relative equality, the state contributes to the *salus populi*. And I have argued that this civic condition is no less transcendental or no more secular than the blessedness promised by the *Ethics*.

---

[50] The supposition that one could achieve happiness in one's lifetime was declared heretical in the Condemnations of 1277. And it was opposed by "Eternalists" in Spinoza's time. See, for instance, Malebranche's claim that "Complete felicity must not be hoped for in this life, because on earth we must not lay claim to infallibility" (Malebranche 1997, 1.1, p. 1).

[51] Nadler 2005, p. 216.

Admittedly, there are limits to the civil contribution to intellectual/ethical perfection. The state cannot substantially facilitate the fullest expression of salvation or blessedness, which consists in the intellectual love of God that springs from the third kind of knowledge (5p36s). Salvation is, after all, "as difficult as [it is] rare" (5p42s). This highest expression of salvation is beyond the reach of the state.[52]

Still, now that we see the vital role that civic institutions and laws play in shaping and reforming of *ingenia*, we can fully appreciate the reasoning behind the bold assertion in TP 5/2–5/3 that the virtue and vice of citizens are primarily a function of state organization (Section 1.3). Character grows out of sociopolitical conditions. Savvy, adaptive, and affectively attuned states can adopt institutions and enact laws that promote virtue and empowerment. Conceiving of the two political treatises as playing complementary roles in the ethical project of *ingenia*-formation reveals the depth of Spinoza's psychological insights and the originality of his politics, which shares methodological roots with the rhetorical approach of Renaissance humanists, but is tied to a distinctly modern metaphysical psychology and a robust, naturalistic ideal of moral perfectionism. It also reveals the coherence of Spinoza's philosophy, as the political works flesh out Spinoza's vision of human liberation, exposing how stunted the account of the *Ethics* is when read in isolation from the political works. Spinoza advances a rich and astute analysis of civil life that – while not without flaws and outmoded commitments – is in many respects well-suited to engage with contemporary political issues and to inform contemporary nonideal theories of governance.

Unfortunately, Spinoza's political thought has yet to receive its due in Anglophone philosophy, where he is still regarded by and large as a Hobbesian. There is reason to hope, though, that as his general profile continues to wax, his political works will garner more attention. When Spinoza finally emerges from out of Hobbes's shadow, he will reveal himself to be a formidable, original, and prescient political thinker supremely worthy of our attention.

---

[52] Nevertheless, the TTP points toward a broader vision of blessedness and salvation than what one finds in the *Ethics*, Spinoza allows that "true salvation" (*vera salus*), "blessedness" (*beatitudo*) and "peace of mind" (*acquiescentia mentis*) (TTP 7.68, iii.111) are available to all insofar as they can apprehend the clear, simple truths taught by Scripture.

References

Akkerman, Fokke. 1985. "Le caractère rhétorique du Traitè théologico-politique," *Les cahiers de Fontenay*, 36–8: 381–90.

Alberti, Leon Battista. 1969. *The Family in Renaissance Florence*. Translated by Renée Neu Watkins. Columbia: University of South Carolina.

1987. *Dinner Pieces*. Translated by David Marsh. Binghamton, NY: Medieval and Renaissance Texts.

Allais, Lucy. 2016. "Kant's Racism," *Philosophical Papers* 1–2: 1–36.

Allison, Henry. 1975. *Benedict de Spinoza*. Boston, MA: Twayne.

Ambedkar, B. R. 1988. "What Path to Salvation?" Speech delivered to the Bombay Presidency Mahar Conference, 31 May 1936, Bombay. Translated by Vasant W. Moon. Edited by Frances W. Pritchett. Available at: www.columbia.edu/itc/mealac/pritchett/00ambedkar/txt_ambedkar_salvation.html (Accessed on February 13, 2018).

Anderson, Elizabeth. 2006. "The Epistemology of Democracy," *Episteme* 3: 9–23.

2010. *The Imperative of Integration*. Princeton, NJ: Princeton University Press.

Appiah, Kwame Anthony. 1996. "Race, Culture, and Identity: Misunderstood Connections," in *Color Conscious: The Political Morality of Race*, Kwame Anthony Appiah and Amy Gutmann (eds.). Princeton, NJ: Princeton University Press.

Aquinas, Thomas. 2008. *Political Writings*. Edited and translated by R. W. Dyson. Cambridge: Cambridge University Press.

Armstrong, Aurelia. 2009a. "Natural and Unnatural Communities: Spinoza Beyond Hobbes," *British Journal for the History of Philosophy* 17(2): 279–305.

2009b. "Autonomy and the Relational Individual: Spinoza and Feminism," in *Rereading in the Canon: Feminist Interpretations of Benedict de Spinoza*, Moira Gatens (ed.). University Park, PA: The Pennsylvania State University Press.

Austin, J. L. 1975. *How to Do Things with Words*. Cambridge, MA: Harvard University Press.

Balibar, Étienne. 1989. "Spinoza: The Anti-Orwell: The Fear of the Masses." *Rethinking Marxism: A Journal of Economics, Culture, and Society* 2(3): 104–39.

1997. *From Individuality to Transindividuality*. Delft: Eburon.

1998. *Spinoza and Politics*. Translated by Peter Snowdon. London: Verso.

2014. "Preface," in Louis Althusser, *On the Reproduction of Capitalism*. London: Verso.

Barbone, Steven and Lee Rice. 2000. "Introduction and Notes to Spinoza's *Political Treatise*." Translated by Samuel Shirley. Indianapolis, IN: Hackett.

Barry, Brian. 1965. *Political Argument*. Berkeley, CA: University of California Press.

Belaief, Gail. 1971. *Spinoza's Philosophy of Law*. The Hague: Mouton.

Ben Ze'ev, Aaron. 1999. "Emotions and Change: A Spinozistic Account," in *Desire and Affect: Spinoza as Psychologist*, Yirmiyahu Yovel (ed.). New York: Little Room Press, 139–54.

Bennett, Jonathan. 1984. *A Study of Spinoza's Ethics*. Indianapolis, IN: Hackett.

Berlin, Isaiah. 1993. "A Reply to David West," *Political Studies* 41: 297–8.

Blits, Jan. 1989. "Hobbesian Fear," *Political Theory* 17(3): 417–31.

Blom, Hans. 1993. "The Moral and Political Philosophy of Spinoza," in *The Renaissance and Seventeenth Century Rationalism*, G. H. R. Parkinson (ed.). London and New York: Routledge, 313–48.

    1995. *Causality and Morality in Politics: The Rise of Naturalism in Dutch Seventeenth-Century Political Thought*. Utrecht: Universiteit Utrecht.

Blom, Hans and Lauren Winkel (eds.). 2004. *Grotius and the Stoa*. Assen: Royal Van Gorcum.

Bonadeo, Alfredo. 1969. "The Role of the 'Grandi' in the Political World of Machiavelli," *Studies in the Renaissance* 16: 9–30.

Brennan, Geoffrey and Philip Pettit. 2005. "The Feasibility Issue," in *The Oxford Handbook of Contemporary Philosophy*, Frank Jackson and Michael Smith (eds.). Oxford: Oxford University Press, 258–79.

Brooke, Christopher. 2012. *Philosophical Pride*. Princeton, NJ: Princeton University Press.

Butterfield, Herbert. 1962. *The Statecraft of Machiavelli*. New York: Collier Books.

Cameron, Evan. 2010. *Enchanted Europe: Superstition, Reason and Religion, 1250–1750*. Oxford: Oxford University Press.

Carriero, John. 2005. "Spinoza on Final Causality," *Oxford Studies in Early Modern Philosophy* 2: 105–47.

Carruthers, Mary. 2008. *The Book of Memory: A Study of Memory in Medieval Culture*, 2nd Edition. Cambridge: Cambridge University Press.

Cassirer, Ernst. 1963. *The Individual and the Cosmos in Renaissance Philosophy*. Translated by Mario Domandi. New York: Harper Torchbooks.

Charron, Pierre. 1971. *Of Wisdom [De la Sagesse]*. Amsterdam: Da Capo Press.

Cicero. 1942. *De Oratore*, vol. I. Translated by E. W. Sutton and H. Rackham. Cambridge, MA: Harvard University Press.

    1991. *On Duties*. Translated by M. T. Griffin and E. M. Atkins. Cambridge: Cambridge University Press.

Cohen, Joshua. 1986. "An Epistemic Conception of Democracy," *Ethics* 97: 26–38.

    1989. "Deliberation and Democratic Legitimacy," in *The Good Polity*, A. Hamline and P. Pettit (eds.). Oxford: Blackwell, 17–34.

Collins, Jeffrey. 2005. *The Allegiance of Thomas Hobbes*. Oxford: Oxford University Press.

Coogan, Robert. 1969. "Petrarch and More's Concept of Fortune," *Italica* 46(2): 167–75.

Cooper, Julie. 2013. *Secular Powers*. Chicago: University of Chicago Press.

    2017. "Reevaluating Spinoza's Legacy for Jewish Political Thought," *The Journal of Politics* 79(2): 473–84.

Copenhaver, Brian P. and Charles B. Schmitt. 1992. *A History of Western Philosophy, Vol. 3: Renaissance Philosophy*. Oxford: Oxford University Press.

Corneau, Sorana. 2011. *Regimens of the Mind*. Chicago: University of Chicago Press.

Cox, Virginia. 2010. "Rhetoric and Ethics in Machiavelli," in *The Cambridge Companion to Machiavelli*, John M. Najemy (ed.). Cambridge: Cambridge University Press, 173–89.

Crick, Bernard. 2003. *"Introduction" to Machiavelli, The Discourses*. London: Penguin.

Curley, Edwin. 1990a. *"Homo Audax.* Leibniz, Oldenburg and the TTP," *Studia Leibnitiana* 27: 277–312.

1990b. "Notes on a Neglected Masterpiece [II]: Spinoza's *Theological–Political Treatise* as a Prolegomenon to the *Ethics*," in *Central Themes in Early Modern Philosophy*, J. A. Cover and M. Kulstad (eds.). Indianapolis, IN: Hackett.

1991. "The State of Nature and Its Law in Hobbes and Spinoza," *Philosophical Topics* 19(1): 97–117.

1992. "'I Durst Not Write So Boldly' or, How to Read Hobbes' *Theological–Political Treatise*," in *Hobbes e Spinoza*, Daniela Bostrenghi (ed.). Napoli: Bibliopolis, 497–593.

1995. "Samuel Pufendorf (1632–1694) as a Critic of Spinoza," in *L'hérésie Spinoziste. La discussion sur le Tractatus Theologico-Politicus, 1670–1677, et la réception immédiate du Spinozisme*, P. Cristofolini (ed.). Amsterdam: APA-Holland University Press, 89–96.

1996. "Kissinger, Spinoza, and Genghis Khan," in *Cambridge Companion to Spinoza*, Don Garrett (ed.). Cambridge: Cambridge University Press, 315–42.

Darwall, Stephen. 2012. "Grotius at the Creation of Modern Moral Philosophy," *Archiv Für Geschichte Der Philosophie* 94(3): 296–325.

Davidson, Donald. 1980. "How is Weakness of Will Possible?" in *Essays on Actions and Events*. Oxford: Oxford University Press.

De Dijn, Herman. 2004. *"Ethics* IV: The Ladder, Not the Top," in *Spinoza on Reason and the Free Man*, Yirmiyahu Yovel and Gideon Segal (eds.). New York: Little Room Press, 37–53.

De la Boétie, Étienne. 1942. *The Discourse of Voluntary Servitude*. Translated by Harry Kurz. Indianapolis, IN. http://oll.libertyfund.org/titles/boetie-the-discourse-of-voluntary -servitude. Available at: http://oll.libertyfund.org/titles/2250#Boetie_Discourse1520_9 (Accessed on February 13, 2018).

Debrabander, Firmin. 2007. *Spinoza and the Stoics: Power, Politics and the Passions*. London: Continuum.

Del Lucchese, Filippo. 2009. *Conflict, Power, and Multitude in Machiavelli and Spinoza: Tumult and Indignation*. London and New York: Continuum.

Della Rocca, Michael. 1996a. *Representation and the Mind–Body Problem in Spinoza*. Oxford: Oxford University Press.

1996b. "Spinoza's Metaphysical Psychology," in *The Cambridge Companion to Spinoza*, Don Garrett (ed.). Cambridge: Cambridge University Press, 192–266.

1998. (with Robert Sleigh and Vere Chappel). "Determinism and Human Freedom," in *The Cambridge History of Seventeenth-Century Philosophy*, Michael Ayers and Daniel Garber (eds.). Cambridge: Cambridge University Press, 1195–270.

2008a. *Spinoza*. New York: Routledge.

2008b. "Rationalism Run Amok," in *Interpreting Spinoza: Critical Essays*, C. Huenemann (ed.). Cambridge: Cambridge University Press, 2008.

Den Uyl, Douglas. 1983. *Power, State and Freedom: An Interpretation of Spinoza's Political Philosophy*. Assen, The Netherlands: Van Gorcum and Company.

Douglas, Alexander X. 2015. *Spinoza and Dutch Cartesianism: Philosophy and Theology*. Oxford: Oxford University Press.

Du Vair, Guillaume. 1990. "The Moral Philosophy of the Stoics," in J. B. Schneewind (ed.), *Moral Philosophy from Montaigne to Kant*. Cambridge: Cambridge University Press.

Dunn, John. 1968. "The Identity of the History of Ideas," *The Journal of the Royal Institute of Philosophy* 43: 85–104.

Elster, Jon. 1997. "The Market and the Forum: Three Varieties of Political Theory," in *Deliberative Democracy: Essays on Reason and Politics*, James Bohman and William Rehg (eds.). Cambridge, MA: The MIT Press.

Estlund, David. 1997. "Beyond Fairness and Deliberation: The Epistemic Dimension of Democratic Authority," in *Deliberative Democracy: Essays on Reason and Politics*, James Bohman and William Rehg (eds.). Cambridge, MA: The MIT Press.

Feuer, Lewis. 1958. *Spinoza and the Rise of Liberalism*. Boston, MA: Beacon Press.

Flanagan, Owen. 1993. *Varieties of Moral Personality*. Cambridge, MA: Harvard University Press.

Fontana, Biancamaria. 2008. *Montaigne's Politics: Authority and Governance in the Essais*. Princeton, NJ: Princeton University Press.

Frankena, William K. 1963. *Ethics*. Englewood Cliffs, NJ: Prentice-Hall.

Frankfurt, Harry. 1998. "Coercion and Moral Responsibility," in Frankfurt, *The Importance of What We Care About*. Cambridge: Cambridge University Press.

Franklin, Julian. 1991. "Sovereignty and the Mixed Constitution: Bodin and His Critics," in *The Cambridge History of Political Thought 1450–1700*, J. H. Burns (ed.). Cambridge: Cambridge University Press, 298–328.

Freudenthal, Jakob. 1899. *Die Lebensgeschichte Spinoza's in Quellenschriften, Urkunden and Nichtamtlichen Nachrichten*. Leipzig: Verlag Von Veit.

Fricker, Miranda. 2014. "What's the Point of Blame? A Paradigm Based Explanation," *Nous* 50(1): 165–83.

Frijda, Nico. 1999. "Spinoza and Current Theory of Emotion," in *Desire and Affect: Spinoza as Psychologist*, Yirmiyahu Yovel (ed.). New York: Little Room Press, 235–61.

Gabbey, Alan. 2008. "Spinoza, Infinite Modes, and the Infinite Mood," *Studia Spinozana* 16: 41–65.

Garber, Daniel. 2005. "'A Free Man Thinks of Nothing Less Than Death': Spinoza on the Eternity of the Mind," in *Early Modern Philosophy: Mind, Matter and Metaphysics*, Christia Mercer and Eileen O'Neill (eds.). New York: Oxford University Press, 103–18.

Garrett, Aaron. 2003. "Was Spinoza a Natural Lawyer?" *Cardozo Law Review* 25(2): 627–41.

2012. "Knowing the Essence of the State in Spinoza's *Tractatus Theologico-Politicus*," *European Journal of Philosophy* 20(1): 50–73.

Garrett, Don. 1994. "Spinoza's Theory of Metaphysical Individuation," in *Individuation in Early Modern Philosophy*, Kenneth F. Barber and Jorge J. E. Gracia (eds.). Albany, NY: State University of New York Press, 73–101.

1996. "Spinoza's Ethical Theory," in *Cambridge Companion to Spinoza*, Don Garrett (ed.). Cambridge: Cambridge University Press, 267–314.

2002. "Spinoza's Conatus Argument," in *Spinoza's Metaphysics: Central Themes*, John I. Biro and Olli Koistinen (eds.). Oxford: Oxford University Press, 127–58.

2009. "Spinoza on the Essence of the Human Body and the Part of the Mind That Is Eternal," in *The Cambridge Companion to Spinoza's Ethics*, Olli Koistinen (ed.). Cambridge: Cambridge University Press, 284–302.

2017. "Representation and Misrepresentation in Spinoza's Philosophy of Mind," in *The Oxford Handbook of Spinoza*, Michael Della Rocca (ed.). Oxford: Oxford University Press, 190–203.

Garver, Eugene. 1987. *Machiavelli and the History of Prudence*. Madison, WI: University of Wisconsin Press.

Gatens, Moira. 1995. *Imaginary Bodies: Ethics, Power, and Corporeality*. London: Routledge.

Gatens, Moira and Genevieve Lloyd. 1999. *Collective Imaginations*. New York: Routledge.

Gauthier, David. 1986. *Morals by Agreement*. Oxford: Oxford University Press.

2001. "Hobbes: The Laws of Nature," *Pacific Philosophical Quarterly* 82(3–4): 258–84.

Geuss, Raymond. 2008. *Philosophy and Real Politics*. Princeton, NJ: Princeton University Press.

Grey, John. 2014. "Spinoza on Composition, Causation, and the Mind's Eternity," *British Journal for the History of Philosophy* 22(3): 446–67.

Groenhuis, Gerrit. 1981. "Calvinism and National Consciousness: The Dutch Republic as the New Israel," in *Britain and the Netherlands, Vol. 7, Church and State Since the Reformation*, A. C. Duke and C. A. Tamse (eds.). The Hague: Nijhoff, 118–33.

Grofman, Bernard and Scott Feld. 1988. "Rousseau's General Will: A Condorcetian Perspective," *American Political Science Review* 82(2): 567–76.

Guicciardini, Francesco. 1965. *Ricordi [Maxims and Reflections]*, Series C. Translated by Mario Domandi. Philadelphia, PA: University of Pennsylvania Press.

Haakonssen, Knud. "Divine/natural Law Theories in Ethics," in *The Cambridge History of Seventeenth-Century Philosophy*, Michael Ayers and Daniel Garber (eds.). Cambridge: Cambridge University Press, 1317–57.

Habermas, Jurgen. 1996. *Between Facts and Norms: Contributions to a Discourse Theory of Law and Democracy*. Cambridge, MA: MIT Press.

Haitsma Mulier, Eco. 1980. *The Myth of Venice and Dutch Republican Thought in the Seventeenth Century*. Translated by Gerard T. Moran. Assen: Van Gorcum.

Hanasz, Waldemar. 2010. "Machiavelli's Method Revisited: The Art and Science of Modeling," *Review Journal of Political Philosophy* 8(1): 1–32.

Harris, Errol. 1984. "Spinoza's Treatment of Natural Law," in *Spinoza's Political and Theological Thought*, Cornelis de Deugd (ed.). Amsterdam: North-Holland Publishing, 63–72.

Haserot, Francis. 1973. "Spinoza and the Status of Universals," in *Studies in Spinoza: Critical and Interpretive Essays*, S. Paul Kashap (ed.). Berkeley, CA: University of California Press, 43–67.

Hübner, Karolina. 2014. "Spinoza on Being Human and Human Perfection," in *The Ethics of Spinoza's Ethics*, Matthew Kisner and Andrew Youpa (eds.). Oxford: Oxford University Press, 124–42.

2015. "Spinoza on Negation, Mind-dependence and the Reality of the Finite," in *The Young Spinoza: A Metaphysician in the Making*, Yitzhak Melamed (ed.). Oxford: Oxford University Press, 221–37.

2016. "Spinoza on Essences, Universals, and Beings of Reason," *Pacific Philosophical Quarterly* 97: 58–88.

Huebner, Bryce. 2009. "Troubles with Stereotypes for Spinozan Minds," *Philosophy of the Social Sciences* 39(1): 63–92.

Hume, David. 1975. *An Enquiry Concerning Human Understanding in Enquiries Concerning Human Understanding and Concerning the Principles of Morals*, L. A. Selby-Bigge (ed.), 3rd Edition. Revised by P. H. Nidditch. Oxford: Clarendon Press.

Irwin, Terence. 2009. *Development of Ethics: A Historical and Critical Study*, vol. 2. Oxford: Oxford University Press.

Israel, Jonathan I. 1995a. *The Dutch Republic: Its Rise, Greatness, and Fall, 1477–1806*. Oxford: Clarendon Press.

1995b. "The Banning of Spinoza's Works in the Dutch Republic 1670–1678," in *Disguised and Overt Spinozism Around 1700*, Wiep van Bunge and Wim Klever (eds.). Leiden: Brill, 1–4.

2001. *Radical Enlightenment: Philosophy and the Making of Modernity 1650–1750*. Oxford: Oxford University Press.

2002. "Religious Toleration and Radical Philosophy in the Later Dutch Golden Age (1668–1710)," in *Calvinism and Religious Toleration in the Dutch Golden Age*, R. Po-Chia Hsia and H. F. K. Van Nierop (eds.). Cambridge: Cambridge University Press, 148–58.

2010a. *A Revolution of Mind: Radical Enlightenment and the Intellectual Origins of Modern Democracy*. Princeton, NJ: Princeton University Press.

2010b. "The Early Dutch and German Reaction to the *Tractatus Theologico-Politicus*: Foreshadowing the Enlightenment's More General Spinoza Reception," in *Spinoza's Theological–Political Treatise: A Critical Guide*, Yitzhak Y. Melamed and Michael Rosenthal (eds.). Cambridge: Cambridge University Press, 72–100.

2011. *Democratic Enlightenment: Philosophy, Revolution, and Human Rights*. Oxford: Oxford University Press.

James, Susan. 1996. "Power and Difference: Spinoza's Conception of Freedom," *The Journal of Political Philosophy* 4(3): 207–28.

2009. "Shakespeare and the Politics of Superstition," in *Shakespeare and Early Modern Political Thought*, David Armitage, Conal Condren, and Andrew Fitzmaurice (eds.). Cambridge: Cambridge University Press, 80–98.

2010. "Narrative as the Means to Freedom," in *Spinoza's Theological–Political Treatise: A Critical Guide*, Yitzhak Y. Melamed and Michael Rosenthal (eds.). Cambridge: Cambridge University Press, 250–67.

2011. "Creating Rational Understanding: Spinoza as a Social Epistemologist," *The Aristotelian Society Supplementary Volume* 85: 181–99.

2012. *Spinoza on Philosophy, Religion, and Politics*. Oxford: Oxford University Press.

Kahn, Victoria. 2014. *The Future of Illusion*. Chicago: The University of Chicago Press.

Kingston, Rebecca. 2008. "The Political Relevance of the Emotions from Descartes to Smith," in *Bringing the Passions Back In*, Rebecca Kingston and Leonard Ferry (eds.). Vancouver: UBC Press, 108–25.

Kisner, Matthew. 2010. "Perfection and Desire: Spinoza on the Good," *Pacific Philosophical Quarterly* 91(1): 97–117.

2011. *Spinoza on Human Freedom*. Cambridge: Cambridge University Press.

Klein, Julie. 2014. "'Something of it Remains': Spinoza and Gersonides on Intellectual Eternity," in *Spinoza and Jewish Philosophy*, Steven M. Nadler (ed.). Cambridge: Cambridge University Press, 177–203.

Kneale, Martha. 1969. "Eternity and Sempiternity," *Proceedings of the Aristotelian Society* 69: 223–38.

Kossmann, E. H. 1987. "The Singularity of Absolutism," in E. H. Kossmann, *Politieke theorie en geschiedenis. Verspreide opstellen en voordrachten.* Amsterdam: U.B. Bakker.
    2000. *Political Thought in the Dutch Republic. Three Studies.* Amsterdam: Koninklijke Nederlandse Akademie van Wetenschappen.

Kramer, Matthew. 2003. *The Quality of Freedom.* Oxford: Oxford University Press.

Lærke, Mogens. 2010. "G.W. Leibniz's two readings of the *Tractatus Theologico-Politicus,*" in *Spinoza's Theological–Political Treatise: A Critical Guide,* Yitzhak Y. Melamed and Michael Rosenthal (eds.). Cambridge: Cambridge University Press, 101–27.
    2014. "Spinoza's Language." *Journal of the History of Philosophy* 52(3): 519–47.

Laursen, John Christian. 1992. *The Politics of Skepticism in the Ancients, Montaigne, Hume, and Kant.* Leiden: Brill.
    1996. "Spinoza on Toleration: Arming the State and Reining in the Magistrate," in *Difference and Dissent: Theories of Toleration in Medieval and Early Modern Europe,* Cary J. Nederman and John Christian Laursen (eds.). Lanham, MD: Rowman & Littlefield, 185–204.

LeBuffe, Michael. 2009. "The Anatomy of the Passions," in *The Cambridge Companion to Spinoza's Ethics,* Olli Koistinen (ed.). Cambridge: Cambridge University Press, 188–222.
    2010a. *From Bondage to Freedom: Spinoza on Human Excellence.* Oxford: Oxford University Press.
    2010b. "Change and the Eternal Part of the Mind in Spinoza," *Pacific Philosophical Quarterly* 91(3): 369–84.

Lesser, Alexander. 1931. "Superstition," *Journal of Philosophy* 28: 617–28.

Lin, Martin. 2006a. "Teleology and Human Action in Spinoza," *Philosophical Review* 115(3): 317–54.
    2006b. "Spinoza's Account of Akrasia," *Journal of the History of Philosophy* 44(3): 395–414.

Lipsius, Justus. 1970. *Sixe Bookes of Politickes or Civil Doctrine.* Translated by William Jones. New York: Da Capo Press.
    2006. *Of Constancy.* Translated by Sir John Stradling. Edited by John Sellars, Exeter: Bristol Phoenix Press.

Lloyd, Genevieve. 1986. "Spinoza's Version of the Eternity of Mind," *Spinoza and the Sciences* 91: 211–33.

Lord, Beth. 2011. "Between Imagination and Reason: Kant and Spinoza on Fictions," in *Inventions of the Imagination: Romanticism and Beyond,* Richard T. Gray, Nicholas Halmi, Gary J. Handwerk, Michael A. Rosenthal, and Klaus Vieweg (eds.). Seattle: University of Washington Press, 36–53.
    2014. "Spinoza, Equality, and Hierarchy," *History of Philosophy Quarterly* 31(1): 59–77.
    2016. "The Concept of Equality in Spinoza's Theological–Political Treatise," *Epoche: A Journal for the History of Philosophy* 20(2): 367–86.

Lordon, Frédéric. 2014. *Willing Slaves of Capital: Spinoza and Marx on Desire.* Translated by Gabriel Ash. London: Verso.

Lucretius. 2006. *De Rerum Natura.* Translated by W. H. D. Rouse. Cambridge, MA: Harvard University Press.

Malebranche, Nicolas. 1997. *The Search After Truth*. Edited and translated by Thomas M. Lennon and Paul J. Olscamp. Cambridge: Cambridge University Press.

Marshall, Eugene. 2008. "Adequacy and Innateness in Spinoza," *Oxford Studies in Early Modern Philosophy* 4: 51–88.

2013. *The Spiritual Automaton: Spinoza's Science of the Mind*. Oxford: Oxford University Press.

Matheron, Alexandre. 1969. *Individu et Communauté chez Spinoza*. Paris: Les Editions de Minuit.

1986. "Spinoza et la décomposition de la politique Thomiste: Machiavélisme et utopie," in *Alexandre Matheron, Anthropologie et Politique au XVIIe Siècle: Études sur Spinoza*, Paris: J. Vrin, 49–79.

1990. "Le Problème de L'évolution de Spinoza *Du Traité Théologico-Politique au Traité Politique*," in *Spinoza: Issues and Directions*, E. Curley and P. F. Moreau (eds.). Leiden: Brill, 258–70.

2011. "L'indignation et le *conatus* de l'État spinoziste," in *Études sur Spinoza et les philosophies de l'âge classique*, Alexandre Matheron (ed.). Lyon: ENS, 219–229.

McGrade, A. S. 1982. "Rights, Natural Rights, and the Philosophy of Law," in *The Cambridge History of Later Medieval Philosophy*, Norman Kretzmann, Anthony Kenny, and Jan Pinborg (eds.). Cambridge: Cambridge University Press, 738–56.

McShea, Robert. 1968. *The Political Philosophy of Spinoza*. New York: Columbia University Press.

1969. "Spinoza on Power," *Inquiry* 12: 133–43.

Melamed, Yitzhak. 2010. "Spinoza's Anti-Humanism: an Outline," in *The Rationalists: Between Tradition and Innovation*, Carlos Fraenkel, Dario Perinetti, and Justin E. H. Smith (eds.). Dordrecht: Springer.

2013a. *Spinoza's Metaphysics: Substance and Thought*. Oxford: Oxford University Press.

2013b. "Charitable Interpretations and the Political Domestication of Spinoza, or, Benedict in the Land of the Secular Imagination" in *The Methodology of the History of Philosophy*, Mogens Lærke, Justin E. H. Smith, and Eric Schliesser (eds.). Oxford: Oxford University Press, 258–77.

Mendelssohn, Moses. 2012. *Morning Hours in Last Works*. Translated by Bruce Rosenstock. Champaign, IL: University of Illinois.

Miller, Jon. 2003. "Spinoza and the Concept of a Law of Nature," *History of Philosophy Quarterly* 20(3): 257–76.

2012. "Spinoza and Natural Law," in *Reason, Religion, and Natural Law: From Plato to Spinoza*, Jonathan A. Jacobs (eds.). Oxford: Oxford University Press.

2015. *Spinoza and the Stoics*. Cambridge: Cambridge University Press.

Mills, Charles. 2005. "'Ideal Theory' as Ideology," *Hypatia* 20(3): 165–83.

Milton, J. R. 1998. "Laws of Nature," in *The Cambridge History of Seventeenth-Century Philosophy*, Michael Ayers and Daniel Garber (eds.). Cambridge: Cambridge University Press, 680–701.

Montaigne, Michel de. 1958. *The Complete Essays*. Translated and edited by Donald Frame. Palo Alto, CA: Stanford University Press.

More, Sir Thomas. 1997. *Utopia*. Mineola: Dover.

Moreau, Pierre-François. 1994. *Spinoza, l'expérience et l'éternité*. Paris: Presses universitaires de France.

Mout, M. E. H. N. 1997. "Limits and Debates: A Comparative View of Dutch Toleration in the Sixteenth and Early Seventeenth Centuries," in *The Emergence of Tolerance in the Dutch Republic*, C. Berkvens-Stevelinck et al. (eds.). Leiden: Brill, 37–47.

Mueller, Carol. 2004. "Ella Baker and the Origins of 'Participatory Democracy,'" in *The Black Studies Reader*, Jacqueline Bobo, Cynthia Hudley, and Claudine Michel (eds.). New York: Routledge, 79–90.

Nadler, Steven. 1999. *Spinoza: A Life*. Cambridge: Cambridge University Press.

   2002a. *Spinoza's Heresy: Immortality and the Jewish Mind*. Oxford: Oxford University Press.

   2002b. "Eternity and Immortality in Spinoza's *Ethics*," *Midwest Studies in Philosophy*, 26: 224–44.

   2005. "Hope, Fear, and the Politics of Immortality," in *Analytic Philosophy and History of Philosophy*, Tom Sorell and G. A. J. Rogers (eds.). Oxford: Oxford University Press, 201–17.

   2011. *A Book Forged in Hell: Spinoza's Scandalous Treatise and the Birth of the Secular Age*. Princeton, NJ: Princeton University Press.

   2013. "Scripture and Truth: A Problem in Spinoza's *Tractatus Theologico-Politicus*," *Journal of the History of Ideas* 74(4): 623–42.

   2014. "Virtue, Reason and Moral Luck: Maimonides, Gersonides, and Spinoza," in *Spinoza and Medieval Jewish Philosophy*, Steven Nadler (ed.). Cambridge: Cambridge University Press, 152–76.

Negri, Antonio. 1991. *The Savage Anomaly*. Translated by Michael Hardt. Minneapolis, MN: University of Minnesota Press.

   1997. "*Reliqua Desiderantur*: A Conjecture for a Definition of the Concept of Democracy in the Final Spinoza," in *The New Spinoza*, Warren Montag and Ted Stolze (eds.). Minneapolis, MN: Minnesota University Press, 219–46.

Nelson, Eric. 2007. "The Problem of the Prince," in *The Cambridge Companion to Renaissance Philosophy*, James Hankins (ed.). Cambridge: Cambridge University Press, 319–37.

Newlands, Samuel. 2015. "Spinoza's Early Anti-Abstractionism," in *The Young Spinoza: A Metaphysician in the Making*, Yitzhak Y. Melamed (ed.). Cambridge: Cambridge University Press, 255–71.

Noreña, Carlos G. 1989. *Juan Luis Vives and the Emotions*. Carbondale: Southern Illinois University Press.

Nussbaum, Martha. 2001. *Upheavals of Thought: The Intelligence of Emotions*. Cambridge: Cambridge University Press.

Parchment, Steven. 2000. "The Mind's Eternity in Spinoza's *Ethics*," *Journal of the History of Philosophy* 38(3): 349–83.

Pender, Stephen. 2005. "Between Medicine and Rhetoric," *Early Science and Medicine* 10(1): 36–64.

Petrarch. 1991. *Remedies for Fortune Fair and Foul*. Translated by Conrad Rawski. Bloomington, IN: Indiana University Press.

Pitkin, Hanna. 1984. *Fortune Is a Woman: Gender and Politics in the Thought of Niccolò Machiavelli*. Chicago: University of Chicago Press.

Plotinus. 1964. *The Essential Plotinus*. Translated and edited by Elmer O'Brien. Indianapolis, IN: Hackett.

Pocock, J. G. A. 1975. *The Machiavellian Moment: Florentine Political Thought and the Atlantic Republican Tradition*. Princeton, NJ: Princeton University Press.

　　1987. "Spinoza and Harrington: An Exercise in Comparison," *Bijdragen en Mededelingen betreffende de Geschiedenis der Nederlanden* 102: 435–49.

Poppi, Antonio. 1988. "Fate, Fortune, Providence and Human Freedom," in *The Cambridge History of Renaissance Philosophy*, Charles B. Schmitt and Quentin Skinner (eds.). Cambridge: Cambridge University Press, 641–67.

Preus, J. Samuel. 2001. *Spinoza and the Irrelevance of Biblical Authority*. Cambridge: Cambridge University Press.

Prokhovnik, Raia. 1997. "From Democracy to Aristocracy: Spinoza, Reason and Politics," *History of European Ideas* 23(2–4): 105–15.

　　2004. *Spinoza and Republicanism*. London and New York: Palgrave Macmillan.

Price, H. H. 1964. "Half-Belief," *Proceedings of the Aristotelian Society, Supplementary Volumes* 38: 149–62.

Raphael, D. D. (ed.). 1991. *British Moralists 1650–1800, Vol. I. Hobbes–Gay*. Indianapolis, IN: Hackett.

Rawls, John. 1971. *A Theory of Justice*. Cambridge, MA: Harvard University Press.

Revault d'Allonnes, Myriam. 1999. "Affect of the Body and Socialization," in *Desire and Affect: Spinoza as Psychologist*, Yirmiyahu Yovel (ed.). New York: Little Room Press, 183–90.

Rosenthal, Michael. 1997. "Why Spinoza Chose the Hebrews: The Exemplary Function of Prophecy in the *Theological–Political Treatise*," *History of Political Thought* 18(2): 207–41.

　　2001. "Tolerance as a Virtue in Spinoza's *Ethics*," *Journal of the History of Philosophy* 39(4): 535–57.

　　2003a. "Spinoza's Republican Argument for Toleration," *The Journal of Political Philosophy* 11(3): 320–37.

　　2003b. "Persuasive Passions: Rhetoric and the Interpretation of Spinoza's *Theological–Political Treatise*," *Archiv für Geschichte der Philosophie* 85(3): 249–68.

Ross, W. D. 1988. *The Right and the Good* (Reprint). Indianapolis, IN: Hackett.

Russell, Bertrand. 2009. *The Basic Writings of Bertrand Russell*. London: Routledge.

Russell, Paul. 2010. *The Riddle of Hume's Treatise: Skepticism, Naturalism, and Irreligion*. Oxford: Oxford University Press.

Rutherford, Donald "Spinoza's Conception of Law: Metaphysics and Ethics," in *Spinoza's Theological–Political Treatise: A Critical Guide*, Yitzhak Y. Melamed and Michael Rosenthal (eds.). Cambridge: Cambridge University Press, 143–67.

Santos Campos, Andre. 2012. *Spinoza's Revolutions in Natural Law*. London: Palgrave Macmillan.

Schama, Simon. 1987. *The Embarrassment of Riches*. New York: Alfred A. Knopf, 231–4.

Scott, Jonathan. 2002. "Classical Republicanism in Seventeenth Century England and the Netherlands," in *Republicanism: A Shared European Heritage* (2 vols.), Martin Van Gelderen and Quentin Skinner (eds.). Cambridge: Cambridge University Press.

Seigel, Jerrold. 1966. "'Civic Humanism' or Ciceronian Rhetoric? The Culture of Petrarch and Bruni," *Past and Present* 34: 3–48.

Seneca, Lucius Annaeus. 1917. *Ad Lucilium Epistulae Morales [Epistles]*, vol. 1. Translated by Richard M. Gummere. Cambridge, MA: Harvard University Press.

1920. *Ad Lucilium Epistulae Morales [Epistles]*, vol. 2. Translated by Richard Gummere. Cambridge, MA: Harvard University Press.

Shapiro, Lisa (ed. and trans.). 2007. *The Correspondence Between Princess Elisabeth and René Descartes*. Chicago: University of Chicago Press.

Sharp, Hasana. 2005. "Why Spinoza Today? Or, a Strategy of Anti-Fear," *Rethinking Marxism: A Journal of Economics, Culture, and Society* 17(4): 591–608.

2011. *Spinoza and the Politics of Renaturalization*. Chicago: University of Chicago Press.

2012. "Eve's Perfection: Spinoza on Sexual (In)Equality," *Journal of the History of Philosophy* 50(4): 559–80.

2013. "Violenta Imperia Nemo Continuit Diu," *Graduate Faculty Philosophy Journal* 34(1): 133–48.

Sidgwick, Henry. 1962. *The Method of Ethics*. London: Macmillan.

Skinner, Quentin. 1978. *The Foundations of Modern Political Thought*, vol. 1. Cambridge: Cambridge University Press.

1984. "The Idea of Negative Liberty: Philosophical and Historical Perspectives," in *Philosophy in History*, Richard Rorty, J. B. Schneewind, and Quentin Skinner (eds.). Cambridge: Cambridge University Press.

1996. *Reason and Rhetoric in the Philosophy of Hobbes*. Cambridge: Cambridge University Press.

1998. *Liberty Before Liberalism*. Cambridge: Cambridge University Press.

2000. *Machiavelli: A Very Short Introduction*. Oxford: Oxford University Press.

Slomp, Gabriella. 2000. *Thomas Hobbes and the Political Philosophy of Glory*. New York: St. Martin's Press.

Smith, Steven B. 1997. *Spinoza, Liberalism, and the Question of Jewish Identity*. New Haven, CT: Yale University Press.

2003. *Spinoza's Book of Life: Freedom and Redemption in the Ethics*. New Haven, CT: Yale University Press.

Sommerville, J. P. 1991. "Absolutism and Royalism," in *The Cambridge History of Political Thought 1450–1700*, J. H. Burns (ed.). Cambridge: Cambridge University Press, 347–73.

Soyarslan, S. Forthcoming. "Spinoza's Critique of Humility in the Ethics," *The Southern Journal of Philosophy*.

Steinberg, Diane. 2005. "Belief, Affirmation, and the Doctrine of *Conatus* in Spinoza," *The Southern Journal of Philosophy* 43: 147–58.

Steinberg, Justin. 2008. "On Being *Sui Iuris*: Spinoza and the Republican Idea of Liberty," *History of European Ideas* 34(3): 239–49.

2009. "Spinoza on Civil Liberation," *Journal of the History of Philosophy* 47(1): 35–58.

2010a. "Benedict Spinoza: Epistemic Democrat," *History of Philosophy Quarterly* 27(2): 145–64.

2010b. "Spinoza's Curious Defense of Toleration," in *Spinoza's Theological–Political Treatise: A Critical Guide*, Yitzhak Y. Melamed and Michael Rosenthal (eds.). Cambridge: Cambridge University Press, 210–30.

2013. "Imitation, Representation, and Humanity in Spinoza's *Ethics*," *Journal of the History of Philosophy* 51(3): 383–407.

2014. "Following a *Recta Ratio* Vivendi: The Practical Utility of Spinoza's Dictates of Reason," in *The Ethics of Spinoza's Ethics*, Matthew Kisner and Andrew Youpa (eds.). Oxford: Oxford University Press, 178–96.

2016. "Affect, Desire, and Judgement in Spinoza's Account of Motivation," *British Journal for the History of Philosophy* 24(1): 67–87.

2018a. "Two Puzzles Concerning Spinoza's Conception of Belief," *European Journal of Philosophy* 26(1): 261–82.

2018b. "Spinoza and Political Absolutism," in *Spinoza's Political Treatise: New Assessments*, Hasana Sharp and Yitzhak Melamed (eds.). Cambridge: Cambridge University Press.

Steinberg, Justin. Forthcoming. "Spinoza on Bodies Politic and Civil Agreement," in *Spinoza and Relational Autonomy: Being with Others*, Aurelia Armstrong, Keith Green, and Andrea Sangiacomo (eds.). Edinburgh: Edinburgh University Press.

Strauss, Leo. 1965. *Spinoza's Critique of Religion*. Translated by E. M. Sinclair. Chicago: University of Chicago Press.

1988. *Persecution and the Art of Writing*. Chicago: University of Chicago Press.

2003. *Why Societies Need Dissent*. Cambridge, MA: Harvard University Press.

Sunstein, Cass. 2002. "The Law of Group Polarization," *The Journal of Political Philosophy* 10(2): 175–95.

Sunstein, Cass, David Schkade, and Reid Hastie. 2007. "What Happened on Deliberation Day?" *California Law Review* 95: 915–40.

Tuck, Richard. 1987. "The 'Modern' Theory of Natural Law," in *The Languages of Political Theory in Early–Modern Europe*, Anthony Pagden (ed.). Cambridge: Cambridge University Press, 99–119.

Van Bunge, Wiep. 2001. *From Stevin to Spinoza: An Essay on Philosophy in the Seventeenth-Century Dutch Republic*. Leiden: Brill.

Van Gelderen, Martin. 1992. *The Political Thought of the Dutch Revolt 1555–1590*. Cambridge: Cambridge University Press.

1993. "The Machiavellian Moment and the Dutch Revolt: The Rise of Neostoicism and Dutch Republicanism," in *Machiavelli and Republicanism*, Gisela Bock, Quentin Skinner, and Maurizio Viroli (eds.). New York: Cambridge University Press, 205–23.

Velema, Wyger. 2002. "'That a Republic is Better than a Monarchy': Anti-Monarchism in Early Modern Dutch Political Thought," in *Republicanism: A Shared European Heritage* (2 vols.), Martin Van Gelderen and Quentin Skinner (eds.). Cambridge: Cambridge University Press, 9–25.

Verbeek, Theo. 2003. *Spinoza's Theologico-Political Treatise: Exploring 'The Will of God.'* Aldershot: Ashgate.

Viljanen, Valtteri. 2011. *Spinoza's Geometry of Power*. Cambridge: Cambridge University Press.

Viroli, Maurizio. 2002. *Niccolò's Smile*. New York: Hill and Wang.

Walker, Leslie. 1950. *"Introduction" to The Discourses of Niccolò Machiavelli*. Translated and edited by Leslie Walker. New Haven, CT: Yale University Press.

Warrender, Howard. 2000. *The Political Philosophy of Hobbes*. Oxford: Oxford University Press.

Wernham, A. G. 1958. "Notes and Introduction," in *Spinoza: The Political Works* A. G. Wernham (ed.). Oxford: Clarendon Press.

Williams, Bernard. 1995. "Internal Reasons and The Obscurity of Blame," in *Making Sense of Humanity and Other Philosophical Papers*, Bernard Williams (ed.). Cambridge: Cambridge University Press, 35–45.

Wilson, Catherine. 2008a. *Epicureanism at the Origins of Modernity*. Oxford: Oxford University Press.

2008b. "From Limits to Laws: The Construction of the Nomological Image of Nature in Early Modern Philosophy," in *Natural Law and Laws of Nature in Early Modern Europe: Jurisprudence, Theology, Moral and Natural Philosophy*, Lorraine Daston and Michael Stolleis (eds.). Farnham: Ashgate: 13–26.

Wilson, Margaret. 1999. "Spinoza's Causal Axiom," in Margaret Wilson, *Ideas and Mechanism*. Princeton, NJ: Princeton University Press, 141–65.

Wirszubski, Chaim. 1950. *Libertas as a Political Idea in Rome during the Late Republic and Early Principate*. Cambridge: Cambridge University Press.

Wright, Richard. 1966. *Native Son*. New York: Harper and Row.

Yates, Francis. 1966. *The Art of Memory*. Chicago: University of Chicago Press.

Youpa, Andrew. 2007. "Spinoza's Theory of Motivation," *Pacific Philosophical Quarterly* 88(3): 375–90.

2010. "Spinoza's Theories of Value," *British Journal for the History of Philosophy* 18(2): 209–29.

Yovel, Yirmiyahu. 1989. *Spinoza and Other Heretics*. Princeton, NJ: Princeton University Press.

2004. "Incomplete Rationality," in *Spinoza on Reason and the Free Man*, Yirmiyahu Yovel and Gideon Segal (eds.). New York: Little Room Press, 15–35.

Index